THE SUMMONING OF NOMAN

The True Story of My Parallel Life

Orest Stocco

THE SUMMONING OF NOMAN

Copyright © 2015 by Orest Stocco

ISBN 978-1-926442-08-2

Edited by Penny Lynn Cates

Cover Design by Penny Lynn Cates

ALSO BY OREST STOCCO

NOVELS

The Golden Seed
Tea with Grace
Jesus Wears Dockers
Healing with Padre Pio
Keeper of the Flame
My Unborn Child
On the Wings of Habitat
What Would I Say Today If I Were to Die Tomorrow?

NON FICTION

The Lion that Swallowed Hemingway
The Sum of All Spiritual Paths
Do We Have An Immortal Soul?
Stupidity Is Not a Gift of God
Letters to Padre Pio
Old Whore Life
Just Going with the Flow
Why Bother? The Riddle of the Good Samaritan
The Pearl of Great Price
In the Shade of the Maple Tree

"Dreams are the guiding words of the soul. Dreams pave the way for life, and they determine you without you understanding their language."

C. G. Jung

Table of Contents

1. *The Key to My Dreams Is My Dreams*

While working on the last chapter of my book *Old Whore Life, Exploring the Shadow Side of Karma* ("Does the World Need to Be Saved?"), I was strongly nudged to go online and do some research on C. G. Jung, the founding father of Analytical Psychology, who had a great influence upon my life. My research led to Jungian analyst Marion Woodman and her Jungian analyst brother Fraser Boa's long documentary *The Way of the Dream*, which I watched in two sittings with undiminished fascination. This inspired me to start a new dream journal, which I began February 3, 2012.

Fraser Boa's conversation with Dr. Marie-Louise von Franz rekindled my interest in recording my dreams, which I've done off and on for the past forty years; but this time I wanted to make an in-depth study of my dreams, because all of my research on Jung and the psychology of dreams caused a paradigm shift in my understanding of dreams.

Dr. Marie-Louise von Franz was a Jungian analyst who worked closely with C.G. Jung in Switzerland. In fact, she wrote the chapters "The Process of Individuation" and "Science and the Unconscious" of the book edited and introduced by C. G. Jung, *Man and His Symbols* which I had read several times; and her intuitive gift for dream interpretation in *The Way of the Dream* impressed me so much that I dug up all of my books on dreams and C. G. Jung to re-read, beginning with *Our Dreaming Mind,* a sweeping exploration of the role that dreams have played throughout history, by Robert L. Van De Castle, Ph. D.

I thoroughly enjoyed this book the first time I read it, but as I began to read *Our Dreaming Mind* over again it held a whole new fascination for me because of the shift I had in my perspective on the dynamic process of dreaming.

If I may, there is an esoteric dimension to the study of dreams that goes back to ancient times. I had seven past life regressions seven years ago, and I learned that I was a student of the legendary Greek philosopher Pythagoras. Aside from teaching philosophy, mathematics, and his theory of music he also taught a mystery teaching in secret which included the spiritual component of the dreaming process (he taught us in our dreams).

The mystery teaching that Pythagoras taught centuries ago continues to be taught today in the teachings of the Way of the Eternal, which I reconnected with while I was studying Gurdjieff's teaching; so I viewed my dream life from the esoteric perspective of my new spiritual path, which diminished my appreciation of the Jungian perspective on dreams. But while listening to Dr. von Franz talking about the archetypal nature of dreams I had a shift in consciousness and realized that **the spiritual and psychological perspectives on dreams were merely two facets of the same dynamic**; and this inspired me to start a new dream journal so I could explore what my dreams were trying to tell me.

I've been having dreams of my home town of Nipigon, Ontario for a long while now, for years in fact; and I have never been able to understand why. While working on my novel *Healing with Padre Pio*, which was inspired by the ten spiritual healing sessions that I had with a psychic medium who channeled Ascended Master St. Padre Pio, I learned something that took me completely by surprise—**I am reliving my same life over again, but only this time I am living it to achieve a different outcome.**

In effect, I lived my life once in my hometown of Nipigon in Northwestern Ontario, Canada (I died in Nipigon), but according to St. Padre Pio I returned to my same life to live it over again because I was not happy with the first outcome; and this time around I left my hometown of Nipigon and am living in Georgian Bay, South Central Ontario.

This opens the door to the concept of parallel worlds; and the more I thought about this, the more I suspected that I'm having all these dreams of my hometown because I have a lot of karma there that I'm working off in my dream life.

In my spiritual path, working off karma in our dream life speaks to one of the spiritual functions of our dreams; but as much as I accepted this spiritual aspect of my dreams I still could not put my finger on just what kept pulling me back to my hometown in my dreams—because I was getting sick and tired of my hometown dream life.

Maybe this quandary pulled me back to C. G. Jung, because my research on Jung inspired me to start a new dream journal to study my dreams. *"Perhaps my dreams can tell me why I keep going back to my hometown in my dream life,"* I said to myself; and I started my new journal, and within three days my dreams gave me my first clue. Friday, February 3, 2012; I recorded my first dream:

I'm vague on the details of my dream last night, but it had to do with my inner and outer life. My inner life was rich with my studies of the ancient secret spiritual teachings, which focused on the alchemy of the spirit, and my life was symbolized by a beautiful house, with the interior all white and clean; and although my outer life was successful, my outer-life success did not compare to my inner-life success, and my family felt I could have done a lot better. My family could not see my inner-life success. They could only see my outer life, and they could not understand why I spent so much of my life with my inner-life interests, and they were disappointed in me. They felt that I had invested way too many years in something that did not show materially, and I puzzled and alienated them.

This dream gives me a better picture of why I felt I didn't belong with my family. Not that I didn't love my family, but because I did not resonate with the same material interests that my family had. In many ways I was a loner, even though I tried to fit in. I couldn't understand what it was about me that made me different until I hit high school where my inner life began to demand more of my attention with writers like Hemingway, Joyce, and Maugham. I started reading literature in grade school, at one point reading one book a day; and when I was fifteen I ordered the encyclopedic set of books called *The Great Books of the Western World*. That sealed the fate of my inner life: I wanted to become a writer.

It's not my place to prove or disprove the existence of parallel worlds (better minds than mine will have to tackle this concept), but for the sake of inquiry into my dream life I'm going to accept what St. Padre Pio told me and posit that I have lived my life as Orest Stocco once already and am reliving my life in a parallel world today.

This boggles my mind; but I hope my dreams will make sense of it over time. I'm taking my cue from C. G. Jung who had complete confidence in the power of dreams to bring to light the mysteries of life. "Dreams are the speech of my soul. Dreams pave the way for life, and they determine you without you understanding their language," he wrote in his book *Dreams*. He also wrote in his iconic memoir *Memories, Dreams, Reflections*: "My life is the story of the self-realization of the unconscious."

And no wonder; he spent his whole life trying to understand the individuation process of the collective unconscious. Jung believed that the path leading to self-realization and personal wholeness could be discovered, and his belief was affirmed by a dream that he had just before he died. In his dream he saw "high up in a high place," a boulder lit by the sun. Carved into the boulder were the words: "Take this as a sign of the wholeness you have achieved and the singleness you have become" (*Our Dreaming Mind*, p.145).

I spent the most fertile years of my life looking for a path to wholeness and singleness of self, because I had a sexually

4

traumatizing experience in my early twenties that convinced me I was not myself, and I spent years looking for the path to my true self; and only when I discovered Gurdjieff and his concept of the false personality, which was later affirmed by Jung's concept of the shadow, did I begin to understand the sexual experience that shocked my conscience awake and catapulted me into my quest for my true self.

Since this is a narrative of my dream life, it's only fair to mention that I met G. I. Gurdjieff in my dreams a few times. Gurdjieff was long dead when I met him in my dreams shortly after I "chanced" upon P. D. Ouspensky's book *In Search of the Miraculous* in my second year of philosophy studies at university, which was a thorough account of Gurdjieff's teaching as experienced by Ouspensky himself. Ouspensky belonged to Gurdjieff's inner circle of students, and I wanted to become a member of his inner circle; so I asked Gurdjieff in my dream the first time I met him if he would accept me into his inner circle, but he said that I wasn't ready yet. "Need more work on self," he said.

I put his teaching of "work on oneself" to practice the best way I knew how when I left university in my third year to start my own contract painting business (I did not know anyone else who had even heard of Gurdjieff, let alone practiced his teaching), and two years later I met him again in a dream and asked to be accepted into his inner circle, and he said yes. This dream still brings tears to my eyes.

Gurdjieff and I were in the center of the large circle of his students. I was kneeling, and Gurdjieff was standing over me with his hands on my shoulders. His bald dome shone in the daylight, and he had a big white handlebar moustache. I looked up into his incredibly magnetic eyes, and they were so full of love that I burst into tears.

"Now work. Become real man," he said, in his Pidgin English; and work I did—*on myself!* To use St. Paul's phrase, I "died daily" until I gave birth to my spiritual self, just as Jesus promised. ***"Whoever finds the interpretations of these sayings will not*** *taste death,"* said Jesus in the *Gospel of Thomas,* and I found the correct interpretation and released the inherent power of self-transformation as I *lived* the sayings; that's how I came to the realization that one does not find his true self, but *becomes* his true self.

In essence, with Gurdjieff's teaching and the sayings of Jesus I sped up what Jung called the natural process of individuation. According to Gurdjieff, nature will only evolve man so far and no further. To continue evolution and realize personal wholeness we have to take evolution into our own hands. This is what Gurdjieff's teaching helped me to do. But I had trouble understanding Gurdjieff's concept of the false personality, which is why the omniscient guiding force of life introduced me to Jung's psychology of the self.

It's hard to believe that there is an omniscient guiding force of life that points us in the right direction whenever we stray too far from our destined purpose, but I have experienced too many coincidences in my search for the Way (the path to personal wholeness) to not believe it. This guiding force has been called Providence, Divine Spirit, guardian angels, the invisible Hand of God, the Way, and the Tao; but by whatever names it is known, I *know* that we are not alone in our journey through life.

We may not be aware of it, but it's always there; and one way that it speaks to us, aside from signs, symbols, coincidences, and book angels (some people hear a voice), is by inner nudges. It prods our shins from the inside, as it were, and speaks to us in silence. We can call it instinct, "the still small voice within" as Eileen Caddy, one of the founding members of the Findhorn Community called it, strong hunches, gut feelings of certainty, or whatever; but I have experienced these inner nudges all of my life, and when I listen to them whole new vistas open up to me, like my recent nudge to study my dream life.

Saturday, February 4, 2012; I recorded the second dream in my journal, which to my surprise gave me the second clue that I was looking for:

I'm in my hometown of Nipigon in my dream. I'm at the post office. I want to pick up my mail, but I do not have my post office key. I ask the girls behind the counter if they would get my mail for me. They cannot give it to me without my key. I have to go home to see if I can find it, or order a new key. There is something in my mail box that is of special interest, but I don't have the key to see what it is.

I've been dreaming of my hometown for quite some time now, and I'm getting very tired of it actually. Either I still have a lot of karma to work off in that town, or I haven't learned something that I'm supposed to learn. Perhaps I don't have the "key" to my problem yet. Could my dream be telling me that I have to have the "key" to get the "message" that will solve my riddle? Maybe my dreams will give me the key.

I felt confident in my interpretation, but obviously I wasn't confident enough because the omniscient guiding force of life gave me the confirmation I needed to take my dreams with utmost seriousness. I had three more dreams the next night, and they puzzled me to confusion. All I could do was guess at what they meant.

In my first dream, which again was rather vague, I was in some kind of sexual relationship. I don't know who I was having sex with, but for some odd reason the image I got was that I was having sex with life; and as I had sex with life, I was being initiated into what was called "the Wisdom."

I had just finished writing my book of spiritual musings on "old whore life," which was my metaphor for the cruel, vicious shadow side of karma that we refuse to acknowledge; so I suspect that my creative unconscious created an image of me having sex with life (I got "screwed" so often by life that I dubbed life an "old whore" that loves to screw us of our virtue), and in the process I was initiated into the wisdom of how life works—i.e., the wisdom of how we get back what we sow; which is why I was inspired to write *Old Whore Life: Exploring the Shadow Side of Karma*. I wanted to reveal the repressed dark side of our karmic personality.

In my second dream I'm having sex again, but this time with an old high school flame (she's an older woman in my dream); but once again, this is not just ordinary sex. I get the impression that I am "superimposing" myself upon her, and inoculating her with "the Wisdom." It's like she's in that other world of my first lifetime and I'm in my new life in this parallel world, and I'm bridging the two worlds by having sex with her in my dream (as though the dream spans both parallel worlds), and as we're having sex I'm inoculating her with "the Wisdom."

My impression is that I'm helping to raise the consciousness of life in my first lifetime in Nipigon, given that the first time I lived my life I did not find my true self, but this time I did; which means that I have been initiated into the wisdom of life *("the Wisdom," or the Way)* in this parallel lifetime, and by having sex with my old high school flame I inoculated her consciousness (the archetypal feminine) with the wisdom of the Way to help raise the spiritual consciousness of my first parallel world.

And in my third dream I'm in my hometown again (you can appreciate why I'm getting tired of my hometown dreams): *I'm driving my work van* (which gives me the feeling that I'm in my second life and not my first life because I don't think I had my painting business in my first life), *and I can see that there is a long line of vehicles waiting for the train to cross the tracks. The CPR tracks divide the town of Nipigon, and there has always been the perception that people who lived on the north side of the tracks were higher class than those who lived on the south side. I lived in the south side, in a section of town that was called "D.P. Ville," where new immigrants seemed to gravitate. But I get out of the line and move closer to the front, so when the train crosses the tracks I'm one of the first to cross over. I pull in front of a man whom I knew to be an aggressive trucking contractor who had made good in life. He is driving a big boat of a car, like the kind they had in the sixties, and he gives me a look when I pulled in front of him. My painting van is in good running condition* (which is odd, because I often have dreams of my van not being in the best condition)*, and I cross over and then wake up from my three dreams.*

I believe this dream speaks to my life number two, and crossing the tracks symbolizes that I'm going to be coming into some success on the other side of the tracks; otherwise I don't know what the dream speaks to. I know that my dreams are speaking to something, because from these three dreams I got definite confirmation for my first dream clue.

When I woke up from my three dreams I got dressed, booted my computer and went downstairs to make coffee. I lay on the sofa waiting for the coffee maker to drip enough coffee for a full cup, and I thought of my dreams so I could record them in my journal.

I knew there was a message in them, and just as I said the word *message* I thought of my dream of the post office. I didn't have the key to get my mail, which I associated with an important message in my mail box, and this image called up one of my dream books that I was re-reading—*Dreams are Letters from the Soul,* by Connie Kaplan, and I almost jumped off the couch I was so excited—because the coincidence of not having my key for my mail box in my dream and a book called *Dreams are Letters from the Soul* was the confirmation I needed that **the key to my dreams is my dreams**; and I knew it would only be a matter of time before the Dream Weaver would send me a "letter" that would explain why I keep going back to my hometown in my dreams and resolve the riddle of my parallel lives.

2. *My Dream in Annecy, France*

"As each plant grows from a seed and becomes in the end an oak tree, so man becomes what he is meant to be. He ought to get there, but most get stuck," said Carl Jung in an interview that I came across on the Internet; and he devoted his life to helping people get unstuck so they could continue on their journey of self-realization and wholeness.

Jung called this journey of the self the individuation process, and whether we like it or not we are all hard-wired to individuate. This defines the essence of man. We are destined to become who we are, just as the acorn seed is destined to become an oak tree and not a monkey; which means that no two people will individuate in exactly the same way. This is why Jung concluded that each person is his own path to wholeness.

"These leaves, our bodily personalities, seem identical," said Rumi, *"but the globe of soul-fruit we make, each is elaborately unique."* And herein lies the mystery of the process of individuation, what Carl Jung called the central archetype of man—the self.

What is the self? That's the question. In Jungian terms the self is a matrix of consciousness that is aware of its own existence. It is the reflective "I" of man. But where does this "I" come from? And how does it come to be? And for what purpose?

These questions haunted me all of my life. I may not have phrased them as cogently (Paul Gauguin did a painting called: *Where do we come from? What are we? Where are we going?*), but it was this longing to know who I was that set me on my quest which brought me to Gurdjieff's teaching that opened the door to the mystery of the self.

I found Gurdjieff in my second year of philosophy studies at university, but the omniscient guiding force of life set the stage for me to find his teaching. It knew what path I needed to find my true self, and from behind the scenes Divine Spirit choreographed my life to set me on my journey of self-realization and wholeness.

Jung came to realize through his patients that the individuation process is precipitated by a life-changing experience like the sudden death of a loved one, marriage breakup, the loss of one's job, threat of death by unexpected illness, or even a near-death experience—whatever; the trauma of such an experience is enough to break down the psychic structure of one's personality and give one room to grow in self-realization consciousness so he can continue his journey to wholeness. That's precisely what happened to me.

I became possessed by an irresistible archetypal force one night in my early twenties that compelled me to have a sexual experience that brutally shocked my conscience awake; and self-revulsion and shame combusted the fire of my quest for self-realization consciousness—*because I knew that the person who did what he did that night was not me!* It was me, but not me; and I could not live with myself. So I sold my pool hall and vending machine business and fled to France to begin my quest for my true self.

One evening in France while doing a meditation on a maple leaf I had an experience that was to change the rest of my life: as I imagined myself crawling up the hollow veins of the leaf, starting at the hollow opening of the stem, up and through each vein, I suddenly became one with the Oneness of the Universe, and this opened up the chakra at the base of my spine and awakened the kundalini; and the "serpent fire" crawled up the canal of my spine and lodged itself into my brain and set my mind on fire.

I had no paper handy to record the experience, so I recorded it on the blank pages of the novel I was reading: *Wuthering Heights*, by Emily Bronte, which I still have as proof of the experience. It was dated October 21, 1968. But now that I had this inexhaustible supply of creative kundalini energy at my disposal, the omniscient guiding force of life saw that I was ready to take the next step on my journey of self-discovery, and shortly after I accidentally awakened the "serpent fire" I had a dream that became my inspiration to return to Canada and go to university to study philosophy to continue my quest for my true self.

In my one room apartment in the beautiful Alpine city of Annecy, I had the most amazing dream. *In my dream I left my body and entered into the mind of every person in the world. I took every question that every person in the world had ever asked, and by the magic of dreams I rendered them all down to one question: why am I?* And thus was my spiritual compass set, and I began my quest proper for my true self...

It took many years to answer my dream question, but only after I had found the answer to the question that had thrust me on my spiritual quest in the first place—*who am I?* Because I certainly was not that person who did what he did that godforsaken night.

I had to find out *who I was* before I could answer *why I was*, and what a journey it was to get to that place where I could answer the question that haunts every single person in the world. I could never understand why my quest for my true self had to be so hard; impossible, to be absolutely truthful, as the symbol of the "squared circle" that appeared to me one night at university proved, but the answer did finally come to me while reading yet one more book on Gurdjieff's teaching—*The Teachers of Gurdjieff,* by Rafael Lefort.

The "squared circle" mandala symbol that appeared to me out of thin air that night foretold the impossible nature of my quest for my true self. This happened in my second year at university. Three men and I (two other adult students and a man from Nipigon who was supply teaching in Thunder Bay) were renting a house for the school term. It was late at night, and I was in my bedroom. I had devoured Ouspensky's book *In Search of the Miraculous,* and I knew in my heart that this was the path for me; but as much as I resonated with Gurdjieff's teaching I just did not "get it," as the phrase goes, and this made me so mad that I threw Ouspensky's book at the wall of my bedroom and lay on my bed in total disgust. And that's when the miraculous vision of my life happened.

I lay on my bed with the lights out trying to make sense of my reason for studying philosophy, because it seemed that the more I studied the mother of all disciplines the more I was cast adrift in a sea of infinite speculation, and I began to feel that I was wasting my time because I had an irrepressible urgency to find my true self; that's why I put so much stock in Gurdjieff's teaching. But I could not penetrate his transformative system of "work on oneself," and I wallowed in self-pity that night. And that's when it happened.

Just above eye level a blue dot appeared in midair at the foot of my bed and remained suspended for a few seconds; and then the blue dot grew into a donut-shaped circle about three feet in diameter and stayed suspended. And then a dot of yellow light appeared at the top, in the middle of the circumference of the circle, and the dot of yellow light grew into a bar of yellow light as it expanded down the circumference of the blue circle to form a straight line, and then it made a right angle and formed another straight line, and then another, and another—forming a perfect square within the circle.

The "squared circle" of yellow and blue light stayed suspended in midair long enough for me to pinch myself several times to see if I was dreaming, and then it disappeared before my eyes right back into the pitch darkness of my room.

I had just witnessed the symbolic squaring of the circle; but it took years for me to realize that I had been destined to do the impossible and find my true self and answer the question that lies buried in the mind of every person in the world—*why am I?*

But why did I have to suffer so much to "square the circle" to find my true self? What made my quest so different from other seekers? I didn't have a clue, until one day I read in my Gurdjieff book what a Sufi mystic told the author about there being two

13

kinds of spiritual quests in life: one quest through the consciousness of one's *being*, and the other quest through the consciousness of one's *non-being*—and guess which quest I was on?

The consciousness of one's *being* is one's authentic self, and the consciousness of one's *non-being* is one's inauthentic self; and although we are all authentic-inauthentic in our ontological makeup, some of us are more centered in one aspect of our personality than others. In effect, some people are more false and others more real.

I didn't know it, but I was centered in the consciousness of my inauthentic self; which is why I suffered so much in my quest for my true self—because I had to suffer the unending anguish of transforming the consciousness of my false self. This is why I was led to Gurdjieff's teaching of "work on oneself," because it was tailor-made for me. But I could not penetrate the secret of "working on oneself," which is why I was nudged to go for one of my long walks the weekend after my vision experience to think things out.

I drove to my home in Nipigon and went for a long walk where I often went for my philosopher's walks, down the CN railroad tracks at the back of our house to the little black bridge and onto the breakwater that separated the Nipigon Bay from the Nipigon River; and while standing on the breakwater I looked heavenward and pleaded with the Almighty Creator. *"God,"* I said, with my heart in my throat, *"I know that we get nothing for nothing in this world, or any world for that matter; so please tell me, what price truth?"*

I didn't expect God to answer me, and I just stared at the fast-flowing water of the Nipigon River as it ran swiftly past me on its way to Lake Superior; and this brought to mind the Preacher's words in *Ecclesiastes*, which I quoted from memory: *"What profit hath a man of all the labor which he taketh under the sun? One generation passeth away, and another generation cometh; but the earth abideth forever...all the rivers run into the sea, yet the sea is not full; unto the place whence the rivers come, thither they return again."*

And for some reason known only to the omniscient guiding force of life the tragic play *Oedipus Rex* came to my mind. King Oedipus had passed an edict that whoever was responsible for the plague that had befallen his kingdom would be banished, and he learned from his soothsayer that he was responsible for the plague because he had committed the heinous crime of murdering his father and defiling his mother's bed. Out of shame and guilt, Oedipus blinds himself and banishes himself from his own kingdom; and no sooner did this play come to mind and I knew what price I had to pay for the truth that I sought.

That's how I created my *Royal Dictum*—my edict of self-denial that I began to live the moment I stepped off the breakwater and onto the mainland. I wrote my edict down in my little pocket notebook, and I vowed that for the rest of my life I would "banish myself out of the kingdom of my own senses." *In effect, I denied myself the pleasures of life.*

And thus began my inner journey to my true self, the inner journey that my family and friends could not see because Gurdjieff made me take a vow of silence. I met him in a dream when I finally broke the code of "work on oneself" with my *Royal Dictum*, and he accepted me into his inner circle on a vow of silence; and the more I "worked" on myself with his teaching and my *Royal Dictum*, the more I awakened to the Word within; and this opened up the hidden wisdom of the sayings of Jesus like the petals of a rose.

But along the way I got stuck, because the more I "worked" on myself the more sensitive I became to human nature. I began to "see" the elusive false nature of man; but I couldn't make sense of it. And then the omniscient guiding force of life introduced me to C. G. Jung and his psychology of the self, and I learned about the repressed shadow side of the human personality and the collective Archetypal Shadow known to the world as the Devil; and I began to make psychological sense of my unbelievable journey to my true self.

I "died" to myself, and I "found" myself as Jesus promised if one found the correct interpretation of his sayings (*"He that findeth his life shall lose it; and he that loseth his life for my sake shall find it,"* said Jesus; Math. 10:39); so my quest for my true self took me through the many stages of self-transformation all the way to spiritual self-realization consciousness that I experienced one day in my mother's kitchen while she was kneading bread dough on the kitchen table, and this gave me such a clear perspective on the process of individuation that Carl Jung came to me in a dream four years ago to talk about my "Soul talk" book *The Way of Soul*, which was about Soul's journey through life. My book wasn't even transcribed yet, but on the Other Side it was published and Jung wanted to talk to me about the "alpha and omega of the self" that I had expounded upon in *The Way of Soul*.

I was so excited by my dream with Carl Jung that I made him central to my novel *The Waking Dream*; but I can talk about this at the appropriate time. For now, let me continue with the concept of the inner journey, of which dreams play the most vital role.

3. *My Inner Journey*

Without dreams we wouldn't have an inner life, and without an inner life we would be no different than any other animal. This does not mean that animals don't dream, which we can never know for sure (I believe they do); but because animals don't have a reflective self-consciousness (some primates do, and according to the latest research dolphins also have self-recognition), they don't share the same kind of dreams that we have. Or do they?

When we were building our new house in Georgian Bay our married young home builder told us that they were going to get rid of one of their cats. He was going to have her put down, which made Penny cringe. She told him that she would ask me if we could take the cat in, which she did, and I said yes.

The day before we got Hu-Lynn (that's the new name we gave the cat) Penny had a dream about her. Penny said to her in the dream, "Hey pussycat, how come you're not very playful?" And the cat replied, "I'm not used to playing."

"But Brian said he played with you all the time," Penny said.

The cat looked into Penny's eyes, and said, "Somebody's lying."

Penny was laughing so hard she woke me up. I woke her up and asked why she was laughing, and she shared her dream. When she told our young contractor her dream the next day his face turned all red because he had been found out. **Dreams don't lie.**

We've had Hu-Lynn for eight years now, and she's become very special to us. We believe she came into our life so she could grow enough in consciousness to make the quantum leap in individuation and reincarnate in her next life as a human being.

Penny has had dreams of a small boy several times now, which she believes to be our cat Hu-Lynn reincarnated in the body of a human being...

Animals are Soul too, and Soul is always in the process of individuating. Jung never spelled it out, but Soul is the collective unconscious; and the purpose of life is to individuate the collective unconsciousness until it gives birth to a reflective self, which I experienced in one of my past-life regressions to my first primordial human lifetime on earth.

The year before Penny and I moved to Georgian Bay I self-published two novel memoirs, *What Would I Say Today If I Were to Die Tomorrow?* and *On the Wings of Habitat, A Volunteer's Story*, which we launched simultaneously at the Nipigon Arena on Labor Day weekend, September 2002.

On the Wings of Habitat was inspired by my volunteer work with Habitat for Humanity; and *What Would I Say Today If I Were To Die Tomorrow?* was inspired by a woman who had been diagnosed with cancer and was given one year to live.

Ruth Picardie wrote *Before I Say Goodbye* so she could tell her children everything that she wanted to tell them but couldn't. I nearly jumped off the couch when I read this, because in one moment of synoptic awareness I saw my whole book *What Would I Say Today If I Were to Die Tomorrow?* and I wrote it in just six weeks!

I put myself under the sword of Damocles the whole time I wrote my novel memoir, because I wanted to experience what it was like to live with the threat of death hanging over my head; and this gave me such courage to speak my mind (I had nothing to lose because I was going to die tomorrow) that what I wrote so offended the good Christian people of my hometown that Penny and I had to relocate for peace of mind.

That's how we ended up in Georgian Bay. But this move was orchestrated by the omniscient guiding force of life, because the coincidence that I experienced when I drove down to Georgian Bay to find a building lot for our new house blew my mind—*to the point where I became convinced that it was not a mere coincidence, but divine intervention.*

This remarkable coincidence convinced me once and for all that we are all guided by Providence. Not that I didn't believe in God; I most certainly did. In fact, when the time is right I will share my experience of looking into the Face of God. I was one of the thirty birds in the Sufi allegory *The Conference of the Birds* that completed their quest for God and looked into the Face of God; but suffice to say now that the miraculous coincidence that I experienced convinced me that there are invisible forces working behind the scenes of life that help us realize our pre-destined purpose of total self-realization consciousness.

The Saturday morning that I was leaving to drive to Georgian Bay to look for a building lot for our new house, Penny and I hugged and kissed; and with tears in her eyes she said to me, "Find us a nice lot O, please."

What Would I Say Today If I Were to Die Tomorrow? revealed the dark shadow side of my hometown personality, and the good Christian people at Penny's workplace saw themselves in the community's shadow self and took out their anger on her, even accusing her of writing my book; and she was anxious to quit her job and relocate. I loved her so much that her request moved me to take a stand with God. *"Give me a sign which lot to buy,"* I demanded of God. I didn't care if God struck me down right then and there. *"Give me an unequivocal sign or don't even bother!"*

I was angry. I had written a book that had awakened my readers to the shadow side of life, which I felt was a significant spiritual service to life, but what the good Christian people were doing to Penny (one co-worker spit in her face) had taken its toll on us, and I had to get her out of that toxic situation; so I had my back to the wall. *"Either you give me an unequivocal sign which lot to buy, or don't even bother,"* I repeated; and I hugged and kissed Penny once more and drove the thousand miles to Georgian Bay.

Penny's friend, our home builder's father from Wasaga Beach and I checked out all the lots in the area that Penny and I had researched on the Internet, but none spoke to me; and then Penny's friend said, "I have a contractor friend who said there's building lots in Tiny Beaches. Want to check it out?"

We did; but the drive down to Tiny Beaches felt like we were going to the boonies, and I said to myself, *"Good God, where am I going to be taking Penny?"*

Being new to the area, I didn't know that we were headed for prime Georgian Bay cottage country, and it unnerved me to see so few houses; but then we came upon what looked like a small subdivision, with street signs. This gave me some relief.

We drove around the subdivision, and we did spot some lots for sale and I took down some numbers. We continued looking. And then it happened. We came upon a street called STOCCO CIRCLE. Stocco is my last name, and "O" is my nickname.

My heart stopped. I couldn't believe it. I stared at the sign incredulously. I got out of my friend's truck and looked at the sign to make sure my eyes weren't deceiving me, but they weren't. *"Please God,"* I pleaded, *"let there be a lot for sale on this street."*

There was only one lot for sale, which I learned later had just gone up for sale that week, and five thousand dollars below our allotted budget, and I bought it; and we got a mortgage on our triplex in Nipigon and built our new house on STOCCO CIRCLE, the street with my name. And if that wasn't divine intervention, I don't know what is.

And it came as no surprise to hear Penny say, after living in our new house for a few years and being acquainted with the whole Simcoe County, "I love where we live, O. Of all the places down here, I like our area the best."

I silently thanked God...

Getting back to my regression to my first primordial human life on earth and my other past lives most relevant to my spiritual quest, like my lifetime as Phaedrus, student of Pythagoras in ancient Greece; my lifetime as Samuel the Essene, during the time of Jesus; my lifetime as Salaam the Sufi in medieval Persia; my extreme lifetime in Paris, France as a sexually and morally depraved man out to avenge myself with God and Jesus and the Holy Mother Church that had betrayed my love for the woman I was to marry; my lifetime with Penny as Don Giovanni in Genoa, Italy that karmically compelled us to meet again in this life; and my immediate past life in London, England as Daniel Wellington, Earl of Wellington Manor that set the stage for my current life to connect with the secret teachings of the Way in Gurdjieff's teaching. These lives had an enormous effect upon my current life, and by the time I wrote *What Would I Say Today If I Were To Die Tomorrow?* I had found my true self; so I had solved the riddle of my life that I had set out to solve.

I had answered the question *who am I?* many years before I had my regressions, and I had also answered man's most haunting question, *why am I?* But there were still a few pieces to the puzzle that were missing. That's why the omniscient guiding force of life provided me with the opportunity to find them in my re-awakened desire to learn about my past lives when Penny and I relocated to Georgian Bay.

Ever since I read Jess Stearn's book on the lives of Taylor Caldwell (*The Search for the Soul: Psychic Lives of Taylor Caldwell*), I wanted to write a book on my own past lives; and the opportunity presented itself when I met a woman in Orillia who was a member of our spiritual community who told us she did past-life regressions.

Long story short (I wrote a novel called *Cathedral of My Past Lives*, but I have put it aside until I feel it's ready to be published), in one of my regressions I was brought back to the Body of God where all souls come from, In the Body of God, which in our spiritual path is called the Ocean of Love and Mercy. I experienced myself as an atom of God; but I did not have self-consciousness. I had Soul consciousness, but no self-consciousness. And in this same regression I was brought back to my first primordial human life on earth where I experienced the actual dawning of my own reflective self-consciousness.

I experienced the birth of my reflective self. I was the alpha male of a group of ten or twelve hominids, and for some reason (which I explain in *Cathedral of My Past Lives*) I broke free of my group consciousness and experienced the birth of my own reflective self-consciousness; and as rudimentary as my reflective self was, I *knew* that I was separate from my group consciousness; and this had a very strange effect on me.

My attention was now focused inward instead of outward; and from that lifetime on my reflective self grew and evolved with each new life that I was born into, until centuries later in my current life I had evolved enough in self-consciousness to take evolution into my own hands with Gurdjieff's teaching, my *Royal Dictum*, and the sayings of Jesus and consciously participated in my own individuation process and gave birth to my spiritual self one fine day in my mother's kitchen.

There was only one more piece missing for me to see the big picture of life, but I had that mysterious piece locked away in the back of my mind with an experience that I had many years ago when I first began living Gurdjieff's teaching.

It was early spring. I was sitting on a chair at the back of our family home. I leaned my chair back and rested my head against the warm stucco of the house and closed my eyes to soak in the warm rays of the sun. I drifted off.

Slowly, without any thoughts on my mind whatsoever, I began to drift back through time. I wasn't paying attention to what was happening, I just went with it; and I drifted back through the weeks, months, years, decades, millenniums, and eons—*all the way back to when there was absolutely no life on the planet at all.*

And then I saw the gases of the barren Earth rise up to meet the gases of the sky, and as they mingled they formed tiny nuclei which I learned years later must have been amino acids, the first building blocks of life, because in that moment of their creation I felt myself entering into the life process—**and I knew that this was the genesis of life on Planet Earth.**

Soul consciousness entering into the amino acids to begin the life process was the third and final piece to the puzzle of life (the first piece was coming from the Body of God as an un-self-realized atom, or soul seed; and the second piece was the dawning of my reflective self-consciousness); but it took several years of creative writing after my regressions to connect all the dots that formed a picture of the Divine Plan of God.

Once the picture formed in my mind I could not deny what I saw: **God created life so God could individuate through life and grow in God-realization Consciousness.** In a word, God created life to give birth to God—which was exactly the same conclusion that C. G. Jung came to with his unbelievable confrontation with the unconscious that he recorded in *Liber Novus*, his iconic *Red Book* that his family finally gave permission to publish half a century after Jung's translation to the Other Side.

God sends its un-self-realized atoms into the lower worlds to grow and evolve in consciousness so they can give birth to a new "I" of God, and the new "I" of God grows and evolves through the natural individuation process of life until it realizes total self-identity, which is spiritual self-realization and God consciousness. *This is why we are!*

4. *The Mystery of the Way*

When I learned that Carl Jung believed that the essential principle of individual consciousness is to become itself, which is to individuate the self, I breathed a sigh of relief because he confirmed what I had discovered for myself. I found my own path, actively participated in my own individuation process, and *became* my true self.

"Unconscious wholeness therefore seems to me the true *spiritus rector* of biological and psychic events. Here is a principle which strives for total realization—which in man's case signifies the attainment of total consciousness," wrote Jung in *Memories, Dreams, Reflections* (p. 324). But how can man do this if not by finding the Way?

"Whosoever drinketh of the water that I shall give him shall never thirst; but the water that I shall give him shall be in him a well of water springing up into everlasting life," said Jesus (John 4: 14). I "drank" in the "water of everlasting life" that Jesus talked about as I "worked" on myself with Gurdjieff's teaching and the sayings of Jesus, but this is such a mystical experience that it is almost impossible to put to words.

This is why I enjoyed talking with St. Padre Pio when he was channeled for my spiritual healing sessions, because his suffering for Jesus had awakened him to the Word within also and we had a meeting of minds on the mystery of the Way.

"Life is a journey of the self," St. Padre Pio told me, which resonated completely with my conviction that life is an individual journey (the Sufis have a saying that there are as many ways to God as there are souls of man); but when I was nudged to re-study Jung's psychology of the individuation process and listen to the conversation that Fraser Boa had with Dr. Marie-Louise von Franz in the documentary *The Way of the*

Dream, a light went on in my mind and I realized that **dreams are the Way**.

Dreams are not the only way, but they are the Way for Jungians like Dr. Marie-Louise von Franz just as Gurdjieff's teaching of "work on oneself" was the Way for me, and painting can be the Way for the artist (as Jerry Wennstrom tells us in his book *The Inspired Heart*), and writing poetry can be the Way for the poet (as David Whyte tells us in his book *Crossing the Unknown Sea*), and music can be the Way for the musician (as Victor L. Wooten's autobiographical novel *The Music Lesson* exemplifies), and "entering the castle" can be the Way for anyone, as Caroline Myss teaches with workshops on her book *Entering the Castle: Finding the Inner Path to God and Your Soul's Purpose*—meaning, each person becomes their own Way when they tap into the "water of everlasting life" within with their individual passion for life, regardless which path one chooses to take.

But how can this be? What is this mysterious quality about the Way that manifests itself in every soul accordingly, and in some cases like the founder of *Sacred Activism* Andrew Harvey combust one's soul with the Holy Fire of God? And just how does it manifest itself? That's the mystery many people become aware of but can't explain; which may very well be the connecting theme of *The Summoning of Noman*.

I found the Way, and I *know* what the Way is. I have italicized the word "know" on purpose to distinguish knowing from realization. It is one thing to know something mentally, but it's quite another to have the realization of what one knows. Realization is born of experience, and it is a *knowing* on the deepest level possible—the Soul level. This is the kind of *knowing* that Gnostics called gnosis. As Spinoza expressed it, **"understanding is not understanding until you experience it."**

So what have I realized about the Way that may explain the omniscient guiding force of life—because that's what the Way is, the all-knowing guiding force of life?

When Canadian artist Robert Bateman came to an impasse with his art, the omniscient guiding force of life came to his aid and set him back on track. He was painting abstract art for years, but he outgrew the path of painting abstract art and one day stood back and looked at the last piece he had just painted, studied and pondered it and then said to himself, *"Is that it? Is that all there is to art?"* And he fell into a deep slump.

That's what happens when one comes to an impasse on the path they are on; but then something happens to set us straight, as it did Robert Bateman. He was nudged to go to a viewing of Andrew Wyeth's work across the border in the states, and as he studied the American realist painter's art he had a revelation, which he called his road to Damascus.

"I found my way!" he exclaimed, on the biography channel; and he went back to his roots and became one of the world's foremost nature artists. In fact, the fire of his passion for painting nature burned so deeply in his soul that he became an active environmentalist who generously devoted his time, talent, and money to help save our environment—a*nd this opens up the door to the mysterious redemptive power of the Way.*

Just listen to Andrew Harvey talking about "sacred activism," or Caroline Myss talking about "entering the castle"—they are burning with a passion to save the world; but does the world really need to be saved? That's the question I asked in the last chapter of my book, *Old Whore Life, Exploring the Shadow Side of Karma;* and the answer that my Muse gave me was that the world is what it is, and if it's not one thing it's going to be another; meaning, we do what we can to realize the ideal of our path and let the universe unfold as it will. In Jung's words, "The goal is important only as an idea; the essential thing is the *opus* which leads to the goal: *that* is the goal of a lifetime!"

"I want you to tell him that what he is talking about is a question of trust," St. Padre Pio told Angie (her fictional name) who was channeling him for my spiritual healing when I confronted him on the question of Christ's crucifixion. I wanted him to tell me that Jesus' death on the cross did not absolve us of our sins, because I knew that he knew that karma was a personal responsibility; but I was much too spiritually naïve to appreciate why Jesus died on the cross, and St. Padre Pio had to patiently wean me in my understanding.

In short, we have to trust the omniscient guiding force of life. We have to trust that there is order to the universe, and things are as they are because this is the way they are supposed to be in the Divine Plan of God, and as difficult as it was for me to wrap my mind around this by the time I came out of my healing sessions with St. Padre Pio I understood exactly what he meant, because my passion to be right in my spiritual conviction was tempered by the enormous power of his redemptive love for humanity.

"There is no one way," he told me; but I did not entirely grasp what he meant by this simple statement. Only after the healing grace of his redemptive love slew the spirit of my vanity did I begin to appreciate that **all ways *are* the Divine Plan of God**; and the most that we can do is to live our own way with passion and integrity, and trust God.

Frank Sinatra tells us in his song that he did it his way, and many people who realize their life's dream will tell you that they did it their way; but what is the defining factor of the Way that makes it a universal path? What is this mystery that we call the Way?

When I outgrew Gurdjieff's teaching I did not want to move on to another path more suited to my new state of consciousness (this happens to most people who outgrow their path, especially Christians), despite the fact that I had already found my new path when I reconnected with the secret teaching that Pythagoras taught me in my past lifetime in ancient Greece; so the omniscient guiding force of life stepped in to set me straight.

Robert Bateman was nudged to view Andrew Wyeth's work, which set him on his road to Damascus, and the omniscient guiding force of life gave me a dream that shattered my psychic (unconscious) dependence on Gurdjieff, which gave me the freedom to step onto my new path without the guilt of betraying Gurdjieff.

Whenever I dreamt of Gurdjieff he was always dressed in white, and there was always a glow of benevolence about him; but this time I dreamt of him dressed in black, and there was an ominous air about him that scared me, especially his big dark eyes and black moustache. He looked absolutely menacing. Upon reflection I came to the conclusion that the Dream Weaver had spun that dream to liberate me of the psychic hold that I had upon myself with my loyalty to Gurdjieff and the Work.

Gurdjieff was my salvation. If it wasn't for his teaching I don't know how I would have worked my way through my false self; so I didn't want to move on to the spiritual path that would take me the rest of the way to wholeness and singleness of self. But I experienced the dark side of Gurdjieff's personality in my dream, and I got frightened.

But my attachment to Gurdjieff was so strong that even that dream wasn't enough for me to let go of the Work and move on; so the Dream Weaver spun another remarkable dream to help make up my mind: I met Dr. Maurice Nicoll in my dream, who on the Other Side was an initiate of the new spiritual teaching that I was reluctant to embrace.

Doctor Nicoll was one of my favorite teachers of Gurdjieff's System, and I devoured his five volume set of books called *Psychological Commentaries on the Teachings of Gurdjieff and Ouspensky*, and I especially relished his books *The New Man* and *The Mark* because they spoke to my fascination with the secret aspect of Christ's teaching that I had awakened to; and I woke up from my dream with the conviction that Gurdjieff had served his purpose in my quest for personal wholeness, and that it was time for me to move on to my new spiritual path of the Way of the Eternal as Dr. Maurice Nicoll had done.

With a heavy heart I said goodbye to Gurdjieff, promising him that one day I would make a trip to Fontainebleau-Avon, France and lay a single yellow rose on his gravestone; and I dropped Gurdjieff's teaching and became an initiate of the Way of the Eternal, which has proven to be the path best suited for my spiritual growth. And this opens the door to one of the unfathomable mysteries of the Way—*dreams as a gateway to other worlds.*

5. *When the Student is Ready*

Dr. Maurice Nicoll was an exceptional man. He was kind, generous, and humble with everyone who came into his life; and it's not surprising that he should move on to the higher teachings of the Light and Sound of God in the Way of the Eternal.

The Work made him ready for the most direct path to God, and he came to me in my dream to inform me that I was also ready; that's why he convinced me that I had to let go of my emotional attachment to Gurdjieff and the Work.

Dr. Nicoll had a medical practice on Harley Street in London where he was known as London's leading neurologist and one of Britain's leading psychologists. He studied under C. G. Jung in Switzerland and was a Jungian analyst before discovering the Work through P. D. Ouspensky. He said that meeting Carl Jung was the first important event of his life, and he wrote one of the first books on Jungian dream interpretation—*Dream Psychology*, which I read along with Nicoll's other books. He and his wife spent part of their honeymoon with Emma and Carl Jung, and he remained lifelong friends with the man who also had an enormous impact upon my life and whom I was also privileged to meet on the Other Side in a dream to talk about my book *The Way of Soul*.

I don't recall my whole dream with Dr. Nicoll, but he left a lasting impression. The goodness that shone through in his books was so palpable in the person of my dream that he convinced me it was time to let go of the Work and move on to my new path. He was delighted that I had found it. Curiously enough though, the Way of the Eternal had not yet been brought out to the modern world when Dr. Nicoll died in 1953. It wasn't introduced until 1965; which meant that he must have found it on the Other Side.

But what was so special about the Work that it made us ready for the most direct path to God? It has become a cliché among seekers that when the student is ready the teacher will appear, but as cliché as this may be it is still true; and what makes a student ready for his new teacher is his state of consciousness.

Consciousness determines our station in life. This is where expressions like "misery loves company" and "birds of a feather flock together" come from. The level of our consciousness attracts our life because of the Spiritual Law of Attraction; and the Work (along with my *Royal Dictum* and the sayings of Jesus) had transformed my consciousness enough for me to gravitate to the spiritual teachings of the Light and Sound of God.

What exactly did the Work do for me, then? And why did I have such fascination for Gurdjieff and his remarkable teaching? If we are attracted to the teaching that best serves our state of consciousness, what state of consciousness was I in when I found Gurdjieff's mystifying teaching of self-transformation?

I was in my second year at university when Gurdjieff's teaching came into my life. I became friendly with another philosophy student, who hailed from Toronto. When he came back to university from the Christmas break he brought a book for me that he felt would interest me. This book was *In Search of the Miraculous, Fragments of an Unknown Teaching*, by P. D. Ouspensky. That's how I "discovered" the Work.

But what was my state of consciousness at the time that this teaching should fall into my lap, as it were? What made me ready for the Work?

By the middle of my second year of studies I began to feel a dreading sense of despair, because philosophy wasn't taking me where I wanted to go. I wanted to find my true self; that's why I went to university. I thought philosophy would help me, but I began to sense myself drifting off into a sea of endless, albeit brilliant speculation; and there just seemed to be no end to philosophy.

I was in a state of confusion, and the more I drifted out on this sea of Sartre-Camus-Russell-Nietzsche-Hegel-Kierkegaard-Schopenhauer-Descarte-Locke-Hume-Kant-Spinoza-Hobbes and endless speculation, the more I lost my bearings; that's why the omniscient guiding force of life brought my teacher to me, because I had to get my bearings to find my true self, and Gurdjieff's teaching would bring order into my life and ground me.

Obviously, the mystique that surrounded George Ivanovitch Gurdjieff cast a spell on me; but it was his teaching that spoke to my soul. I was quickly getting lost at sea, and the Work came into my life like a fresh wind that caught my sails; but I would not get back to *terra firma* unless I began to "work" on myself; so I delved into the Ouspensky's book and did my best to put Gurjdieff's transformative teaching to practice.

Gurdjieff spent years searching for the meaning of life, and he travelled far and wide to get an answer to his question *"what is the sense and significance of life on the earth in general and of human life in particular?"* He studied many teachings and was initiated into some of the most secret mystery schools; and when he found what he was looking for he put his esoteric knowledge and gnostic understanding into a teaching that he called the Fourth Way, which he also called the Work, "work on oneself," the System, and my favorite name for his remarkable teaching of self-transformation, "the way of the sly man."

The "sly man" is someone who has discovered the secret of how to "catch" that special energy that one needs to grow in spiritual consciousness. I had a past lifetime as an Essene during the time of Jesus, and I studied the secret teaching of self-transformation at the Essene community at Qumran, and I was taught how to "catch" this special energy that we called "the sweet nectar of life," so I had a pre-conscious knowledge of Gurdjieff's System that I awakened to as I "worked" on myself with his teaching.

The central idea of the Work is that humanity is asleep and must awaken through intense self-observation. One must die to oneself and the thousand and one attachments that one has made in life so that a new real "I" can emerge. That resonated with me, because it spoke to my voracious need to find my true self.

But Gurdjieff's teaching was extreme. So extreme in fact that many of his students left the Work brokenhearted. And some had emotional breakdowns, not to mention students that were so stressed by the Work that they took their own life.

The Work was not an easy teaching to live, which is why Ouspensky finally broke off with Gurdjieff and moderated the Work, and which Dr. Nicoll moderated even further with his great compassion for seekers. But what made Gurdjieff's teaching so extreme?

Gurdjieff called his teaching "esoteric Christianity," and by that he meant that it wasn't religion as such, but an inner meaning of what Jesus taught his disciples in secret; a teaching about the inner evolution of humanity. Gurdjieff believed that not everyone was born with an immortal soul. Only certain people had an embryonic soul, which they created out of extraordinary life circumstances; and he provided these special circumstances with the Work. That's what made his teaching so extreme—because it demanded an impossible level of effort and commitment to create one's own soul.

I was willing to pay any price to find my true self; that's why I took to the Work with such abandon, and I could feel the results of the Work almost immediately. It seemed to satisfy me on a very deep level, and the more I "worked" on myself the more committed I became to living the Work—to the point where I became pathological in my efforts to transform my consciousness and "create" my own soul.

I was willing to pay any price to find my true self; that's why I created my *Royal Dictum*. But I hit a brick wall. I left university in the second semester of my third year and after several jobs started my own contract painting business, which was perfect for "working" on myself because the Work was best lived out in the real world.

Life was my teacher, and I could practice the techniques for self-transformation anywhere under any conditions, which often presented me with more challenges than I could handle. The basic technique was *self-observation*. I had to become aware of myself under all circumstances, and I had to practice the technique of *non-identifying* with my negative emotions—which included all of my desires that I denied with my *Royal Dictum*.

I had to do the impossible. But despite my Herculean efforts, I could not "catch" enough energy to "create" my own soul, and I fell into such despair that I didn't know where to turn. I felt lost and abandoned. And then it happened.

I was sitting in my basement bedroom in my parent's home wallowing in despair. I had Beethoven's Ninth Symphony playing to pick up my dejected spirit, and then the omniscient guiding force of life spoke to me for the first time. I heard a voice in my mind ask me the question, *"Why do you lie?"*

I was shocked into awareness. The voice was real. I heard it as plain as if the person was standing beside me. It was a male voice asking me why I lied; and that simple question had enough energy to fuel my quest for years, all the way to my true self, because in my efforts to answer that question I had to work my way through the false consciousness of my *non-being*—the archetypal shadow consciousness of all my past lives!

Carl Jung said that it takes great moral effort to see one's shadow, but so Gurdjieffian were my efforts to catch myself in a lie that I developed a sixth sense and began to see everybody's shadow, and I could even see the Archetypal Shadow.

"Satan, you are so crafty that I know not which is you and which is me," I wrote in my journal, when I finally saw the archetype of all shadows; and so effective did I become at "dying" to my false self that I gave "birth" to my true self in my mother's kitchen one fine summer day while she was kneading bread dough on the kitchen table.

So Gurdjieff's teaching had served its purpose, and in that same kitchen where I gave birth to my spiritual self I was introduced to the Way of the Eternal when one of my distant cousins and initiate of the Light and Sound of God came to pay my mother a visit and fill up her five gallon blue jug with tap water to bring to her summer cottage.

By "chance" I happened to pop home from a job I was working when she was visiting my mother, who was sitting at the kitchen table, and I stood in the same doorway where I had experienced my own immortality when my cousin asked me if I believed in reincarnation. I wasn't sure where she was going with that, because my cousin was rather "peculiar," but I told her that I did.

"Have you heard of a teaching called the Way of the Eternal?" she asked.

"No. What's it about?" I asked.

"It's based on karma and reincarnation. It's the most direct path to God. I have some books at the cottage if you're interested. Drop by later."

I did. That's how I found my new teacher. I was ready, and the omniscient guiding force of life brought my new path right to my house!

On February 10, 2012 I recorded the following dream: *I'm a teacher, counselor, and guide to a group of twenty to thirty students. We're on a school bus going somewhere. I don't know where, but these are not ordinary students. Each student is gifted in a special way, and I am teaching and guiding them in their studies to bring out their special gift. In another sequence I'm back in school, a university setting, and I'm studying again.*

The gifted students symbolize those individuals that are ready for the teaching that will help them grow in who they are; and being true to the Law of Attraction, I'm the teacher that has come into their life to teach them what they need to know to grow in their unique individuality. Their special gift suggests that they are karmically ready for the teaching that will connect them with their inner self. And finding myself back in university tells me that I'm also embarking on a new learning curve with my new book *The Summoning of Noman, The True Story of My Parallel Life.*

6. *Are Dreams a Gateway to the Inner Worlds?*

The mystery of life is the mystery of the self. Solve the mystery of the self, and we solve the mystery of life. That's why Carl Jung came to me in a dream. He had read my "Soul talk" book *The Way of Soul* on the Other Side, and he wanted to discuss what I knew about what he referred to as "the alpha and omega of the self."

But was it Carl Jung that I met in my dream, or was he an archetypal manifestation of my unconscious? That's one question about dreams that Jungian dream interpretation doesn't answer, because it opens up the question of soul and the afterlife.

In the famous BBC "Face to Face" interview late in his life Jung was asked by John Freeman if death was the end, and he gave a cautious, psychologically-couched answer about the peculiar nature of the psyche that suggests it lives on after death; but in my dream Jung laughed at the game he had to play with the public about the immortal soul of man just to preserve the scientific credibility of his psychology. That's why a few months before he died he wrote to an English correspondent, *"I have failed in my foremost task to open people's eyes to the fact that man has a soul, that there is a treasure buried in the field."*

I was shocked to learn that my "Soul talk" book *The Way of Soul* was published on the Other Side, because I hadn't even transcribed the tapes yet. I had only begun transcribing the first tape, and *The Way of Soul* was a long way from becoming a publishable book; so what does it mean to have Jung come to me in my dream to talk about a book that was published over "there" but not "here"?

What is "there" and what is "here"? Are they two separate worlds? And do dreams bridge these two worlds? Are dreams a gateway to the inner worlds?

This is what Pythagoras taught, which I wrote about in *The Waking Dream*. This novel was scheduled to be published by the same publisher that put out my novel *My Unborn Child*, but I asked to be released from my contract because I didn't feel comfortable with the direction my editor wanted to take *The Waking Dream*.

Pythagoras taught us (a small group of students that studied the Way with him in secret, which incidentally was not in Greece; Pythagoras was living in Italy at the time) that dreams were a gateway to the inner worlds; and when I reconnected with the same teaching when I found The Way of the Eternal I was once again initiated into the secret way of dreams. That's why I drew a distinction between the Jungian interpretation of dreams and my spiritual path—until I was nudged to do more research on Jung and the way of dreams and realized that both interpretations were true—meaning, **dreams are both a manifestation of the unconscious and a gateway to the inner worlds.**

But how can this be? Did I meet Gurdjieff on the Other Side in my dreams? Did I meet Dr. Nicoll on the Other Side in my dream? Were Gurdjieff and Nicoll manifestations of my unconscious, or were they real individual souls? Or both?

Dr. Nicoll could not have been an initiate of The Way of the Eternal when he was alive, because this ancient spiritual path was not introduced to the modern world until 1965, and he died in 1953. But there he was in my dream trying to convince me that I had outgrown the Work and it was time for me to move on, as he had done—which brings up another question: does life on the Other Side continue from where we leave off here, because Dr. Nicoll had dropped the Work and was now living The Way of the Eternal?

Carl Jung was still curious to know about the "alpha and omega of the self"; that's why he wanted to talk about my book *The Way of Soul*. Was he continuing his research on the Other Side, or was his appearance in my dream an archetypal manifestation of my own creative unconscious to further my own individuation process?

When I dropped out of university because I felt that I had been cast adrift in a sea of endless philosophical speculation that was taking me further away from my true self, I made myself a solemn promise to build my life upon the truth that I experienced and not anyone else's truth; that's why I had such a passion for the Work—because it engaged me with the real world, and my relationship with life initiated me into the mysteries of life.

This is what my third dream in my journal revealed (February 5, 2012), that my intercourse with life initiated me into "the Wisdom." And my "wisdom" informed me that dreams are a gateway to the Other Side, because everything that I have learned about myself on my quest for my true self tells me that **we are all born with a spark of divine consciousness** (contrary to what Gurdjieff believed); that **we grow and evolve through many incarnations** (which I proved for myself with my past-life regressions) **until we realize our true self** (which I experienced in my mother's kitchen); and that **our dreams are the inner path to our true self.** And when we die we continue our life on the Other Side, just as my dreams of Gurdjieff, Nicoll, and Jung proved to me; and if that isn't proof enough for me, St. Padre Pio verified this in my spiritual healing sessions.

In my final session I thanked St. Padre Pio for everything he had done for me (I did get a spiritual healing), and then he thanked me—*because he said that our sessions were helping him in his own studies.* This told me what I already knew, that when we cross over to the Other Side we continue with our personal interests until we are ready to be reborn to tie up our karmic loose ends in the physical world; or, if we are evolved enough, we can choose to stay on the Other Side or move on to another world to serve God in the Divine Plan of expanding the Consciousness of God.

St. Padre Pio opened up my world. I went into my spiritual healing sessions with such spiritual conceit that only the humility of a Saint who had suffered the holy wounds of Jesus Christ for fifty years could break down my vanity; and I came out of my ten spiritual healing sessions a different person—*with my tail between my legs!*

Padre Pio is more than a Saint; he's an Ascended Spiritual Master. I came to that conclusion after three sessions because of the way he came through for me. I asked him some hard questions about Christianity, and his answer to my question about sin proved to me that he had transcended the dogmatic consciousness of his Roman Catholic faith and was speaking from a higher spiritual plane. "From my place of all knowing and all seeing, there is no sin," he replied to my outrageously bold question.

I pressed him on that point because it was pivotal that I cleared up this whole issue of sin and damnation, which meant that Jesus did not die for the sins of the world, as the Catholic Church taught, but for other reasons that St. Padre Pio helped make clear for me; but I have explored this in my novel *Healing with Padre Pio* and I need not explicate here.

I simply wanted to make the point that our life continues on the Other Side when we have shuffled off this mortal coil, and we can journey to the Other Side in our dreams, which many of my dreams have confirmed; but like Carl Jung, I now believe that by following the messages of our dreams we can shine a light on our path to wholeness, which is why I was inspired to start keeping a new dream journal.

7. The Summoning of Noman

I left university in my third year of studies because I could not trust where philosophy was taking me. From one perspective, it was foolish to not finish and get my degree; but I was so driven to find my true self that I had to go where the "scent" took me. Like the hound in Francis Thompson's poem "The Hound of Heaven," when I was commanded by the Call of God, I had to go—*"Rise, clasp my Hand, and come!"*

It wasn't until I had seven past life regressions many years after I left university that I understood why I was driven with such pathological need to find my true self, but I did have a waking dream experience in high school that not only foretold but combusted my quest for my true self. This was the experience of writing a poem called *Noman*.

I was in grade twelve. Our English teacher asked the class to write a poem and he would select the best one for the yearbook. I had discovered literature by the time I reached grade twelve, and I read a great deal. I didn't know what it was about literature that attracted me, but it seemed to call me; like it had its own distinct voice.

I didn't know what the voice of literature was in grade twelve, but I do now; it's the voice of the Way. It's the voice of truth. **"Poetry,"** said the poet Adrienne Rich, **"is an act of the imagination that transforms reality into a deeper perception of what is."** This holds true for all literature, because this mysterious, often impenetrable **what is**, is the essential truth of the human condition—however the human condition manifests; be it a small, insignificant experience, a great romance, or a tragic, life-changing catastrophe.

"Art" (literature) said the author of *Out of Africa*, Karen Blixen, **"is the truth above the facts of life,"** which speaks to Adrienne's Rich's definition of poetry; but so far above the facts of life was the symbolic truth of my poem *Noman* that it took years to make sense of it. Once I did however, I saw my whole experience as a waking dream that spoke to my quest for my true self through the recalcitrant consciousness of my *non-being*, which was symbolized by the false self of Everyman—meaning, the archetypal Noman.

A waking dream is like a night dream, only it happens out here in our everyday conscious life; but it stands out from our everyday experiences. We may not recognize a waking dream when we experience it, but **we have waking dreams when the unconscious wants us to know something about ourselves that our conscious mind resists**.

Waking dreams presupposes the individuation process of the inner self, that spark of divine consciousness in everyman that is teleologically driven to return to God. But this journey to God is long and arduous, and only when the self has realized the fruit of the individuation process—which is to become a selfless self, as St. Padre Pio confirmed in one of my spiritual healing sessions— will the self realize its spiritual destiny.

Late in his life Jung was informed by his dream that he had "achieved wholeness and singleness" of self, which meant that he had integrated himself into one individual self and realized the purpose of his own individuation process; but he wasn't finished yet. He was still driven by the imperative of his Soul self to realize his pre-scripted purpose of spiritual self-realization and God consciousness; this is why he came to me in my dream.

Jung wanted to learn what I knew about Soul's journey home to God, which was the theme of my book *The Way of Soul* that he had read on the Other Side; and this is what my poem *Noman* was about—Soul's archetypal journey through the false consciousness of its *non-being*, or inauthentic self. Noman was everyman's false self, and the Archetypal Noman possessed my soul; that's why I *had* to write that poem!

Writing *Noman* was a waking dream. Unfortunately I don't have a copy of my poem, and the only lines that I remember are the closing two lines, which are so powerful that I can only reveal them after I have provided the proper context; but someday I may solicit the assistance of a good hypnotherapist to recover my poem, because it was so fraught with symbols that I would love to study that poem today from the perspective of having solved the purpose of life, which is to expand the consciousness of God.

I do however recall the narrative of my poem, and only after some deep thought did it occur to me that *Noman* was set free from the profound depths of my unconscious because I had opened the trap door to the collective psyche of man with my "inspired" reading of the medieval morality play *Everyman* several days (or perhaps weeks; it is too far back to remember precisely when I read the play) before writing my poem *Noman*.

This Christian morality play must have touched my soul so deeply that my creative unconscious took this opportunity to wake me up to my spiritual situation, and I woke up one morning with the most burning desire to write a poem—and out spewed *Noman* in a torrential flood of uncontrollable passion. I was totally possessed by my daemon, and I experienced every word that poured out of me—*because I was Noman!*

In the anonymous play *Everyman*, God sends his messenger Death to summon Everyman (every person in the world) for a reckoning; but Everyman is not ready to die, and he asks Death for more time to prepare himself to meet God.

Death refuses, and Everyman panics. He asks his friends (symbolized in the person Fellowship) to accompany him, but they turn him down; then he asks his family (Kindred and Cousin), but they too refuse; and then he asks Goods (the material possessions that he has stored), but Goods refuses also.

Now desperate, Everyman asks Good Deeds, who wants to accompany him but cannot because he is too weak (symbolizing that Everyman had not done many good deeds in his life); but Good Deeds introduces Everyman to his sister Knowledge, who says she can help him by taking him to Confession. Everyman weeps with joy.

Confession tells Everyman that he will give him the precious gift of penance if he will confess his sins. Everyman calls upon the Lord to forgive his sins, and then Knowledge informs him that Good Deeds is strong enough now to accompany him, telling Everyman that he is now prepared for eternity, and Knowledge outfits Everyman with the robe of contrition to wear on his journey to eternity. The robe signifies repentance.

Good Deeds introduces Everyman to Discretion, Strength, his Five Wits, and Beauty and asks them to accompany Everyman on his journey. Knowledge then tells Everyman that he must receive the last sacrament of the Church, which he receives, and Discretion, Strength, Five Wits, and Beauty go with Everyman to his grave but refuse to accompany him to the afterlife. But Good Deeds says, "Nay, Everyman. I will bid with thee." Knowledge stays behind; only Good Deeds accompanies Everyman to the afterlife.

That's the story of *Everyman*. In my narrative poem *Noman*, God's messenger informs me that God wants a reckoning, and I am brought to the Court of God. God says to me, "Noman, hast thou my fish's scale?" I answer that I do not have it, and God sends me into the "abyss with four corners" (the world) to find the "fish's scale" and return it to God.

God imposes conditions upon my return to the "abyss with four corners." I have three days to search for the "fish's scale" in the "abyss," but it takes one whole day to search each "corner" of the "abyss." This means that if I do not find God's "fish's scale" within my allotted three days, I will have failed because there would still be one corner left to search.

So I go back to earth in search of the "fish's scale" (which I deciphered years later to mean my lost soul) in the first "corner." (The four corners of the "abyss" symbolize the four points of the compass: North, South, East, and West; and they also, as I later came to realize, symbolize the four planes of consciousness of the lower worlds of God—the physical, astral, causal, and mental planes). And at the end of the first day I can hear God's booming voice: "NOMAN, HAST THOU MY FISH'S SCALE?"

44

THE SUMMONING OF NOMAN

I answer that I do not have it, and I proceed to look in the second "corner." I don't remember what I found in the first "corner," nor in the second, but it wasn't my lost soul; and once again, at the end of the second day God shouts: 'NOMAN, HAST THOU MY FISH'S SCALE." Again I say no, and proceed to the third "corner."

Once again, I cannot remember what I found in the third "corner" (aside from a very vague memory that had to do with my mother), but at the end of the day God once again shouts down to me: "NOMAN, HAST THOU MY FISH'S SCALE?"

I do not have it, and I am summoned back to God's Court. I tremble before God as I wait for God to pronounce sentence. God condemns me to the fourth corner for eternity to find my lost soul, and as I fall from heaven into the abyss I shout:

"Open you vile, voracious, loveable sweet whore!
God, why hast thou forsaken me?"

Thus ends my poem *Noman*, with me wandering throughout my little corner of the world in search of my lost soul. This is a powerful waking dream. This is an eruption of the archetypal false self of man into the full light of conscious awareness, and like all big dreams that come from the collective unconscious it is fraught with such symbolic meaning that it took years to make sense of it—*but only after I had found my lost soul!*

But why did I shout what I did as I fell from heaven? Why would I call life a "vile, voracious, loveable sweet whore"? I was a virgin when I wrote this poem. Was this my "inspired" motivation for writing my book of spiritual musings, *Old Whore Life: Exploring the Shadow Side of Karma*? Why was I so angry at life? Why was I so angry at God?

This is why I went for a spiritual healing with Ascended Master St. Padre Pio on August 9, 2010 (followed by nine more sessions), because I had so much anger in me. I relate my experience in my novel *Healing with Padre Pio*, and I'm happy to say that St. Padre Pio did heal me of my anger issues with God and the Roman Catholic Church—*which I finally learned were a carry-over from my past lifetime in Paris, France.*

Although the Noman of my poem is the archetypal false self of every soul in the world, it was *specifically* my false self as well; that's why my poem was fraught with such volcanic daimonic energy. Noman was the collective false self of all my past life personalities, the archetypal shadow of every personality that I have lived in this "abyss with four corners" that we call life.

I was Noman, and I was everyman's archetypal shadow; and when I was condemned to the world for eternity to find my lost soul, I symbolized everyman's quest for salvation—hence the outrage that Noman expresses when he falls from heaven, because Noman cannot understand how God could be so unfair. It's like Noman was asking, "what have I done that God would condemn me forever to the fourth corner of the abyss?"

To answer that I have to ask myself, *"what happened to me that made me so angry at God?"* And the answer lies in my past lifetime in Paris when I came to be known as *"le salaud de Paris,"* the infamous "scoundrel of Paris," because the universal story of Soul's individuation through life is told through the individual life of every soul, and as *Noman* spoke my personal journey through life so too did it speak every soul's journey through the consciousness of *non-being*—meaning, the false self of man.

But not every soul that journeys through the consciousness of *non-being* achieves wholeness and singleness of self. I did, but Jung did not. In his lifetime as the psychoanalyst C. G. Jung, the central archetype of his life (his Soul self) chose to achieve wholeness and singleness of self through the consciousness of his *being*—meaning, his authentic, or real self, which Jung called his "I am" consciousness; whereas in my current lifetime (my parallel life, that is) my Soul self chose to individuate through the consciousness of my *non-being*—meaning, my inauthentic, or false self.

It took years to part the veil of this elusive mystery, but I finally saw that we can choose the path that we want to achieve wholeness and singleness of self: the path of *being* or *non-being*.

This presupposes karma and reincarnation, the twin spiritual laws that determine our two destines in life—our personal destiny, and our spiritual destiny.

Jung's psychology doesn't include this understanding, which makes it that much more difficult to see the big picture of our journey through life (and, no doubt, the reason Jung came to me in my dream to talk about *The Way of Soul*); but my symbolic poem *Noman* sheds light on the individuation process from the spiritual perspective of Soul's journey through life, because *Noman* speaks to the archetypal false consciousness of man's unresolved karmic, or shadow self—meaning, man's *non-being*.

This is all very confusing, but once I saw that every new life we live creates a new personality the veil finally parted, because with each personality we also create a shadow self, which is the repressed side of our personality; and when we die our personality does not die with our physical body, it is stored in our unconscious mind. So when we are reborn into life we bring the unconscious memory of all our past life personalities with us—like the memory of my past lifetime as the infamous "scoundrel of Paris."

If what St. Padre Pio said about me choosing to live my same life over again to obtain a different outcome is true (which I believe to mean breaking the cycle of karma and reincarnation that I failed to do in my first lifetime as Orest Stocco), I can proudly say that I achieved that goal by taking evolution into my own hands with Gurdjieff's teaching that awakened me to the Word that brought me to my true self.

In effect, I found my lost soul that was trapped in the unconscious memory of all my past life personalities; and having found my lost soul I am very conscious of the process that brought me to my true self. This is why Jung wanted to talk with me about *The Way of Soul,* because I explained how I managed to bring my karmic destiny into alignment with my pre-scripted spiritual destiny and gave birth to my spiritual self.

Because we have free choice we determine our own karmic destiny; but because we are all atoms of God we are also pre-scripted to realize our spiritual destiny just as the acorn is genetically encoded to become an oak tree. This means that **we have two destinies: one that we create ourselves through karmic choices, and one that is hard-wired by God for us to return back to God**; and until we learn how to align our two destinies we will never break the recurring cycle of karma and reincarnation and return God's "fish's scale"—meaning, our lost soul. This was Noman's dilemma!

When I fell from heaven I raged at God for forsaking me; but God had not forsaken me at all—*because it was my own karmic destiny that had condemned me to the fourth corner of the abyss!*—which is why I have always thought of my hometown of Nipigon as a small corner of hell. And only I could liberate myself!

But I had to find my lost soul to liberate myself. This is why I believe I chose to be reborn into my same life again, because it offered a golden opportunity to break the cycle of my eternal return to the "abyss." And I believe the daimonic eruption of my poem *Noman* was my entry point into my parallel life, because the moment my archetypal false self was set free I became a slave to my karmic destiny and had no choice but to go on a quest for my lost soul. I simply could not put it off for another lifetime!

Thus began my parallel life...

8. *From Noman to I Am*

Monday, March 19, 2012. I had my first dream last night that indicates I am reliving my same life over again in a parallel world. *In my dream, a woman that I know said to me, "There are two of you." I am astounded by her comment, because I seem to know that there are two of me in my dream also; that is, I have the knowledge that I have lived my same life before, and I say to her, just to make certain that she is sure of what she said: "Are there two of anybody else?' And she replies, "No; I only see two of you."*

This was my first real dream confirmation of my parallel lives, insomuch that this woman confirmed that I was two people, both the same person (which I remember were both in my hometown of Nipigon). How she came to know this is still a mystery, but I got the impression that she must have seen my two same bodies together, because I recall that when I asked her if there were two of anybody else I remember her pinching somebody in the thigh to see if he was two people too, but he wasn't; and then she said that only I was two people, both the same person. Was the Dream Weaver giving me dream confirmation of my two lives in parallel worlds?

I don't know; but I have the strongest suspicion that writing my poem *Noman* was not something that I had done in my first lifetime as Orest Stocco. I have no way of proving this, of course; but knowing what I know now about archetypes from my study of Jung's psychology of the unconscious, I know that I became possessed by the archetype of man's false self, which my creative unconscious symbolized in the person Noman. And the moment I became possessed by my archetypal false self my life changed completely, because from that moment on I became possessed by an inexplicable impulse to be false—*thereby creating the moral conflict that was to haunt me the rest of my life.*

This is why I'm convinced that I had to complete my individuation process through the consciousness of my *non-being*, or false self; whereas Jung completed his individuation process through the consciousness of his *being*, or real self (until he lost his way, which he relates in *The Red Book* when he asks, "my soul, my soul, where are you?").

While researching Jung I came upon a full interview in which Jung revealed that he was centered in the consciousness of his *being*: "Can I take you back to your childhood?" the BBC interviewer John Freeman asked Jung. "Do you remember the occasion when you first felt consciousness of your own individual self?"

"That was my eleventh year," Jung replied, after careful thought. "There I was certainly on my way to school; I stepped out of a mist. It was just as if I had been walking in a mist and I stepped out of it, and I knew I am. I am what I am. And then I thought, what have I been before? And then I found that I had been in a mist..."

This perception that Soul can choose to individuate through the consciousness of its *being* or *non-being* explains why some people can be the way they are; why some people can be so damn natural and drip with so much authenticity that it makes one green with envy, and why other people can be so false and untrustworthy that it can destroy one's faith in human nature; but it's all because of the path that one has chosen to individuate the central archetype of their life, which Jung called the self and I call Soul self.

Not everyone is centered in the consciousness of their *being* or *non-being*, only those souls that are ready to quicken their individuation process, as Jung and I had done; but if Jung had achieved wholeness and singleness of self as his dream indicated, why did he come to me in a dream to talk about *The Way of Soul*?

What did I know about the "alpha and omega of the self" that Jung didn't? That, really, is the story of my quest for my true self;

because to find my true self I had to answer the question, *why am I?* And this was the journey of my parallel life.

Carl Jung is the only person in my life that I can call a personal hero, because in achieving wholeness and singleness of self he can rightly be called an ideal model for the integrated *being* and *non-being* aspects of our human self; but as satisfying as his psychology of the individuation process may be, it fails to take into account the most vital aspect of man's nature—his spark of divine consciousness.

Not that Jung was unaware of man's spiritual nature; not in the least. He believed that we have a soul, and it lurks in the shadows of his whole psychology; but he failed to acknowledge karma and reincarnation in his understanding of the individuation process—because karma and reincarnation play such a vital role in how Soul individuates through life that we can never make sense of life without factoring them into the equation.

Man is not born a blank slate. He is born with his past, and his past includes every life that he has lived in this world (and other worlds, as some souls have come from elsewhere before they came to Earth). Given my seven past-life regressions, I know that I am an indigenous soul of this planet. I evolved through life to give birth to my reflective self, and I continued to evolve in self-consciousness until I gave birth to my spiritual self, which happened in my mother's kitchen while she was kneading bread dough on the kitchen table; and although I cannot prove this, it is proof enough for me.

It took a few years to work out what happened to me in my mother's kitchen, but eventually I deduced that with all the "work" I had done on myself with Gurdjieff's teaching, my *Royal Dictum*, the sayings of Jesus, and my personal ethic of doing the right-good-honest and just thing, I had transformed my consciousness enough to shift my center of gravity from my *non-being* (inauthentic self) to my *being* (authentic self), and I gave birth to my spiritual self in the process—because I had spiritualized my consciousness enough to gravitate to the Soul plane of consciousness where I experienced my immortal Soul self that memorable day in my mother's kitchen, just as Jesus promised one would if he found the correct interpretation of his sayings!

Quite simply, I had taken the natural individuation process to the next level (what Gurdjieff called taking evolution into one's own hands, which is what Christ's teaching is all about. *"Whoever finds the interpretation of these sayings will not taste death,"* said Jesus in the *Gospel of Thomas*; and not only did I shift my center of gravity from my *non-being* to my *being,* I transcended both my *non-being* and *being* and centered myself in my spiritual self on the Soul plane, which is what Jesus meant by being born again.

Our immortal spiritual self is our Soul self, and realizing our Soul self is what the individuation process leads to; so the natural process of individuation is incomplete until one learns how to spiritualize the consciousness of their human self.

Our human self is born of the consciousness of life and death, which is a consciousness of *being* and *becoming*—or, more precisely, of *being* and *non-being.* This is what attracted me to Sartre and Camus at university. They explored the consciousness of *being* and *becoming* and gave birth to their own philosophies—Sartre creating his philosophy of existentialism, and Camus his philosophy of the absurd; and both believed that we have to posit our own meaning for life, because for them life was contingent and essentially absurd. But that's only because they didn't believe in God and the immortal soul of man, and by logical consequence karma and reincarnation.

This is why Camus came to the conclusion he did in his iconic essay "The Myth of Sisyphus" that "one must imagine Sisyphus happy." *"The struggle itself towards the heights is enough to fill a man's heart,"* he concludes his philosophy; and Sartre brings closure to his philosophy with his clarion pronouncement that "man is a useless passion." *"I am what I am not, and I am not what I am,"* he sums his philosophy; but only because he had trapped himself in the mental consciousness of his human self, which is a consciousness of *being* and *non-being* (hence his great work *Being and Nothingness*); that's why I had to drop both Sartre and Camus, thanking them for their incredible insights into the plight of the existential human condition, and move on. And I "found" Gurdjieff's teaching.

And after living Gurdjieff's teaching of "work on oneself" for a number of years, along with my *Royal Dictum*, the sayings of Jesus, and my personal ethic, I extended the logic of Sartre's philosophy of *being* and *becoming* by adding the missing piece to his despairing philosophy after I experienced my own immortal self in my mother's kitchen: *"I am what I am not, and I am not what I am; I am both, but neither. I am Soul.* And to prove this, on Sunday, February 26, 2012 I had the following dream (remember, dreams don't lie):

In my dream I looked up my name in the Dictionary of Life. The definition of Orest Stocco is Soul. The exact image that I saw was: **Orest Stocco: Soul**.

Soul is spelled with a capital S, not a small s; which draws the distinction between Soul consciousness and a spark of Soul consciousness—meaning, individual soul sparks become Soul (just as Jung drew a distinction between the self of the conscious personality and the Self of the whole personality).

The natural individuation process of life then is about integrating the consciousness of our *being* and *non-being* (authentic and inauthentic selves) until we achieve wholeness and singleness of self; but to realize our pre-scripted spiritual destiny we have to take evolution into our own hands, which is the only way we can give birth to our spiritual self and realize that we are Soul. This is why Jung came to me in my dream to talk about *The Way of Soul*. He wanted to know how I had managed the mystical marriage of my opposites (my *being* and *non-being*) and transcended myself.

Jung was aware of the esoteric purpose of the ancient teachings of Gnosticism and alchemy (both West and East, as he revealed in his commentary to Richard Wilhelm's translation of

The Secret of the Golden Flower), which is to transform the consciousness of our human self and realize our spiritual self; and he incorporated this knowledge into his psychology of the individuation process, which he called the "transcendent function."

Jung deliberately couched his Gnostic wisdom in scientific language to keep his work grounded in empirical science to not threaten the integrity of his fledgling psychology with esoteric spirituality; but I had no reputation to safeguard, and I could write openly in my novels and the poem that expressed my journey from Noman to *I Am*. I lived the inherently self-transcending principles of the Way and realized my Soul self, and I expressed this in the poem that I wrote the night Penny's mother died, on October 30, 1996:

I Am

I felt ashamed of life when I saw her frail body
Fighting for its life in the Emergency Room,
Emaciated and heaving like a bellows for air;
I saw no dignity in the physical struggle
To stay alive, no grace, no love, no honor;
Just a bodily organism in the throes of death.
I walked home alone from the hospital,
The lonely moon as big as the Eye of God
And the stars sparkling like lost souls in heaven,
And I thought of life and death and everything
In between, and in my heart I smiled for all
Of my efforts, struggles, and humiliations to find
My true self, because as I spied death steal my lover's
Mother's life I knew, I simply knew, that I am,
And life is merely something that I do.

But just because I had given birth to my Soul self and was now grounded in the *I Am Principle of Life* didn't mean that I had been blessed with total awareness; I wasn't, because spiritual growth doesn't stop when one has given birth to their Soul self. One is a mere babe in the Soul plane of consciousness, and one has a lot of growing to do yet; but I've already told the story of how I came to this realization in my novel *Keeper of the Flame,* so I need not explicate here. This is the story of my parallel life...

9. *The Missing Piece of the Puzzle*

Until we realize that Soul is who are we will never make sense of life. Soul is the Consciousness of God, and we are a spark of divine consciousness; an atom in the Body of God. This simply means that we are not a physical body that may or may not have an immortal soul; we are Soul that takes on a physical body, and our purpose in life is to grow and evolve in consciousness until we realize our Soul self.

Anyone can dream of looking their name up in the Dictionary of Life, and their name would also be defined as Soul. The Dream Weaver gave me that dream last month because I'm telling the story of how I came to realize my Soul self; which is why St. Padre Pio said in one of my spiritual healing sessions that life is a journey of the self. He also said that life is a voyage of discovery and a journey of peace.

This was my experience. I literally went on a journey in my parallel life by taking an ocean liner from New York City to Naples, Italy, and a bus to Paris, France, and then a train to Annecy in *Haute-Savoie* where I began my quest for my true self; and one stage of the journey led to another until I found my true self. But it wasn't until I came to terms with my past life issues with my Roman Catholic faith that I began my journey of peace.

While researching Jung online one window opened onto another until I came upon Dr. Norman Shealy, the Father of Holistic Medicine. In a video on "The Power of Past Lives", he said: *"There is no other approach that I have experienced as effective as past life therapy in getting people through lifelong and maybe multiple lives of problems."* And the man he was speaking with replied: *"It lets the human mind lift its boundaries and look wherever it needs to look for solutions for whatever bothers you,"* which is precisely what "the sleeping prophet" Edgar Cayce did;

he opened up the way for past life therapy with his thousands of past life readings and healings.

Edgar Cayce would go into a trance, and while in a trance state he tapped into the consciousness of Universal Mind; and from this perspective he was given what was needed to help his clients through their problems. In the book *Edgar Cayce on Dreams*, he was told by Universal Mind that **"dreams work to accomplish two things. They work to solve the problems of the dreamer's conscious, waking life. And they work to quicken in the dreamer new potentials which are his to claim"** (p.16). This was Jung's discovery. In an interview he said, "As each plant grows from a seed and becomes in the end an oak tree, so man becomes what he is meant to be. He ought to get there, but most get stuck."

This is why Jung made dreams central to his therapy. He had intuited the power of dreams to get people unstuck, because **"dreams are a part of a self-regulating, self-enhancing, self-training program, over which the dreamer's own soul ever presides"** (*Edgar Cayce on Dreams*, by Harmon H. Bro, PhD, and Hugh Lynn Cayce, p. 114).

I was stuck; but I was too vain to realize it. I had awakened to the Word. I had broken the code of Christ's sayings. I had found my true self. I had found the secret teachings of the Light and Sound of God, and I was granted the privilege of looking into the Face of God. I was a High Initiate in what claimed to be the most direct path to God, and I was so full of spiritual conceit that I could not see my own vanity; that's why I got stuck and couldn't realize the new potentials which were mine to claim, and Divine Spirit had to intervene to get me unstuck.

When I awakened to the Word by "working" on myself I saw that the Way was everywhere; and the more I saw the Way at work in life, the more I saw that it was Divine Spirit that helped liberate souls from their problems in life. My problem was vanity, which I was blissfully unaware of; that's why the omniscient guiding force of life choreographed my spiritual healing with a gifted intuitive empath and her guide St. Padre Pio.

As often happens, spiritual guidance comes unexpectedly; which was exactly what happened when Penny and I went to the open house that the intuitive empath held when she moved her practice from her home to a public office building. I knew her from a past life reading that she had done for Penny that helped resolve Penny's issues with her deceased mother. She shared her new office space with two other women who both had their own practice unrelated to her spiritual healing and reading practice, and because few people attended the open house the intuitive empath, whom I called Angie St. Claire in *Healing with Padre Pio*, offered to give me a complimentary spiritual healing.

I was reluctant, because I was laboring under the dread that I had a medical situation going on in my life and I was afraid of what she might tell me. Not that I was afraid of dying; I wasn't. I was terrified that I might die before my time and not realize my lifelong dream; so I really didn't want to know. I had too many books to get out and new ones to write, and I didn't want to leave Penny. I wanted us to have a few good years before we moved on to the Other Side, because we had paid too dear a price for the karma-free love that we now had for each other; which was another story waiting to be written.

But I was strongly nudged to have a spiritual healing, and as nervous as I was when Angie told me something about my energies being blocked because I was holding onto some deep emotions for my young brother I got my first glimpse of the opportunity that was to become the seed of my novel *Healing with Padre Pio;* I had family issues that had to be resolved, which I had learned from my regressions stemmed from our aristocratic past life together in the 19th Century London, England and which were exacerbated by the publication of my two novel memoirs that my family took offense to.

During the course of my complimentary healing, Angie told me that St. Padre Pio was one of her spiritual guides. This excited my curiosity, because I knew something of the Saint's life. He was a fellow countryman, and I knew that he was a stigmatic who was often seen in two places at once and that many healing miracles were attributed to him; that's what gave birth to the idea to write a novel on spiritual healing.

After two or three days of pondering whether I should go ahead with it or not, I came to the conclusion that this would be a golden opportunity to heal my issues with my family as well as my wounded Christian soul.

I had left my Roman Catholic faith at an early age to become a seeker, and I learned many years later that in my past lifetime in Paris in the 17th Century I had turned on the Holy Mother Church, on Jesus Christ, and on God; and I knew that it was time to heal myself of all the anger that I still harbored for Christianity. That's why I asked Angie if she would be interested in my project of writing a novel on spiritual healing.

"I would need your permission, your personal guide's permission, and St. Padre Pio's permission. If you all agree, I'd love to pursue a spiritual healing with you," I told her; and she replied that she would do a contemplation on it and let me know. A few days later I got an email from her telling me that they were all in agreement and was looking forward to the project. That's how my novel *Healing with Padre Pio* got to be written.

In all honesty, I did not know that I was stuck in my spiritual path; but the mounting unease with my spiritual community had brought me to a place where I felt out of place with my fellow chelas, especially my fellow High Initiates. I felt that I no longer belonged, and this caused such tension with my spiritual community that something had to give.

I didn't doubt the Way of the Eternal. I believed in it implicitly. I had too many experiences on my spiritual path to doubt its validity; but I didn't feel the same about my spiritual community. It was sadly lacking in the gnostic realization that the Way is an individual responsibility, because it relied too much upon the Inner Master; and because of this blind dependence upon the Inner Master I felt that my community had gotten stuck just as Christianity got stuck when it shifted all the responsibility to Jesus for salvation.

I resonated with the Way of the Eternal because I *knew* that the Way is an individual responsibility, but I no longer resonated with my spiritual community whose mindless mantra *"Just give it to the Master"* irritated the hell out of me. But this only fed my spiritual conceit and set me at odds with my community, and something had to give.

I was too blind to see that I was projecting my own shadow onto the community; but just because I projected didn't make the community shadow less exasperating. It was only too real, especially in High Initiates whose inflated sense of self-importance stank to high heaven; but my spiritual community could not see its repressed shadow personality.

That's why Divine Spirit stepped in so I could continue my journey through life. I had a long way to go to complete the story of my life, but like many High Initiates I could not see through my own vanity because the more spiritually self-realized one becomes, the more nuanced and subtle one's ego is; so the Inner Master introduced me to the venerable Saint of Humility who would prove to be the undoing of my spiritual conceit.

There hasn't been one day since my healing with St. Padre Pio that I do not cringe at the depths of my vanity. *"Why was I so damn vain? How in God's name did I become so spiritually conceited?"* I asked myself. Was it because I had found my true self? Was it because I had looked into the Face of God? Was it because I *knew* that the Way just *Is*? Did this make me so special that I had to be acknowledged for my spiritual consciousness?

My community certainly wasn't supportive of my writing, and I had published *My Unborn Child, Just Going with the Flow*, and *Keeper of the Flame* before I began working on *Healing with Padre Pio*. It was as though my books threatened their sense of spiritual security in the Way of the Eternal. Was this the soul of my conceit?

I didn't know, because I didn't know I was that vain until I met the man (in spirit, that is) who suffered the holy wounds of Jesus Christ for fifty years; the man who said, "I want to inebriate myself with pain" because he could not suffer enough for Jesus.

Only the mirror of St. Padre Pio's humility was pure enough to reflect the depths of my unconscious vanity, and when I got a good look at myself I was so repulsed by what I saw that I wanted to throw up; but the Good Saint had the compassion to tell me that I needed that to get to where I was, which gave me a whole new perspective on vanity. And out of this was born my new, and now favorite saying (after my saying **"stupidity is not a gift of God; it's entirely man-made"**), **"life is a journey through vanity to humility."**

In fact, in my last session I asked St. Padre Pio if he would be willing to do another book project with me, suggesting that my entry point would be the Preacher's words in *Ecclesiastes*, "Vanity of vanities, saith the Preacher, vanity of vanities; all is vanity. What profit hath a man of all the labor which he taketh under the sun?" And he agreed. I am not done with the issue of vanity yet, and I can expect some more surprises.

But that won't be until I finish this book, and quite possibly the next one that was inspired by my reading of Jung's *Red Book* which I received the day before Christmas and finished on New Year's Day, 2013: *The Beauty of Suffering, Reflections on Jung's Red Book*. I'm not quite sure though whether to write *The Beauty of Suffering* before my new project with St. Padre Pio, or after; I'll just have to let my Muse decide for me.

Soul, then, is the missing piece of the puzzle of life. Every person is a spark of divine consciousness that comes into this world to evolve in self-realization consciousness until they are ready to take evolution into their own hands, and this is an individual responsibility that one cannot avoid when the natural process of life makes them ready; and we know we are ready when we come to that fork in the road that calls us to our true self, just as Robert Frost wrote in his iconic poem "The Road not Taken."

"Two roads diverged in a wood, and I— /I took the one less traveled by, /And that has made all the difference," concluded Frost, reflecting the less traveled road that he took when he quit his school teaching job and sold his farm in New Hampshire and moved his young family to England to write poetry. It was a hard decision to make, but walking the road less traveled (which is Frost's metaphor for Soul's call to individuation) is the most difficult decision that one can make in his life.

I know, because I had to make it when I sold my pool hall and vending machine business and went to France to begin my quest for my true self. I was so wrought with emotion from my harrowing sexual experience that godforsaken night that it completely disoriented me, and it took a long time to find some measure of balance—especially after I awakened the "coiled serpent" that set my mind on fire with an insatiable kundalini lust for expression. That's when I got seduced by automatic writing after participating in a foolish Ouija board séance with some friends in Annecy, but which I cannot expand upon now; suffice to say that it took years to calm the raging "serpent fire."

I went out of my mind in my Sufi lifetime in 15th Century Persia, because I was torn apart by the "two stallions of my life"—my love for God and my love for pleasure, so I had an innate awareness of what it meant to be drawn into the hollow chambers of one's mind; but as seductive as the "desires" of my mind were, they could not compromise me enough to be sucked into another lifetime of madness, and I began to channel this irrepressible energy into my quest for my true self with Gurdjieff's teaching of "work on oneself."

It would have been nice if I had been versed in Jung's psychology, but I was destined to have my own naked confrontation with the unconscious; and thank God I came out of it with my sanity intact, as did Jung when he dove into the depths of his own mind with his now legendary *Red Book* confrontation with the unconscious; but I did discover Jung when I needed him to make sense of evil.

I had awakened to the Archetypal Shadow as I "worked" on myself with Gurdjieff's teaching, my *Royal Dictum,* and Christ's sayings, and Jung's psychological insight into Soul's journey through life gave me solace for the rest of my journey. That's why I was so moved when I read what his friend Laurens van der Post wrote in *Jung and the Story of Our Time* how Jung caught his first real glimpse of the individuation process while studying his patients at the Bergholzli Hospital in Zurich: his patients got stuck on their journey through life, and his job as a healer of souls was to get them unstuck.

"This arrest of the personality in one profound unconscious timeless moment of itself called psychosis, he would tell me, occurred because the development of the person's own story had been interrupted, however varied, individual, and numerous the causes of the interruption. All movement of the spirit and sense of beginning and end had been taken away from it and the story, like the sun in the midst of Joshua's battle against the Amorites, suddenly stood still," wrote Laurens van der Post (pages 119-20).

This psychosis is a psychological complex that can only be understood when one realizes as Jung did that every person is their own way to wholeness and singleness of self; meaning, each person's life is their story, and when their story gets interrupted they can end up in a psychiatric hospital, and not until they are reconnected with their life story can they be healed and continue on with their personal story.

That's why Jung chose psychiatry for a profession. In *Memories, Dreams, Reflections* he tells us that he was undecided what he wanted to study for a career; but when he opened up a textbook on psychiatry by Krafft-Ebing as he was preparing for the state exam, he said, "Well, now let's see what a psychiatrist has to say for himself."

Jung read: "It is probably due to the peculiarity of the subject and its incomplete state of development that psychiatric textbooks are stamped with a more or less subjective character." And a few lines further on, the author called psychoses "diseases of the personality." Jung's heart began to pound. "I had to stand up and draw a deep breath. My excitement was intense, for it became clear to me, in a flash of illumination, that for me the only possible goal was psychiatry" (pages 108-9). And on December 10, 1900 Jung took up his position as assistant at Burgholzli Mental Hospital where he made the discovery from his patients that their life story was their most precious possession, whether they knew it or not; and when the development of their story got interrupted—by personal tragedy, or whatever; there are innumerable ways for one's life story to be brought to a sudden stop—they got stuck, as Jung put it; and in extreme cases some committed suicide or ended up in a mental hospital. And Jung, always the compassionate healer, did everything in his power to reconnect his patients with their life story.

I didn't know it, but my life story got stuck. Vanity kept my story from unfolding, and Divine Spirit had to step in to reconnect me with my life story; that's why I had to have a spiritual healing from St. Padre Pio. But to explain how our life story can get interrupted I have to provide a larger context, which will shed light on Jung's process of individuation; and it has to do with the two destinies of man.

I came to this realization because of my seven past life regressions, which fall into the realm of the metaphysical—a term that Jung did everything in his power to avoid. Not that he denied the existence of metaphysical reality; he had to frame the individuation process in a scientific paradigm, which became his empirically based psychology of the unconscious. But then, as Jung knew only too well, life is an individual journey; and whatever I have to say about the individuation process is my "Red Book" experience and mine alone.

I was brought back to the Body of God in my fourth regression, and I experienced myself as an atom of God with Soul consciousness but no self-consciousness; and in the same regression I was brought back to my first primordial human life where I experienced the dawning of my reflective self-consciousness. In effect, I had evolved up the chain of natural evolution into a higher primate where I gave birth to my reflective self; and from lifetime to lifetime I continued to grow in self-consciousness until in my current parallel life I was ready to take evolution into my own hands and continue the next chapter of my life story; and here we come to the mystery of the two destinies of man.

As I experienced in my unbelievable regression, we all begin our existence in the Body of God as atoms of God, or sparks of divine consciousness. God is our essence, and we are all encoded with the DNA of God; so we are all destined to become God-realized Souls. This is our *a priori* spiritual destiny, pre-determined by our divine DNA; but as we evolve through life we give birth to a reflective human self that makes personal choices, and with personal choices comes personal karma, and this creates our karmic destiny.

Our karmic destiny is our life story, because we create it with the choices we make; and the whole purpose of our life is to bring our karmic destiny into alignment with our pre-scripted spiritual destiny, which is total self-realization consciousness. When we stray too far from our spiritual destiny Divine Spirit brings us back, usually kicking and screaming; hence the mystery of our two destinies, because we can be so ego-centered, blind, and headstrong that we just don't want to be aligned with our spiritual destiny. This is what makes for some of the world's best literature in man's struggle with himself; like Goethe's *Faust*, Dante's *Divine Comedy*, Nietzsche's *Zarathustra*, and Jung's *Red Book*.

"At that time, in the fortieth year of my life," wrote Jung in *The Red Book*, "I had achieved everything that I had wished for myself. I had achieved honor, power, wealth, knowledge, and every human happiness. Then my desire for the increase of these trappings ceased, the desire ebbed from me and horror came over me. The vision of the flood seized me and I felt the spirit of the depths, but I did not understand him. Yet he drove me on with unbearable inner longing and I said: 'My soul, where are you? Do you hear me? I speak. I call you—are you there? I have returned. I am here again..." (*The Red Book, Liber Novus*, A Reader's Edition, by C. G. Jung, p. 127).

Thus began Jung's confrontation with the unconscious, his unbelievable quest for his lost soul; and it was lost because his karmic destiny had gone out of alignment with his spiritual destiny, and he had to bring his two destinies into agreement. And his successful quest for his lost soul became the foundation of his psychology of the unconscious and inspiration for the world; *a beautiful, beautiful book!*

Well, I had found my lost soul long before I read *The Red Book*; but my soul got stuck on my spiritual path. Unlike Jung I had not achieved honor, power, wealth, knowledge (a little, to be sure), and every human happiness (some happiness). I had been "bought with a price" and found my true self; but over time I became complacent, which bred the vanity that stopped my life story from unfolding, and so Divine Spirit had to bring me back into alignment with my spiritual destiny; that's why I had to have a spiritual healing with St. Padre Pio—to shed the vanity that kept me stuck!

And once the scales of vanity fell from my eyes the Dream Weaver prepared me for the next stage of my journey through life. In early April 2012 (I don't have the exact day) I had a dream that shed some light on my predicament:

I'm on a train, sitting by the window looking out as the train rolls by a beautifully landscaped estate, which I know is the home of my spiritual community ("that other religion," as St. Padre Pio referred to the new religion of the Light and Sound of God). *The lawns are a lush green, the community building is a huge two or three storey stone building with large windows, very well kept and appealing to the eye; it has a stately appearance about it, giving one the feeling that it is safe to be there. On the grounds there's a beautiful lake with benches here and there for community members to sit and contemplate. Overall, it is very appealing, but I'm on the train leaving this place. I see one student, a male about forty years old, outside looking at me. He has a bewildered look on his face, wondering why I am leaving such a beautiful, clean, safe* place; but as my train rolls on by I have the feeling that as beautiful and safe and wonderful as this place is, I feel that it has invisible walls that keep members trapped inside. I can't explain this, but I know that it's time for me to move on, and I am on the "train of life" going to my next destination—meaning, my next spiritual path, which I know is finally my own path that I have realized out of all the paths that I have lived. I had a sad but happy feeling in my heart.

Now I understand what St. Padre Pio meant when he told me in my last spiritual healing session that I had transcended my own voice and the voice of my community. And then he said something else that shocked me: "Now it is my turn to be in awe of you."

I can't wrap my mind around that, and I won't even try. Suffice to say that the Dream Weaver gave me confirmation for the disquieting feelings I had been avoiding. And to further press the point, he gave me another dream shortly after this dream that **clearly** spelled out my inexpressible feelings about my spiritual community:

I'm standing on a stage, behind and out of sight. I watch as members of my spiritual community come into the hall to listen to the Inner Master's talk. As they walk into the hall I can tell that they are all in some kind of hypnotic spell. When they all sit down the Inner Master walks onto the stage and up to the podium. The Inner Master is the inner form of the Outer Master of the Way of the Eternal. He is dressed in a blue suit. He looks out at all the members, and without saying a word snaps his fingers and everyone wakes up!

Why was my spiritual community asleep? What was the hypnotic spell that they were all under? And why did the Inner Master have to wake them up?

"Dreams are the speech of my soul," said Jung; and these two dreams spoke what I did not have the courage to raise to a conscious level. The Dream Weaver told me what I refused to think about my spiritual community, and I had no choice now but to take the train to the next station. Where that will be, I don't know; but I trust my dreams.

10. *The Shadow Personality*

Dreams don't lie. We may not interpret some dreams correctly, but they do not lie; they reveal what we need to know to continue our journey to wholeness and singleness of self. I was stuck and didn't know it. That's why I was uneasy with my spiritual community, and my dreams told me why. I didn't resonate with my fellow chelas. They seemed to be on a different level. I was told that I was "rude." I replied, "Is it rude to be truthful?"

"To sleep, perchance to dream. Aye, there's the rub," said Hamlet in Shakespeare's iconic *to be or not to be* soliloquy. The truth wakes people up, sometimes rudely; and they react. My insight into my spiritual community's shadow personality made my fellow chelas cringe, and it caused tension; so Penny and I stopped attending our community functions to live the Way of the Eternal in our own individual way; her by *doing*, and me by *being*.

"If life led you to take up an artificial attitude, then you wouldn't be able to stand me, because I am a natural being," said Carl Jung. "By my very presence I crystallize; I am ferment. The unconscious of people who live in an artificial manner senses me a danger. Everything about me irritates them, my way of speaking, my way of laughing" (*Carl Jung, Wounded Healer of the Soul*, by Claire Dunne, p. 22).

The false self cannot stand the real. The real threatens the false self, and the false self reacts because it does not want to be found out. The unconscious shadow personality is the false part of our conscious personality, and it is threatened by anyone who is more grounded in the real than they are; this is why I bothered my fellow chelas.

My essential *being* bothered them; or, to be more specific, if not more mystifying, I had more *spiritual gravitas* than my community could take; but it bothered me that I bothered them, because I could not figure it out. And I had to ask St. Padre Pio why I bothered my fellow chelas, some more than others; especially one person in particular who was so bothered by me that he wrote such a vicious email about me which he shared with our spiritual community that it made me shudder. *"What in God's name did I do to him that he would react with such animus?"* I asked myself; but St. Padre Pio cleared it up for me.

"You chafe people," he said to me; and with respect to the man who had a hate on for me that made me shudder, he told me that this was past-life related. In my immediate past life he and I were on a British navy battle ship. I was a ranking officer, and he wasn't; but he didn't think I deserved my rank because I was an aristocrat. He felt that because I was privileged I had not earned my rank, and he goaded me into a duel. But I unsworded him with ease and humiliated him so badly that he went on to commit suicide; and he brought those feelings for me into this life. That was the source of his animus for me.

But why did I chafe people? Did I humiliate them with the truth? St. Padre Pio told me to **"resist the urge to be right,"** and I knew that the Good Saint was right, because I have been chafing people ever since I found my true self; but I didn't understand why. So I said to him, "Is it because I can see their shadow?"

He acknowledged my insight, and it all fell into place. That's why I resonated so quickly with what Jung said. *"The unconscious of people who live in an artificial manner sense me a danger,"* he said, and the more false one's shadow personality is, the more they sense a danger in me; and they react with unconscious intent, usually with malice, resentment, anger, envy, or jealousy. Like the man who said to me one day, "What the hell are you trying to prove out there, anyway?"

I was in the post office in Nipigon. I was into long distance running then. I had taken up running because I was nudged to do so, and it proved to be exactly what I needed at the time to balance out my energies; and I ran seven miles every evening after work, summer and winter. I did not know the man in the post office. I knew him to see him, but not personally; so his remark took me off guard. It was the middle of winter, and he saw me running on Highway 11 along the Lake Helen shoreline. He was either on his way to his cottage at Polly Lake, or on his way back; and he saw me running with icicles hanging down my face mask that I had fashioned out of my work dust mask which I had on over my balaclava, and he had to tell me what he thought. "Are you crazy?" he asked me.

"Why?" I said, "Just because I like to run?"

"You must be crazy running in that kind of weather," he said, with such disdain in his voice that it wouldn't matter what I said to convince him otherwise; so I didn't bother. I picked up my mail and left.

Long distance running made me more real, more authentic; that's why Dr. George Sheehan, "the guru of running," wrote: *In running I found my salvation.*" He couldn't explain it, but he knew that there was something about running that "saved" him; but this "something" that he couldn't understand I knew to be the Way, because I had awakened to the Way with Gurdjieff's teaching, my *Royal Dictum*, and the sayings of Jesus.

The Way is the path to one's true self, or one's spiritual center if you will; and the Way is everywhere to be found. It is not a specific set of rules to live by that can be found in the sayings of Jesus, the *Tao te Ching,* or Buddha's Eightfold Path; it is the omniscient guiding force of life that is imminently present in life. It is the life force, Divine Spirit, and the redemptive energy of God that Jesus called "water of eternal life," and one can connect with this inherently self-transcending energy with whatever one does—like running.

"In running I found my salvation," said Dr. Sheehan, and I salvaged many a rotten day with a good long distance run along

the Lake Helen shoreline; but I had a dream that told me why running was what I needed at that time in my life. My dream spoke the impenetrable truth that Dr. George Sheehan was unable to conceptualize:

It's a beautiful summer day, and I'm on the highway in front of St. Sylvester's Historic Mission Church that the people of the Lake Helen reserve still used, to which I had volunteered six weeks of my time to paint one summer, and I am beginning my usual run to Five Mile Park and back, a distance of seven miles. As I run down the highway I am aware that I have a ball of string in my mouth. It is made up of tiny pieces of string tied together, and as I run it's like there's an invisible hand in front of me is pulling the string out of my mouth, and the ball gets smaller and smaller the further I run.

That's my dream. It took a while to decode the Soul message of my dream, but it finally came to me one morning while I was reciting the long list of wisdom sayings that I had collected to impress upon my mind before going to work my trade for the day.

I did this ritual three times every morning. I began by reciting my *Royal Dictum*, then Kant's categorical imperatives, and then the following fifty or sixty wisdom sayings that I had collected to remind me throughout the day to aspire to personal excellence. This was the path that I had cultivated to "work" on myself so I could "catch" the life force that I needed to grow in my spiritual self, and I was **pathological** in my commitment. Three years later I was **nudged** to take up long distance running.

I didn't know why, but I just felt that this is what I should do; and so, true to my nature I went out and bought all the books I could find on running and my first pair of New Balance running shoes and latest fashion in sports running wear at PHEIDIPPIDES store in Winnipeg (Pheidippides was an ancient Greek hero who ran the first marathon) while I was visiting my sister, and I began running; first down old bush roads in Nipigon where no one could see me, and when I was ready on the highway along the beautiful Lake Helen shoreline where I continued to run every day until I burnt out eight years later while working a contract on the Lake Helen reserve hanging the drywall, taping, and painting seven new homes; but that's another story for another time that I hope to write, because this was the experience that **woke** me up to the Spiritual Law of Karma. My working title for this story is: "My Thirty-Thousand Dollar Karmic Lesson." (Spinoza was absolutely right: we really do not understand what we know until we have the experience!)

I took up running because Divine Spirit knew that this was what I needed to grow in spiritual consciousness; but I did not understand the reason until the Dream Weaver gave me the dream that explained the metabiological benefits of long distance running.

I coined the word "metabiological" because of my running dream. The pieces of string tied together into a little ball symbolized all of my wisdom sayings that I "mouthed" every morning before going to work; and the ball of string being pulled out of my mouth symbolized that all the wisdom sayings that I "mouthed" every morning were assimilated by my consciousness *as I ran* and coalesced with my *being*. In effect, I *became* my wisdom sayings as I *lived* them every day—which is precisely what Jesus meant when he said that one had to *do* his sayings to build his house upon a rock; meaning, to grow in spiritual consciousness and give birth to our spiritual self we have to *live* his sayings:

"Therefore whoever heareth these sayings of mine, and doeth them, I will liken him unto a wise man, which built his house upon a rock. And the rain descended, and the floods came, and the winds blew, and beat upon that house; and it fell not, for it was founded upon a rock. And everyone that heareth these sayings of mine, and doeth them not, shall be likened unto a foolish man, which built his house upon sand. And the rain descended, and the floods came, and the

winds blew, and beat upon that house; and it fell: and great was the fall of it." (Math. 7: 24-27)

Long distance running helped me to build my house upon a rock, because I assimilated and coalesced the wisdom of those sayings as I *lived* them. If I may play upon an old saying, I not only walked my talk; *I ran my talk!* And the more I grew in *being*, the more authentic and real I became; and I began to chafe people!

That's why I chafed my spiritual community, especially some High Initiates whose inflated sense of self-importance born of their High Initiate status emitted such a foul odor of spiritual elitism that they were hard to suffer. But I bugged them more than they bugged me; and they reacted to me in ways that made some chelas shake their head in wonder, because it was not what our spiritual path was about.

My fellow chelas were under the hypnotic spell of the repressed community shadow personality, which I threatened with my mere presence; and all because they had forfeited their individual responsibility to the Inner Master just as Christians have forfeited their personal responsibility to their lord and savior Jesus Christ.

"I just gave it to the Master," said one chela, speaking of a problem he wanted resolved; and another said, "I gave it to Spirit to work out for me." And the more they forfeited their responsibility to the Inner Master and Divine Spirit, the more they fell under the spell of the community's shadow; that's why I had the dream I did: the Inner Master snapped them out of this spell and woke them up to their responsibility to save themselves.

The Inner Master is the omniscient guiding force of life personified in the image of the Spiritual Leader of the Way of the Eternal, and his spiritual mandate is to guide us on our journey through life. Like he said in one of his talks as the Outer Master, "I can lead a horse to water, but I can't make it drink." He is *the* Way-shower, not a messiah; just as Jesus was a Way-shower and not the messiah. There's a huge difference.

I tried to make this distinction in my novel *Jesus Wears Dockers, The Gospel Conspiracy Story*, which I wrote six or seven years ago and was reluctant to publish until St. Padre Pio encouraged me to get it out because it offered a whole new way of thinking about Christ's gospel to the world. Jesus solicits the help of my fictional self to help him explain the secret meaning of his sayings, which if lived correctly will liberate one from the eternal cycle of life and death—meaning, karma and reincarnation; because neither Jesus nor the Inner Master can liberate us. They can only show us the Way, not live the Way for us.

We have to liberate ourselves, and the only way to do that is to take responsibility for our own life. And if we don't get it right in this lifetime, we will just keep coming back until we do; and getting it right is what living the Way is all about.

This is why I was reborn into my same life as Orest Stocco. I did not get it right in my first life as Orest Stocco, and I returned to try again because of all the lives that I have lived this one offered me the best opportunity to get it right.

11. *A Whole New Look at Reincarnation*

I wouldn't be exploring this dimension of my life had not St. Padre Pio revealed to me that I am living my same life over again to achieve a different outcome. He told me that I have lived my same live over again three separate times, and this is one of those times; but I could not wrap my mind around this for a long time, and not until I began to do some research on parallel worlds did I catch a glimmer of what he was trying to tell me, and I began to look at reincarnation differently.

Actually, it was something that Jesus said in the book that St. Padre Pio suggested that Angie and I should read, *Love without End, Jesus Speaks,* by the artist Glenda Green who painted the portrait of Jesus (*The Lamb and the Lion*) while he manifested in her studio over a period of almost four months, between November 1991 and March 1992. *"The philosophy of reincarnation is not that simple,"* said Jesus. *"It does affirm your immortality, and that is good. However, there's a twist in it which defers your immortality back to structure and linearity, which is not true. Your immortality is not imprisoned within a wheel of life, or pathway of cause and effect. Neither are you the product of linear evolvement. You were created in perfection, and perfect love, and you **do continue** to re-manifest, but it is according to the will of the Father, and according to your own purpose. You actually only have one life! It's just a very long one, with many chapters"* (pages 76-7).

Wow! When I read that I had a dramatic shift in consciousness—from my linear understanding of the process of karma and reincarnation to another yet-to-be grasped process; one which did not follow the chronological order that I had assumed, and thus began my research into parallel worlds and a whole new look at reincarnation.

My belief in reincarnation did not come from books; not at first, anyway. It came from dreams in my youth. While in elementary and high school I had dreams that did not fit into the category of what I considered to be normal dreaming, because they were so real that it was like I was actually there, totally present as another person who was me!

And they certainly did not fit in with my Roman Catholic faith, so it was a good thing that I did not know what they were then. I learned many years later when I found the Way of the Eternal that these kinds of dreams are called "past life recollection dreams," and that we have these dreams because we're ready to move on to a higher path in our journey through life, a path that prepares us for conscious evolution; which means that we're ready to take evolution into our own hands by assuming responsibility for our own karma.

My Roman Catholic faith believed in the forgiveness of sins, so it didn't matter how much negative karma I created I would be forgiven my sins by going to Holy Confession, or saying a perfect act of contrition; a faith which served its purpose until I was strong enough to stand on my own two spiritual legs, as it were. That's why the Dream Weaver let me have those past life recollection dreams—to prepare me for the Way.

Jesus said, *"Many are called, but few are chosen."* This is a very harsh thing to say, but Jesus was a realist of the highest order (which I try to show in my novel *Jesus Wears Dockers*); and he was merely pointing out that one has to be ready to assume the responsibility of taking evolution into their own hands, because this requires a commitment to total accountability that few people can make. But this is the inherent purpose of karma and reincarnation: to make us ready for the Way.

Obviously then, I was ready to take evolution into my own hands in this life. But apparently I did not achieve the goal of spiritual liberation the first time I lived my life as Orest Stocco, so I was reborn into my same life to try again. I gave myself another chance, as it were; and the Dream Weaver paved the way for me with my dreams.

In one dream I'm a fish monger in England. I don't know what century it is, but I'm peddling fresh fish speaking cockney and shouting, "KIPPERS! FRESH KIPPERS! FILLETS!" It was me, but in another body; which I didn't understand.

In another dream I'm in ancient Greece. I'm a nobleman. A statesman, in fact; and I remember talking to the men who had come in from the countryside to help defend our noble city from an impending invasion. "Remember," I said to the men who were now armed and assembled, "you are Athenian soldiers. When you kill, do not kill with savagery; but with the dignity of your noble bearing." I learned many years later when I had seven past life regressions that I served my noble city for thirty years after Pythagoras let me return to Athens to live a life of service so I could begin the long and difficult journey of bringing my karmic destiny into alignment with my spiritual destiny.

Pythagoras was a remarkable Master. He looked into the future and saw my karmic destiny unfolding, and it was to bring me more anguish and suffering because I was karmically programmed to seek out power; so he accepted me into his secret circle to help change the course of my karmic destiny. Thus began my long journey of reconciliation, which culminated in my current lifetime—my second lifetime as Orest Stocco, that is.

In another past life dream I was a North American Indian. This dream was so vivid in sights and sounds and smells that all these years later I can still recall the strong smell of the smoke and hides and sweat of our wigwam village. The odor never went away. It enveloped our village like a permanent fog of human and animal musk; and this life was pivotal in bringing my karmic destiny into alignment with my spiritual destiny.

I was a young man, and it was time to be initiated into manhood; but the ritual for this rite of passage was so painful that I refused to go through with it. The initiation was not unlike the initiation ritual that Richard Harris had to go through in the movie *A Man Called Horse;* so I had two choices: I could remain in the village and be treated like a squaw and serve the women and warrior men, but this was a fate worse than a dog's life; or I could leave the village and live on my own to build up my courage to go through my initiation. I chose the latter, and for one whole winter I lived on my own outside my village.

This was very hard; but my mother would sneak food out to me whenever she could to make sure that I did not starve to death. Nonetheless I did build up enough courage to go through my initiation; and I grew to become chief of my tribe. I was called "Bear Claw," because of the scar that I had on my face from the bear that I killed with my stone knife. I cut off the bear's claw that had left a permanent scar on the right side of my face and hung it around my waist as a talisman. And as chief of my tribe I had the counsel of my shaman, who introduced me to the mysterious world of spirits.

And in another past life recollection dream I was a black slave in the southern state of Georgia. My name was Solomon, and I was known as Solomon the Good Slave; but I had an irrational compulsion to be free, and I ran away from the plantation twice. The second time I was made an example of, and every Sunday morning I was whipped on my bare back in front of all the slaves to keep them in a state of fear and submission.

The pain was unbearable, and the scars never healed in time for my next whipping. But something happened during one whipping that helped bring my karmic destiny into greater alignment with my spiritual destiny: *I had a spiritual awakening.*

With one stinging lash of the whip, like an insight sent from God, I realized that they could whip my body and make my body submit to the slave master's will, but they could not make my soul submit because in my soul I was free. This was my first conscious realization of the distinction between the consciousness of my physical life and the consciousness of my spiritual life; and I *realized* for the first time in all of my incarnations that I was two selves: one human, and one spiritual!

This is why I have never had an attraction to Buddhism, because it does not believe in the concept of the individual soul. In *The Monk and the Philosopher, A Father and Son Discuss the Meaning of Life*, by Jean-Francois Revel and Matthieu Ricard (who was a personal aid to the Dalai Lama), Matthieu Ricard says:

"First of all, it's important to understand that what's called reincarnation in Buddhism has nothing to do with the transmigration of some 'entity' or other. It's not a process of metempsychosis because there is no 'soul.' As long as one thinks in terms of entities rather than function and continuity, it's impossible to understand the concept of rebirth...This, of course, leads to a fundamental question: is there a nonmaterial consciousness distinct from the body? It would be impossible to talk about reincarnation without first examining the relationship between body and mind. Moreover, since Buddhism denies the existence of an individual self that could be seen as a separate entity capable of transmigrating from one existence to another by passing from one body to another, one might well wonder what it could be that links those successive states of existence together."

And his father replies: "That's pretty hard to understand."

Matthieu answers: "In fact, it's seen as a continuum, a stream of consciousness that continues to flow without there being any fixed or autonomous entity running through it."

To which the philosopher father replies: "A series of reincarnation without any definite entity that reincarnates. More and more mysterious."

Here the Buddhist monk son solves the mystery: "It could be likened to a river without a boat descending along its course, or to a lamp flame that lights a second lamp, which in turn lights a third lamp, and so on; the flame in the end of the process is neither the same flame as at the outset, nor a completely different one."

And the skeptic philosopher replies: "Those are just metaphor" (pages 30-1).

And so the dialogue goes on, and it will continue to go on, and on, and on; that's why in my third year I dropped out of university where I had gone to study philosophy to find answers to the question that catapulted me into my quest for my true self: *who am I?*

I knew that the person who did what he did that godforsaken night was me but not me, and I had to find out who the real me was; so out of self-revulsion and shame I sold my pool hall and vending machine business and fled to France to begin my lonely quest for my true self; and in Annecy I accidentally awakened the *kundalini* while meditating on a maple leaf which set my mind on fire, and then I had the symbolic dream that revealed the haunting existential question in the heart of every person in the world: *why am I?*

It's no wonder that I gravitated to the Gnostic teachings central to the mysteries of the Way, because they answered the question of the two selves of man; but still, even these teachings failed to answer my questions satisfactorily. I had to do that on my own.

C. G. Jung, the most articulate modern day exponent on the secret teachings of Gnosticism, was ambivalent about reincarnation:

"The idea of rebirth is inseparable from that of karma. The crucial question is whether a man's karma is personal or not. If it is, then the preordained destiny with which a man enters life represents an achievement of previous lives, and a personal continuity therefore exists. If, however, this is not so, and impersonal karma is seized upon in the act of birth, then that karma is incarnated again without there being any personal continuity...I know no answer to the question of whether the karma which I live is the outcome of my past lives, or whether it is not rather the achievements of my ancestors, whose heritage comes together in me. Am I a combination of the lives of these ancestors and do I embody these lives again? Have I lived before in the past as a specific personality, and I did not progress so far in that life that I am now able to seek a solution? I do not know" (*Memories, Dreams, Reflections,* by C. G. Jung, pages 317-18).

All indications pointed to rebirth for Jung, which he confessed he could well imagine; and near the end of his life he did have a series of dreams that led him to almost embrace reincarnation; but because he never came across such dreams in other persons he had no basis for comparison. "I must confess, however," he admits, "that after this experience (his dreams) I view the problem of reincarnation with somewhat different eyes, though without being in a position to assert a definite opinion" (Ibid., p. 319).

Interestingly enough, his position on reincarnation did not affect his psychology of the individuation process, because for Jung it didn't matter which life one was living; the process of individuation happened during one's current life, and that's what he devoted his whole life to understanding, which made perfect sense to me.

But still, it made more sense to include ones past lives in the individuation process as I was forced to do to reconcile my karmic destiny with my spiritual destiny; that's why I had to have my past life regressions. I had a very strong feeling that my issues with my family were past life related, and I *knew* that Penny and I were brought together by our past life karma, and I also *knew* that my issues with my Roman Catholic faith were much too deep to have been created in my current lifetime; so I had my regressions to find out.

And I was right. I asked the Inner Master to take me back in my regressions to my past lives that most affected my current lifetime; and I began by asking if I could go back to my most immediate past life because I felt that this lifetime would help me come to terms with my family. And it turned out that my whole family and I were together (except for my father who was a commoner) as members of the aristocracy in London, England in the mid-19th Century. I loathed the aristocracy, which reeked of what I scathingly referred to as "the foul stench of honor and deceit," and I became the hated *bête noire* of London's elite.

Once I had this regression the puzzle of my relationship with my family was solved, because in an instant it all made sense. For the first time in my life I understood why my family and I were the way we were, and why there was always an underlying tension between us—the same tension that existed between us in our previous life together; and I continued my regressions with fevered interest because I knew that I was going to solve the deepest mystery of my life—the mystery of *Noman*, which I did when I was regressed to my past lifetime as the *"le salaud de Paris"* in 17th Century Paris, France; because this was my unconscious lustful personality that possessed me that godforsaken night!

In my fourth regression I was brought back to the Body of God where I experienced myself as an atom of God with Soul consciousness but no self-consciousness; and in the same regression I was brought back to my first primordial human life where I had the dawning of my reflective self-consciousness, thereby solving the origin of our individual existence; and with my other regressions I pieced together the historical spectrum of my karmic individuation process which culminated in my current parallel life when I took evolution into my own hands and gave birth to my spiritual self in my mother's kitchen one summer day while she was kneading bread dough on the kitchen table.

No one can imagine how sensitive to the world a newborn spiritually self-realized soul can be until they experience it; and unless they have a spiritual community to support them in their spiritual rebirth life can be unbearably anguishing, as it was for me. That's what induced me to study by correspondence an offshoot Christian solar cult teaching that I found advertised in *Psychology Today* magazine that alleged to nourish one's spiritual self with the Logos supposedly imbued with the rays of the sun; which turned out to be one of the most stupid decisions of my entire life, because I did irreparable damage to my eyes with three stationary solar burns that now made reading very, very fatiguing!

As St. Paul said, one is bought with a price; and the price that I paid to initiate myself into the mysteries of the Way was so dear that I did not even bat an eye when St. Padre Pio, who suffered the stigmatic wounds of Jesus for fifty years, said "You and I are very much alike." We both knew that to enter into the kingdom of heaven one has to be bought with a price, and I had paid the price for my spiritual rebirth; but I was so caught up in the momentum of my quest for my true self that I could not deny the opportunity to speed up my spiritual growth with the Logos simply by ingesting the rays of the sun with the solar techniques provided by the teacher; but little did I realize how dangerous this would be.

Even though it has been thirty-some years since I had that experience, I'm still too close to it to write about it; but one day I will write my novel *The Sunworshipper.* Suffice to say for now that I had a taste of the dark side of life and I have the gnostic experience of the archetypal dark forces of human nature at work in the world, because the moment I shook hands with that solar cult teacher when I flew to Reno, Nevada for a workshop I *knew* that I was in the presence of evil; and I dropped the teaching like a hot potato.

My dreams then were my introduction to reincarnation. The Dream Weaver let me experience my past lives to prepare me for my spiritual quest for my true self, because each life that we live is not our real self, as such; it is only the outer personality of our inner spiritual self that grows in self-realization consciousness through life experience.

The more experiences we have in life, the more we grow in our own identity; or self-realization consciousness. This is the Way of Life, the natural process of creating and resolving karma; but the natural way of karma and reincarnation cannot reconcile our two selves until we take full responsibility for our own karma. This is what Gurdjieff meant when he said that nature can only evolve us so far, and no further; and what the alchemists meant when they said **"man must finish the work which nature left unfinished."**

Nature cannot bring our karmic destiny into agreement with our spiritual destiny, because we have to choose to do that by taking responsibility for our own karma. To continue evolution we have to reconcile our two selves, which is the fundamental premise of Christ's teaching of salvation that I spelled out in *Jesus Wears Dockers;* but not until life has made us ready for the Way. This is the mystery of the individuation process and the reason Carl Jung came to me in my dream to talk about *The Way of Soul.*

I hadn't even transcribed the tapes of my "Soul talk" book *The Way of Soul* (in fact, they're still not transcribed), but my book was published on the Other Side. **This proved to me that our life continues on the Other Side, but in a different dimension of time**; and that we continue to evolve in our own individual identity on the Other Side. This is why Jung wanted to talk to me about my understanding of the individuation process.

I wasn't as well read on Jung as I am now, so I wasn't as conscious of his profoundly gnostic and scholarly understanding of the individuation process (reading his *Red Book* has given me a whole new respect and admiration for him); but the reason my book *The Way of Soul* excited him so much was because it was about my personal experience of the individuation process that I had wrought out of the impenetrable granite of life, which impressed him to high heaven because he knew only too well the price that one has to pay to be initiated into the mysteries of the Way.

In a conversation with the Chilean diplomat and writer Miguel Serrano, Jung and Serrano were talking about the writer Herman Hesse, whom Serrano said underwent analysis with Jung during one of Hesse's dark periods. Jung said, "I met Hesse through a mutual friend who was interested in myths and symbols. His friend worked with me for a while, but he was unable to follow through to the end. The path is very difficult..." (*C.G. Jung and Hermann Hesse, A Record of Two Friendships*, p. 76).

Jung was being professionally discreet, because I suspect he was talking about Hesse and not their mutual friend. Hesse explored myths and symbols in his major works (*Demian, Steppenwolf, Narcissus and Goldmund*, and my favorite *Magister Ludi*), and his belief in the afterlife was pure Buddhism, as he revealed to Serrano when he visited Hesse at his home in Montagnola: "The act of dying is like falling into Jung's Collective Unconscious, and from there you return to form, to pure form" (p. 26); whereas Jung believed that the whole purpose of the collective unconscious was to individuate the central archetype of the Self; which is why he said to Serrano, "The path is very difficult."

The path for Jung was the process of individuation; to realize the Soul self, not to extinguish it into pure form as the Buddhists believed. But the path is the Way, and it is given expression according to one's own unique individuality (which I expound upon in my book *Why Bother? The Riddle of the Good Samaritan*); and Jung found the Way when he had what he called his "confrontation with the unconscious," which he recorded in his "Black Books" that later became *The Red Book* that he could not publish in his lifetime because of the damage it would do to his reputation. And he expended every ounce of his creative energy to give expression to his gnostic understanding of the Way in his psychology of individuation; but it was very, very difficult.

"Nobody understands what I mean," he revealed to Serrano in a far-away voice when they were talking about the mystical marriage of the alchemical union of the two selves, which is the blossom flower of the individuation process. "Only a poet could begin to understand..." (*C. G. Jung and Hemann Hesse, A Record of Two Friendships*, p. 75).

And just a few months before he died Jung wrote to an English correspondent: "I have failed in my foremost task to open people's eyes to the fact that man has a soul, that there is a treasure buried in the field..." That's why he came to me in a dream to talk about *The Way of Soul*; like the Ascended Master St. Padre Pio, he was still working to help heal the wounded soul of the world from the Other Side.

Jung's departure from Freud forced him to forge his own path in depth psychology, and I dropped out of university to forge my own path in life with Gurdjieff's teaching of "work on oneself," which awakened me to the Way; but unlike Jung I did not have a reputation to protect, so I could take creative liberties with my path, as I did in my novels *Healing with Padre Pio* and *Jesus Wears Dockers*, as well as my non-fiction books *Just Going with the Flow*, and *Old Whore Life, Exploring the Shadow Side of Karma*.

I had nothing to lose, so I could afford to be candid about my path. But after thirty-some years I began to feel boxed in by my path, which the Dream Weaver confirmed with the two dreams of my relationship with my spiritual community. In one dream I'm on the "train of life" leaving my community; and in my other dream the Inner Master snaps my community out of the hypnotic spell that the community shadow has over it.

These dreams put me on the horns of a dilemma: do I walk away from what claims to be the most direct path to God and continue on my own (Plotinus said that the journey to God is a flight of the alone to the Alone); or do I stay and suffer the indignity of my spiritual community's shadow personality that is as obvious to me as the shadow cast by one's body in the light of the afternoon sun? Is there a way through the horns of my dilemma?

As I said, when I dropped out of university to forge my own path in life I took a personal vow to build my life upon my own experiences, and I have had too many meaningful experiences to just walk away from the Way of the Eternal; but what choice do I have? After all, my dreams point to walking away. Or do they?

In my first dream I'm on the "train of life" and I'm riding away from the **physical location** of my spiritual community; from the building and community grounds. It does not mean that I am riding away from the **inner teachings of the Way of the Eternal,** which one can never leave because they *are* the Way, which is life itself; and in my second dream the Inner Master snaps my spiritual community out of the spell of its own shadow. Which tells me that it's not my responsibility to wake up my fellow chelas to their own shadow, because that's their responsibility, and the Inner Master's; so what do I choose?

There are two teachings to the Way of the Eternal: the outer, exoteric teachings; and the inner, esoteric teachings. The outer teachings are for public consumption, and the inner teachings are for private consumption—like the dreams of my relationship with my spiritual community, for example. So there is a way out of my dilemma.

I can continue to live the inner teachings of the Way of the Eternal as I am nudged to live them by the Inner Master, who is also the Dream Weaver, and I can participate in the outer teachings if I so choose. This is why it is an individual path. And the purpose of the path is to realize our divine nature, like St. Padre Pio and all Ascended Masters.

My initial belief in reincarnation then was born of my dreams, which was given all the credence I could ask for with all my reading on different spiritual paths, especially Dr. Michael Newton's research on reincarnation and life between lives. His books *Journey of Souls, Destiny of Souls,* and *Memories of the Afterlife* have gone a long way to firming up the case for reincarnation. But when all is said and done, it all comes down to whether one is ready to believe in reincarnation or not; and I was ready.

But I would never have answered the two most problematic questions of my life *(who am I?* and *why am I?)* had I not had seven past life regressions. Unlike Dr. Brian L. Weiss, the respected mainstream psychiatrist who serendipitously stumbled upon reincarnation one day when one of his patients under hypnosis responded to his directive ("Go back to the time from which your symptoms arise...") and was shocked out of his scientific paradigm when she went back to a past life instead of her childhood as he expected, but who even after years of conducting past-life regression therapy still cannot fully embrace the concept of reincarnation because for him it doesn't matter whether his patients' memories come from past lives or the collective unconscious as long as he helps his patients reconnect with their life story, if I may allude to Jung's metaphor for soul healing, reincarnation for me is a fact of life; not a theory to believe in or justify for propriety's sake.

Dr. Weiss has done the world a service with his books, starting with his break-away book *Many Lives, Many Masters*, and like Jung and most professional people who have to maintain credibility in the scientific community he has to be guarded about his beliefs; but I'm just a no-name writer from Georgian Bay, Ontario with no reputation to safeguard, so it doesn't really matter to me what anyone thinks of my belief system; and I believe in reincarnation no less than any other fact of life, like the Earth revolving around the sun. But I've had a shift in my perspective on reincarnation ever since I received a spiritual healing from St. Padre Pio; that's why I'm writing this book on my parallel life.

When it comes to the Way however, I have to say one thing before I express my new perspective on reincarnation which, incidentally, I don't believe I would have arrived at had it not been for my unique relationship with the Way that began when I started living what Gurdjieff called "the way of the sly man," which I can expound upon another time.

Jung told Serrano that only another poet would understand what he was talking about, because it takes the gift of the poet to penetrate the deepest mysteries of the Way; like John Keats, who caught a glimpse of Soul's purpose in life in a letter that he wrote to his brother ("The Vale of Soul Making"); or Wordsworth, who caught Soul's relationship with God in his poem "Intimations of Immortality; or Rumi, whose every poem speaks the Way.

"I, you, he, she, we. /In the garden of mystic lovers, /these are not true distinctions," said Rumi; and, "These leaves, our bodily personalities, seem identical, /but the globe of soul fruit /we make, /each is elaborately /unique" (*The Language of Life*, by Bill Moyers pages 57 and 48 respectively). Rumi is talking about the two selves.

The Way is life itself, then; or what the American poet Adrienne Rich calls "that which is." And "poetry is an act of the imagination that transforms reality into a deeper perception of what is," she adds; which is the closest that one can get to describing the Way of the Poet, whose imperative is to slay the great Slayer of the Real; so it all depends upon one's relationship with life that determines whether one awakens to the Way or not.

Of course, we are all awake; but there are many levels of consciousness. One may take ayahuasca, a botanical brew and a hallucinogen of legendary power and awaken one's mind like the Harvard-trained anthropologist and ethnobotonist Wade Davis (author of *The Serpent and the Rainbow* and *One River*) who said, "Taking those plants (ayahuasca) was profoundly catalytic in my life. I can't imagine I would write the way I write, think the way I think, have the values I have, if I had not had my imagination opened by those transcendent experiences" (*Toronto Star*, January 13, 2012); but awakening one's mind does not necessarily awaken one to the Way. It can, however, as it has many seekers, trap one on the mental plane of consciousness; which is why Jung and I saw eye to eye on Buddhism and why he wanted to talk to me about my book *The Way of Soul*.

"The path is very difficult," said Jung, precisely because one has to break free of the mind. "The Mind is the great Slayer of the Real," said Blavatsky in *The Voice of Silence*. "Let the Disciple slay the Slayer." And that's what living the Way is all about—slaying the great Slayer of the Real; which very, very few people can do. But as the modern day founder of the Way of the Eternal said, if we don't get it right in this life, we will just keep coming back until we do. God is merciful, indeed.

That's why I was reborn into my same life as Orest Stocco, because I had the ideal opportunity to get it right; and I got it right this time because I awakened to the Way, which I could not do in my first life as Orest Stocco. So the question is: just how did I awaken to the Way that allowed me to slay the great Slayer of the Real? Jung tells us how he did it in his iconic *Red Book*; but how did I do it?

I worked out the long answer in my novel *Jesus Wears Dockers*; but the short answer is TRUST. I had to have total and absolute trust in my own intuition to take the road less travelled every time my path brought me to another fork in the road—because not all paths will take one to their true self, just as Jerry Wennstrom realized when he got stuck on his path of art. But so driven was he by his daemonic spirit that he burned all his art, gave away all his possessions, and placed his trust in the Universe to take care of him; which it did for fifteen years, as he tells us in his amazing book *The Inspired Heart*.

The Way is the Way is the Way, and every path leads to the Way; but waking up to the Way is what the struggles of life are all about. ***"Many are called but few are chosen,"*** said Jesus; and all because it takes a special kind of courage to trust oneself totally, as Jung did when he realized that he had lost his own soul and had to find it at all cost.

That's exactly what happened to me in my past life as "Daniel Wellington, the Earl of Wellington Manor" (that's the name that came to me, but I have done no research on it) in London, England; I had compromised my soul to the "foul beast of foppery" and abandoned my hypocritical life and sailed to the new land of the Americas to live as a penitent trapper with the vow to reclaim my lost soul; but after eight years of struggling to survive in the wilderness a bear cut my life short, and I was reborn into this life as Orest Stocco where I continued my quest for my compromised soul and failed. But then in grade twelve I became possessed by my daemonic spirit and wrote my poem

Noman, which I believe was my **choice point of entry** into my parallel life as Orest Stocco.

I cannot wrap my mind around this yet, but I honestly suspect that I crossed over from my first life as Orest Stocco into a parallel universe with my poem *Noman*; because this poem set my daemonic spirit free to possess me, and I had no choice but to become a seeker at such an early age. *I had to find my lost soul or die trying.*

So my perspective on reincarnation has evolved. It has expanded from the linear dynamic of karmic rebirth to include rebirth into one's same life in a parallel universe; but I will have to rely on my dreams to provide more proof, because as far as I know (and I did ask St. Padre Pio about this) there is no information out there yet about this whole new perspective on reincarnation. Indeed, life really is a journey of discovery.

12. *The Mandala of My Life*

When I found the Way of the Eternal—actually, it was the other way around; the Way of the Eternal found me. As I've already said, I came home one day to find my cousin visiting my mother. She was standing at the kitchen sink filling a five gallon blue plastic container with tap water to bring to her cottage. My mother was sitting at the kitchen table. Out of the blue my cousin asked me, "Do you believe in reincarnation?"

I hesitated before answering. My cousin was known to be a bit off the wall; but it was a fair question despite that it came out of nowhere, so I replied, "Yes, of course, and she proceeded to tell me about a teaching called The Way of the Eternal and that she had some books at her cottage if I wanted do drop by later.

Just like that. No further explanation. She filled her jug, thanked my mother, and left; and later that evening after some deliberation I drove out to her cottage and borrowed *The Far Country*, by Paul Twitchell that pulled me in so quickly that I devoured it in two sittings—which was a real feat for me given my impaired eyesight.

When I got to chapter two I read something that made my heart jump. I couldn't believe it. For the first time in my life I found something that spoke to my personal experience with the Way. No one else had even come close.

Rebazar Tarzs, Paul Twitchell's spiritual teacher, is speaking: "Christ said that the way into the Kingdom of Heaven, meaning the Far Country, was within. But he was wrong. He said again in the Gospel of John that He was the Way, as the Christ. And again I say that he was wrong! Now I tell you," Rebazar Tarzs emphasized with his left forefinger. "The way into Heaven IS! This is what I can tell you in so many words—this and this alone, for it is the same as saying that God IS!" (*The Far Country*, p. 31)

Wow! I could not believe what I had just read. For the first time since I had awakened to the Way I had corroborating proof of my experience with the Way.

"The Way just IS!" I exclaimed to myself. "Finally, someone who speaks what I *know* about the Way. I'm home!"

That's how I became acquainted with the Way of the Eternal thirty-some years ago, and I've been an Initiate of this spiritual path ever since—which I nearly walked away from because of my two dreams concerning my spiritual community.

And to think that the only reason I dropped by my cousin's cottage was because I overrode my feelings about her. After dinner that evening I drove to the Texaco Restaurant on the outskirts of Nipigon on the Trans Canada Highway for a cup of coffee. I had no intention of driving to her cottage, because my ego wouldn't allow me to take advice on my spiritual life from my "flaky" cousin; but my better nature took over.

I was well into Gurdjieff's teaching by this time, and I honestly felt that this was my path for life. But I had awakened to the Way, and I knew that life *was* the Way; so my better judgment overrode my feelings for my cousin and I drove to her cottage. As the saying goes, when the student is ready the teacher appears.

I had outgrown Gurdjieff's teaching, but I didn't know it. The omniscient guiding force of life knew it, though; that's why I had the *coincidental* encounter with my cousin at my home. I just *happened* to come home early that day, and she just *happened* to be visiting my mother. Coincidence? Serendipity? Divine intervention?

They're all the same to me, and I no longer question how Divine Spirit works to help souls find their way back home to God. All I know is that I had the wisdom to override my ego and go with my gut feeling and check out this new spiritual path, which wasn't new at all because it stretches far back into antiquity; it surfaces every so often when the world needs it, and Paul Twitchell introduced it to the modern world in 1965.

This teaching connected a lot of dots for me; but it wasn't until I had my regressions when Penny and I moved to Georgian Bay that I finally got to see the Big Picture. Had not the Inner Master taken me back to the Body of God where I experienced myself as an atom in the Body of God with Soul consciousness but no self-consciousness, and then experiencing the birth of my reflective self-consciousness in my first primordial human life I would never have pieced together the puzzle of life.

Actually there was one more piece that I needed to complete the Big Picture, and I had this piece in my memory. I had this experience in my early Gurdjieffian years, but it surfaced after I had my regressions because I needed it to complete the puzzle of life. This was my experience of the genesis of life on Planet Earth.

As I've already said, I was sitting on a chair leaning back so my head rested on the warm stucco wall of our family home. I was wearing my white painter's pants and tea shirt. It was spring, and the sun felt good. It had been a long winter, as they always are in northern Ontario, and the warm spring sun felt good. I let my mind drift off.

Then it happened. I felt myself drifting back through time, further and further back. I drifted back through the months, the years, and the centuries, through millennia, through eons, all the way back to when there was no life on the Earth at all. It was completely barren. And then I saw the gases from the Earth rise to meet the gases in the sky, and when they blended they formed amino acids, the first building blocks of life; and as the amino acids formed I felt myself enter into them, and that's when I experienced the genesis of life on Earth. The moment I entered into the amino acids, life began!

It took many years before I broke the code of this experience. I was watching a science documentary on TV one day and the microbiologist explained how amino acids, the first building blocks of life, were created out of gases that were trapped in a rock billions of years old; but what was I that had entered these amino acids that initiated the life process? How could I be responsible for the genesis of life on Planet Earth?

That's what my past life regression to the Body of God answered for me. The Way of the Eternal maintains that we are Soul, and I had the experience of being an atom of God in the Body of God with Soul consciousness but no self-consciousness; which meant that I was Soul. The Dream Weaver confirmed this several months ago with the definition of my name in the Dictionary of Life—**Orest Stocco: Soul.** So when I entered into the amino acids and initiated the life process, I realized that **life exists because of Soul consciousness.**

This is why the indigenous people of many countries speak of the soul of a tree, the soul of a rock, the soul of a river, the soul of a fish, the soul of a bird and so on—because all of life is Soul in essence; and the purpose in life, as I reasoned after my regression to my primordial human life where I gave birth to my reflective self-consciousness, is to evolve Soul consciousness through the chain of evolution until life gives birth to a new reflective self, which is a new "I" of God. But then what?

Does the self exist after death? That's the big question that haunts everyone. Is the self mortal or immortal? Is it illusory and ephemeral, as Buddhists believe; or is it real and everlasting as the Gnostics believe?

It took years, but I finally solved this riddle when I connected all the dots and saw the Big Picture. Both beliefs are true, because **we have two selves; one illusory and ephemeral, which is our ego self, and one real and everlasting, which is our Soul self.** And we realize our Soul self through the experiences of our ego self. This is how the Divine Plan of God works to expand the consciousness of God, and why man is as important to God as God is to man—just as Jung had worked out with his individuation process.

In a BBC interview late in his life Jung was asked by John Freeman if he believed in God. Jung hesitated for a moment, not expecting such a direct question; then he said, "Difficult to answer. I know. I do not need to believe. I know."

Jung's answer caused some controversy because he was accused of being a mystic Gnostic, which Jung never acknowledged publically because he wanted to maintain his image as an empirical scientist; but his answer was pure Gnosticism whose purpose is to reconcile the two selves of man, which Jung had finally managed to do as the dream he had just before his death confirmed. In it he saw "high up in a high place," a boulder lit by the full sun. Carved into that illuminated boulder were the words: "Take this as a sign of the wholeness you have achieved and the singleness you have become."

This was my journey as well. I became possessed that godforsaken night by my sexually depraved *"le salaud de Paris"* past life personality that compelled me to do something that shocked my conscience awake, and out of self-revulsion I sold my pool hall and vending machine business and fled to France to begin my quest for my true self; because I knew that the person who did what he did that night was me but not me, and I had to solve the riddle of my life because I could not live with myself unless I did. So as original as Jung's journey of self-discovery was with his confrontation with the unconscious, mine was no less so however undignified; but because we had both found the Way, we came to the same gnostic understanding of the individuation process.

We had a meeting of minds, despite his intimidating scholarly writing generously sprinkled with learned Latin phrases (not to mention Greek and French) and encyclopedic knowledge. Jung was classically educated, and he had an incredibly grasp of history; that's why his psychology spans the ages. But then, the Way is the Way is the Way, regardless what epoch; and once one finds the Way and initiates himself into the mysteries of the Way, as Jung did with his confrontation with unconscious and I did with Gurdjieff's teaching of "work on oneself," my *Royal Dictum,* and Christ's sayings, then one has a meeting of minds. Despite how abstruse Jung was at first, I understood him on the level of the Way—because there is a subtext to his formidable writing that shouts the Way loud and clear to all seekers, just as Rumi's poetry shouts the Way in every poem.

When I had my seven past life regressions I had such an explosion of consciousness that I wrote ten books in two years all the while holding down my day job of drywall taping, which was physically very exhausting. I was driven to write, and I wrote every morning from 3:30 to 8:30 before going to work. I couldn't help myself; I *had* to write!

Jung wrote in *Memories, Dreams, Reflections*: "There was a daimon in me, and in the end its presence proved decisive. It overpowered me, and if I was at times ruthless it was because I was in the grips of the daimon. I could never stop at anything once attained. I had to hasten on, to catch up to my vision..." (p. 356).

Neither could I stop. I had all the pieces to the puzzle, and I had to piece them together before my vision expended itself; that's why my daimon drove me with such ferocity that I ended up having two heart attacks (which I foolishly thought were "panic attacks"), and had to have bypass surgery—which I poured into my novel *The Sweet Breath of Life*. But it was my novel *Cathedral of My Past Lives* that gave me my first real glimpse of the Divine Plan of God that resolved the impenetrable mystery of life.

From the perspective of the Divine Plan of God, **all paths are valid; and no one path is truer than another**. Each serves its purpose. As the Sufis say, there are as many paths to God as there are souls; because every soul is its own path to God. And that's the mystery of the Way—to connect us with our Soul self which is divinely encoded and teleologically driven to return back home to God. This is why anyone who dares to live their own life lives the Way, whether they know it or not, because they have tapped into the River of God that flows through their divine nature, as I did with Gurdjieff's teaching.

This is why Jung stressed that every person should live their own life to achieve wholeness and singleness of self, because he knew that we all have our own story to live. This is what Jung meant when he said, "Thank God I'm Jung and not a Jungian." But most of us get disconnected, and this is when life can become very complicated because the natural way of life (karma and reincarnation) will set us right despite ourselves.

Jung tried to uncomplicate life with his psychology; and he helped countless people directly or indirectly to reconnect with their life. In fact, a little known fact about Jung is that he provided the seminal seed for the foundation of Alcoholics Anonymous by advising a man called Rowland H. to appeal to a Higher Power to cure his addiction, because Jung had come to see that one's "craving for alcohol was the equivalent, on a low level, of the spiritual thirst of our being for wholeness, expressed in medieval language: the union with God" (*from Jung's letter to Bill Wilson, founder of AA*). Rowland H. appealed to a Higher Power, was cured of his alcoholism, and told his story to a friend who told it to Bill Wilson, the founder of AA. *God works in mysterious ways...*

Jung had to do service in the Swiss military, and during the First World War when he was Commandant de la Region anglaise des Internes de Guerre (1918/1919) Marie-Louise von Franz writes: "every morning he devotedly and painstakingly sketched a circular drawing in a notebook. After a time he noticed that the form of the drawings appeared to mirror his own subjective condition. If he was 'outside himself' or in a bad mood, then the mandala would be distorted. He writes (*Memories, Dreams, Reflections*): 'Only gradually did I discover what the mandala really is: 'Formation, Transformation, Eternal Mind's eternal recreation' (from Goethe's *Faust*). And that is the self, the wholeness of the personality, which if all goes well is harmonious, but which cannot tolerate self-deception...The self, I thought, was like the monad which I am, and is my world. The mandala represents this monad and corresponds to the microcosmic nature of the psyche...The mandala is the center. It is the exponent of all paths. It is the path to the center, to individuation'" (*C. G. Jung, His Myth in Our Time*, pp. 139-40).

This is the first time that I have found a satisfactory explanation for the spontaneous manifestation of the mandala that I experienced in my second year at university when I was so mad at myself for not "getting" Gurdjieff's teaching of "work on oneself" that I threw Ouspensky's book at my bedroom wall in disgust and lay on my bed to wallow in self-pity. After all these years I now understand what my creative unconscious was telling me with the "squaring of the circle" symbol—*it was the madala of my life's path!*

Jung writes that "the mandala is the path to the center, to individuation," and my mandala, born of my own unconscious need for wholeness and singleness of self that erupted from the depths of my unconscious into a circle of blue light that was squared by a yellow light, was telling me that I had to "square the circle" to get to the center of my being; that I had to do the impossible to find my lost soul; that I had to "die" to my life to "find" my life; that I had to "create" my own soul!

There I was then; studying philosophy at the beginning of my quest and my creative unconscious was telling me that I had to do the impossible to find my true self; but I had no idea what that mandala meant. I didn't even know it was a mandala until I started reading Jung; and even so, all these years later, I didn't discover what my mandala meant until I reread Marie-Louise von Franz's book *C. G. Jung, His Myth in Our Time!*

And now that I understand what my mandala symbolized, I feel like I've been given permission to speak of my own path with the authority of my own individuation process sanctioned by the spiritual wisdom of my creative unconscious, because I did do the impossible; I did transform the consciousness of my non-self and realized my true self; and I did find my lost soul. So when God shouts again, "NOMAN, HAST THOU MY FISH'S SCALE?" I can proudly (and with all the humility in the world) answer, "Yes."

13. *The Way of Soul*

Gurdjieff was wrong. He believed that not everyone has an immortal soul. Only a small number of people have an immortal soul, which they have created out of extraordinary life circumstances; and he believed that by replicating these circumstances by "working on oneself" one can create their own soul. He gave the analogy of an oak tree to explain his belief. Out of the thousands of acorn seeds that fall to the ground, only one or two might take root. This is how nature works. Only one or two people out of millions might take root and grow their own soul. **"Man must finish the work which nature left unfinished,"** said the alchemists. This made Gurdjieff's teaching "impossible" to live.

I didn't know whether to believe Gurdjieff or not; but to play it safe I gave him the benefit of the doubt and "worked" on myself with pathological commitment. Gurdjieff called his teaching "esoteric Christianity," which implied that the teachings of Christ also maintained that not everyone is born with an immortal soul.

Jesus taught the secret teachings of the Way. He spoke to the public in parables and to his disciples in secret. *"Because it is given unto you to know mysteries of the kingdom of heaven, but to them it is not given,"* said Jesus to his disciples (Math. 13: 11). His sayings have both an exoteric and esoteric meaning, and if one learns how to interpret the esoteric meaning of his sayings he will have eternal life, as he promised in the *Gospel of Thomas: "Whoever finds the interpretation of these sayings will not taste death."*

Does this mean that Jesus also believed that not everyone is born with an immortal soul, and by living the correct interpretation of his sayings one could create his own soul?

Is this the real meaning of spiritual rebirth? *"Verily, verily, I say unto thee, Except a man be born again, he cannot see the kingdom of God"* said Jesus, (John 3:3). And *"He that loveth his life shall lose it; and he that hateth his life in this world shall keep it unto life eternal"* he adds later (John 12: 25), giving us the most obvious clue as to how to interpret his sayings correctly, because the life that we have to lose is our ephemeral, human self; and the life that we get to keep is our eternal, Soul self.

As I *lived* the sayings of Jesus the Way revealed itself more and more to me, and I began to suspect that Gurdjieff was wrong to believe that not everyone is born with an immortal soul, because the Way awakened me to the spiritual essence, or Soul consciousness of life; and if Jesus held the same view he was wrong also. Besides, I had an inner awareness of my eternal Soul self with my past life recollection dreams.

And then I found the secret teachings of the Way of the Eternal and learned that we are all Soul, that we are individual atoms in the Body of God, and that our purpose in life is to individuate the consciousness of life to expand the consciousness of God; which meant that Gurdjieff was wrong, and Jesus also if that's what he believed.

The Way of the Eternal resonated with me, and I had no doubt that we are all Soul; and then I had seven past life regressions and experienced myself as an atom of God in the Body of God. I had Soul consciousness but no self-consciousness; and then I experienced myself in my first primordial human life where I gave birth to my reflective self.

These experiences confirmed my belief that we are Soul, and that we evolve through life to individuate the consciousness of life until we realize our Soul self. This happens naturally through karma and reincarnation, as my past life regressions confirmed; but the natural process of evolution can only take us so far, and this is man's dilemma.

How many souls have evolved unconsciously by the natural process of karma and reincarnation and then hit a brick wall because they could not satisfy their longing for wholeness and singleness of self? And how many souls have been shipwrecked on the shoals of life looking for a way to satisfy their longing for wholeness?

The Conference of the Birds tells the story of countless souls that went on a quest to satisfy their longing for God only to be thwarted by the trials and tribulations that they had to face along the way. Only thirty birds completed the journey, and when they looked into the Face of God they saw their own image—their eternal Soul self that they had realized by overcoming their many trials and tribulations to complete their journey.

I was one of the thirty birds. I looked into the Face of God. This was one of the most intense periods of my entire life, if not the most intense. I had started my own contract painting business and was pouring an inordinate amount of energy into making a go of it; I "worked" on myself daily with Gurdjieff's teaching, my *Royal Dictum*, and Christ's sayings with such pathological commitment that I gave birth to my spiritual self in my mother's kitchen; I had been practicing the solar techniques from that offshoot Christian solar cult teaching that did irreparable damage to my eyesight; I had become a chela of the Way of the Eternal and received my Second Initiation; I poured myself into my writing every morning and ran seven miles after work every day; and when I met the Inner Master in a dream one night, I said to him, *"what do I call you?"*

I was so traumatized by the ophthalmologist at the Thunder Bay Clinic who lost his temper and abandoned his professional code of conduct by refusing to treat me when he learned how I got the three solar burns in my eyes (thank God they were stationary and not degenerative; but I didn't find this out for several weeks and I lived in terror of going blind), and I was so devastated when I had to own up to my family for what I had done to my eyes that I had such a bitter taste in my mouth for that solar cult teacher that I never again wanted to consider anyone becoming my Spiritual Master; that's why I said to the

Inner Master the first time I met him in my dreams, *"what do I call you?"*

I could not call him Spiritual Master as my spiritual community did, but he gave me a warm loving smile and placed his arm gently around my shoulders and slowly turned me around; and as we turned, I found myself staring into the Face of God. I cannot describe my experience because it was ineffable. All I could utter was, "GOD I LOVE YOU!"

Two years later it dawned on me that he had answered my question *"what do I call you?"* The Inner Master let me experience his essential nature, which is the Consciousness of God, thereby confirming that he was a God-realized Soul!

But I never called him Master whenever I met him on the Inner Planes. I called him by his spiritual name. However, about ten years later I began to have doubts about my spiritual experience. *"Did I really look into the Face of God?"* I asked myself. I began to doubt my own mind, and this really bothered me because it struck at the very core of my being. I was one of the thirty birds. Or was I?

My doubt was insidious. It ate away at me like a worm, and soon I began to doubt my spiritual path which was my *raison d'être* because all of my questing for my true self had brought me to the Way of the Eternal; and then Providence intervened.

It was Sunday morning. I told Penny I was going for a nice gentle run along the Lake Helen shoreline, where I normally ran every day. As I ran I thought about my experience of looking into the Face of God. It was early summer, and there was a little bite to the air; but running warmed me up and I began to feel good.

That's why I went for a daily run. Running had a metabiological effect on me, and regardless how I felt going into my run I always felt good after my run. This was the magic of long distance running, and why Dr. George Sheehan could proudly boast that in running he had found his salvation. I knew exactly what he meant, but little did I expect that I would experience salvation from my demon doubt that morning.

I was approaching the long curve on the highway where a giant pine tree had washed up onto the shoreline and had been there for years, its trunk and roots and branches all washed a clean dirty gray by the weather, but I saw that some Canada Geese were huddled around the length of the tree and the thought came to me: *"Wouldn't it be something if there were thirty birds there? That would confirm that I did look into the Face of God."* And of course I had to stop to count the birds: "1, 2, 3, 4, 5..."

I counted twenty-five, and my heart sank. Close, but not close enough; but I wanted to make sure, so I counted again. This time I counted twenty-seven. I counted two more times to make certain, and my heart sank again. Then I was nudged to jump up onto the guard rail so I could have a complete view of the tree and Canada Geese, and I spotted two more; which made twenty-nine. I counted three more times to be certain, but there were only twenty-nine Canada Geese—one bird shy of vindication. My heart sank.

I jumped off the guard rail and started running down the road. I wanted to cry. How could that happen? Why would God tease me like that? And then out of the blue it hit me and I shouted, "I'M THE THIRTIETH BIRD!"

I could not believe it! So certain was I of the symbolic validation of my experience of looking into the Face of God that it left absolutely no crack for doubt to ever worm its way into my mind again, and I could not wait to share my unbelievable coincidence with Penny—which for me was not coincidence at all, but what Jung called the "synchronistic principle" and what I have come to simply call the Way of Soul!

"Life is a journey of the self," said St. Padre Pio, the Ascended Master who blessed me with a spiritual healing; but there will be those that will doubt it was St. Padre Pio that the gifted psychic medium channeled for my novel *Healing with Padre Pio*, as there will be those that will doubt my experience of looking into the

Face of God. But there's good reason why people doubt the spiritual life, and it took me years to figure out why.

Because of karma, life is inherently self-correcting; and every belief that we have that is founded upon a false premise will eventually be found out. It is *ipso facto,* because Soul is the essential nature of life, and Soul is *that which is.* "Reality, truth, and existence are synonymous," said Paul Twitchell, and regardless how long it takes false beliefs will eventually collapse by the weight of their own nothingness.

This makes life very interesting, because we never know for certain what is true and what is false. Life is a perpetual winding and weaving and twisting and grinding of the true and false, and it's up to us to make sense of it all; and some of us do make sense of it, and some of us don't. *"God is in his heaven and all is right with the world,"* says one poet; and another says, *"Life is a tale told by an idiot full of sound and fury signifying nothing."* It all depends upon one's state of consciousness. And this is the mystery of the two selves of man that I was destined to resolve in my current parallel life.

In my dialogue with the archetypal Jesus that I called upon from the fertile depths of my creative unconscious for my novel *Jesus Wears Dockers* we went into great detail on how to resolve the two selves of man so one can enter into the kingdom of heaven (Christ's metaphor for spiritual consciousness), and the essential principle for this miraculous resolution is the Way which is central to Christ's sayings, Gurdjieff's teaching, Gnosticism, Alchemy, Sufism, Taoism, Buddhism, Christianity, Judaism, Islam, Hinduism, and all paths really because the Way is life—*every single facet of it.*

This is why I call the Way the omniscient guiding force of life; which means that the Way is as much about the false nature of life as it is the real, because **the Way is all about the resolution of opposites.** This is what Jung realized with his confrontation with the unconscious; and his psychology of individuation is all about bringing resolution to the opposing natures of our individuating self-consciousness (our *being* and *non-being*). But I would never have made any sense of this without coming to grips with the Way of Soul, which is the Way of all ways and archetypal path that every soul is destined to live.

I resolved this mystery when I connected the missing pieces to the puzzle of life and worked out the Divine Plan of God. The missing pieces were the answer to Gauguin's questions: *Where do we come from? What are we?* And *where are we going?* My regression to the Body of God answered the first question; my experience of being an atom of God with Soul consciousness but no self-consciousness answered the second question; and my experience of looking into the Face of God after I had given birth to my Soul self answered the third question; so I had personal experience of the Way of Soul, which gave my spiritual perspective gnostic authority, just as Jung's confrontation with the unconscious that he recorded in *The Red Book* gave his psychology of individuation gnostic authority.

Jung lived his own path to the Way, and I lived mine; and just as it took volumes of words for Jung to give expression to his gnostic knowledge of the Way, which he did everything in his power to frame within an empirically based psychology, it took me volumes of words to work out my own individuation process in my writing. I wrote book after book to express the vision I had caught a glimpse of with my past life regressions, and finally I began to see that Soul evolves through life in three stages, which I came to call the Three Circles of Life. And I called these three stages the Divine Plan of God.

The First Circle of Life is the exoteric stage, where the atom of God is introduced into life, *as I experienced with the genesis of life on Earth;* and from life form to life form Soul evolves, constellating more life consciousness with each life it lives until it evolves into a life form that is capable of constellating enough life consciousness to become aware of itself for the very first time, *which I experienced in one of my regressions when I had the dawning of my reflective self-consciousness in my first human lifetime as a higher primate;* and then Soul continues to evolve in self-consciousness until it can evolve no further through the natural process of karma and reincarnation and must look for the Way to complete its destiny to spiritual self-realization and God consciousness, *which I did in my current parallel life.* I was reborn into my same life to take evolution into my own hands and complete my spiritual destiny that I left incomplete the first time I lived my life as Orest Stocco; and I began to fulfill my spiritual destiny with Gurdjieff's teaching, my *Royal Dictum*, and the sayings of Jesus.

So the First Circle of Life is all about natural evolution, which is directed by the Spiritual Laws of Karma and Reincarnation. We grow and evolve in our own individuality through the karma that we create and resolve with each life we live; but when we have evolved to the point where natural evolution can no longer satisfy our spiritual need for total self-realization consciousness we have to take evolution into our own hands. In effect, we become seekers; and what we are looking for is the Way.

This is the Second Circle of Life, which is the mesoteric stage of evolution that is characterized by karmic awareness. We now know that choices have karmic consequences, and we look for a path that will liberate us from the negative consequences of life; but the mesoteric stage is so difficult to live that few people make it to the Third Circle of Life.

The Conference of the Birds allegorizes the mesoteric stage of evolution, and the thirty birds that saw their Soul self in the Face of God were granted permission to enter into the Third Circle of Life to continue their journey to God-realization consciousness; so the key to the mesoteric stage of evolution is spiritual rebirth, as Jesus said; or, as Gurdjieff believed, "creating" one's own soul. In either case, the journey to one's Soul self is not an easy journey. As Jung said to Miguel Serrano, "The path is very difficult."

In fact, it is so difficult that clever people have tried to short circuit the entire mesoteric stage of evolution. In the mesoteric stage we take full responsibility for our own karma and look for the best way to resolve it. Christianity short circuits this "fear and trembling" stage of evolution by proclaiming that Jesus died on the cross to atone for the sins of the world. This clever doctrine that inspired my book *Jesus Wears Dockers, The Gospel Conspiracy Story* is founded upon the premise that sins can be forgiven, which goes contrary to the immutable Law of Karma. This is why I abandoned my Christian faith. I felt suffocated by all the unresolved karma of my past lives, and I had to find a path that would let me breathe; which I did when Divine Spirit introduced me to Gurdjieff's teaching.

Gurdjieff taught a mesoteric teaching of spiritual growth, because it taught one how to take evolution into his own hands by transforming the consciousness of his false self for the specific purpose of "creating" one's own soul. I lived Gurdjieff's teaching with such pathological commitment that I gave birth to my Soul self, so I know that it works; but once I worked out the Divine Plan of God I had a larger context to explain Gurdjieff's teaching: one does not "create" his own soul, as such; one shifts his center of gravity from his ephemeral human self to his eternal Soul self, which appears to be a spiritual rebirth but isn't. It's a shift in I-consciousness from our lower to higher self; or, to put it in the simplest terms possible, spiritual rebirth is a shift in I-consciousness from ego to Soul.

Making this shift in I-consciousness can be very difficult; but it all depends upon one's karmic path. Mine was so difficult that I had to "square the circle" to find my true self; and Jung's path was so difficult that there were times he thought he was losing his mind. But he didn't. He made it through to the other side and recorded his journey through the mesoteric stage in *The Red Book*, which tells the incredible story of his confrontation with the unconscious that provided him with the seed material for all his future writing—three of my favorite books being *Modern Man in Search of a Soul*, *The Undiscovered Self*, and his autobiographical memoir *Memories, Dreams, Reflections*.

The Way of Soul then begins in the Body of God where we all come from as atoms of God with Soul consciousness but no self-consciousness; and we evolve through the exoteric first stage of evolution from life form to life form until we are born into a life form that can constellate enough consciousness for the atom of God to become aware of itself for the first time in its existence, as I experienced in my first primordial human life when to my utter confusion I had the dawning of my reflective self-consciousness.

Once Soul gives birth to a new "I" of God it continues to grow and evolve in its own individuality according to the karma that it creates by the choices it makes, because with choice comes personal karma. Soul is not conscious enough to be aware of the karmic consequences of its choices, but as it evolves through the exoteric stage of evolution it becomes increasingly more conscious until one day it dawns upon us that there is a direct relationship between choice and our life—meaning, we create the life we have by the choices we make; thereby alerting us to the mesoteric second stage of evolution.

The self that we give birth to in the first stage of evolution is our reflective human self-consciousness; it is not our Soul self, as such. It takes many more incarnations before our human self constellates enough consciousness to become aware of our Soul self, as I did in my past lifetime as Solomon, the Good Slave.

I had constellated enough consciousness to realize that I had a soul that was separate from me, but I also realized that my soul was at the mercy of my outer life; and to realize my freedom I had to master my outer life, which I could not do in that lifetime because I was a slave subject to my master's wishes. But I could devote my life to God, though; which was the only way that I could become master of my pitiful life of bondage.

Mastering life is the final stage of the First Circle of Life, because it awakens one's soul to the responsibility that comes with taking control of one's own life; and it will only be a matter of time before one realizes that he is the author of his own karmic destiny, however fortunate or unfortunate it may be. And from lifetime to lifetime one's soul will grow in the consciousness of its own individuality until it can no longer suffer the burden of its own life; and it will begin to look for a way out of the prison of its own consciousness—which is why

Gurdjieff said that his teaching was for those who despaired their life. Just like me. I despaired my life so much that I had to find my true self or die trying. And Jung also. As successful as he was, he despaired his life; and he had to find his lost soul.

Late in his life, in the aftermath of World War II, Carl Jung wrote *The Undiscovered Self* in response to the apocalyptic mood of the times. In the forward to the 2010 Bollingen Series edition of *The Undiscovered Self*, "Reading Jung After *The Red Book*," Jungian scholar and editor of *The Red Book* Sonu Shamdasani writes: "he (Jung) argued that the only solution to the seemingly catastrophic developments in the world lay in the individual turning within and resolving the individual aspects of the collective conflicts...What was required was a psychology that facilitated self-knowledge by reconnecting individuals with their dreams and the symbols that spontaneously emerged from within—which was the theme of Jung's last written work, *Symbols and the Interpretation of Dreams*."

Jung was acutely conscious of the distinction between the outer personality and the unconscious inner self, and it was his mission to provide a psychology to resolve the inherent conflict of our two selves. That was the only way to resolve world conflicts. "Most people confuse 'self-knowledge' with knowledge of their conscious ego-personalities," he wrote in *The Undiscovered Self*. "Anyone who has any ego-consciousness at all takes for granted that he knows himself. But the ego only knows its own content, not the unconscious and its contents" (p.5); which in effect means that we do not really know who we are.

Soul is who we are, as one of my dreams recently confirmed; and dreams don't lie. Soul is our unconscious inner self, and every time we are reborn into life we create a new ego personality; but what happens to our past life ego-personalities? Do they die with our body, or do they survive in our unconscious Soul memory?

Everything indicates that our past life personalities exist in our unconscious self, and these personalities affect our current life—as the sexually depraved personality of my past life in Paris in the 17the Century affected me when it burst out of the unconscious that godforsaken night and shocked my conscience awake; and my past life personality in Genoa, Italy when I dishonored my wife (Penny in my current life) and was karmically bound to resolve my betrayal in this life; and my hypocritical lifetime in London's aristocracy that bound me to my family in my current life; and so on.

We cannot escape our past lives. They come back to haunt us; and they will continue to haunt us until we resolve them of all the karma that keeps them from being integrated into our individuating Soul self. This is the aspect of the individuation process that Jung failed to take into account in his psychology of the self, and with good reason; the times were not evolved enough yet to include past life therapy in his psychology.

Fortunately for Jung our past lives speak to us through our dreams, so in one way it doesn't really matter if we remember our past lives or not; but it goes a long way to solving the riddle of who we are, what we are, and where we are going. This is why Jung came to me in a dream one night to talk about my book *The Way of Soul*.

14. *The Omniscient Guiding Force of Life*

I could not pass up the opportunity to ask Ascended Master St. Padre Pio the question about the immortal soul of man, because I truly wanted to know what Jesus believed. Being in a place of all knowing and seeing, he could answer my question.

My curiosity was not idle by any means. I was reborn in my mother's kitchen when I experienced my immortal Soul self. I *knew* that I would never die, and from that moment on I have never doubted that *I am*. But I had lived the Way consciously to realize my Soul self, and I wanted to know if one was born with an immortal soul or not.

St. Padre Pio's answer was short and sweet. He said that we are all a part of the divine Whole, so how could we not be born without a divine nature? This divine nature is what John Keats called "sparks" of God, and "atoms of perception" born into life to "acquire" their own identity—meaning, their own Soul self. Keats called this "Soul-making," Jung called it the individuation process, and I have called it the Way of Soul.

The Way of Soul takes these "sparks" of God through the three stages of evolution: the First, Second, and Third Circles of Life. Nature evolves the individuating "sparks" of God through the exoteric first stage; but to evolve through the mesoteric second stage of life we have to transform the consciousness of our exoteric self, which is made up of the consciousness of *being* and *non-being*; only then will we be allowed to enter into the esoteric third stage of conscious evolution.

Shakespeare gave us a profound glimpse into the dual nature of human consciousness in Hamlet's famous *to be or not to be* soliloquy. I spent years of unbelievable Gurdjieffian effort to shift my center of gravity from my lower self (my *being* and *non-being*) to my higher self—from my ego to Soul, if you will. Gurdjieff called this shift in consciousness "creating one's own soul," and Jesus called it being "born again." In the Way of the Eternal it is called "spiritual self-realization consciousness."

This is the great mystery of life that I returned to resolve in my parallel life. I'm still having dreams of my life in my hometown of Nipigon, the people I knew there, and especially dreams of my family and family home. Just last night (Sunday, January 27, 2013) I had another dream of our family home. My mother had two young men clean the house for her, and it was spotless; and I remember being in the kitchen with some people I knew and having a cup of coffee into which I inadvertently poured some maple syrup thinking that it was a bottle of Anisette and then calling my cup of coffee "a serendipity drink." I took that to be the Dream Weaver's way of telling me that serendipity plays an important role in our life, because quite often serendipity changes the course of our life.

I wrote a spiritual musing called "Chance or Divine Intervention?" for my third volume of spiritual musings (*Stupidity is Not a Gift of God*), which was inspired by Robert H. Hopcke's book *There Are No Accidents, Synchronicity and the Stories of Our Lives*, because I wanted to show with my own experiences of synchronicity that there is an omniscient guiding force in life that watches over us; but this is a difficult concept to get across apart from sounding like a religious zealot who relegates his whole life to "the will of God." It certainly is God's will that guides us; but in a very special way that allows us the dignity of free choice. And it is this "special way" that I had awakened to by "working" on myself with Gurdjieff's teaching, my *Royal Dictum,* and the sayings of Jesus.

In the Bollingen Series edition with a forward by Sonu Shamdasani, *Synchronicity, An Acausal Connecting Principle,* Carl Jung (who coined the term "synchronicity" for meaningful coincidences) wrote: "Chance, we say, must obviously be susceptible of some causal explanation and is only called 'chance' or 'coincidence' because its causality has not been discovered. Since we have an inveterate conviction of the absolute validity of causal law, we regard this explanation of chance as being quite adequate" (p. 7).

This cause-effect paradigm rules out an acausal principle, which intrigued Jung his whole life. This is why he was so fascinated with the *I Ching,* the *Book of Changes.* He writes: "The function on which the use of the *I Ching* is based at first sight appears to be in sharp contrast to our Western way of scientific causal thinking... The science of the *I Ching,* indeed, is not based on the causal principle, but on a principle (hitherto unnamed because not met with among us) which I have tentatively called the synchronistic principle...because the causality principle seemed to me to be inadequate for the explanation of certain remarkable phenomenon of the unconscious. Thus I found that there are psychic parallelisms which cannot be related to each other causally, but which must stand in another sort of connectedness. This connectedness seemed to me to lie mainly in the relative simultaneity of the events, therefore the expression 'synchronistic'" (from his memorial to Richard Wilhelm: *The Secret of the Golden Flower,* translated by Richard Wilhelm and commentary by C. G. Jung, p. 141).

What is this mysterious "synchronistic principle"? Jung never quite resolved this mystery to his satisfaction because he could not stick his neck out and openly admit to the "unscientific" transcendent factor responsible for synchronicity; but I have, which I will relate in a subsequent chapter "The Synchronistic Principle." So, again, what is it?

It is the Way of Soul, the omniscient guiding consciousness of life that transcends the causal principle and renders the cause-effect paradigm totally inadequate to explaining the human condition, because the causal principle does not take into account the spiritual nature of man. I cannot prove this, of course, except with my own experiences with the Way of Soul; but then, didn't Gurdjieff say that there is only self-initiation into the mysteries of life?

It all comes down to a question of individual consciousness, which is determined by the stage of one's journey through life;

and as long as one is stuck in the exoteric first stage of evolution he will never rend the veil of the mind and see the acausal synchronistic principle of the Way of Soul at work in life.

One has to enter through Christ's "strait gate" of the "narrow way" that constitutes the mesoteric second stage of evolution to awaken to the Way of Soul; which is why I chose to be reborn into my same life again. I had a golden opportunity to initiate myself into the second stage of evolution and resolve the mystery of my life, which I did not take advantage of in my first lifetime; but how can I be certain that I am living my parallel life now?

What is certain for me may not necessarily be certain for anyone else, but from the day that I began writing *The Summoning of Noman* I have been focused on the mystery of my two lives as Orest Stocco, and I *know* now that I am living my parallel life. I have italicized the word *know* to indicate that indescribable gnostic awareness that Gnostic scholars like Stephan A. Hoeller and Elaine Pagels are still trying to come to terms with; and I got my first clue from a curious dream that I had a few years ago when I asked myself the question, *"what would my life have been like if I had taken that course?"*

Carl Jung told me in my dream experience with him that to understand a dream we have to see it in context. In other words, a dream is born of its context; and when we have the context the dream will reveal its meaning. What, then, was the context of the dream that answered my question *"what would my life have been like if had taken that course?"*

The context is simple enough, but the dream that it gave birth to opens a window onto the unfathomable mystery of the Way of Soul that cannot be penetrated by the exoterically minded person; only a mesoterically minded initiate of the Second Circle of Life can make sense of how the omniscient guiding force of life plays its part to help us on our pre-destined spiritual journey to total self-realization consciousness, and initiating myself into the mesoteric stage of evolution is what my parallel life has been all about.

This, then, is the context of my dream that reveals how the omniscient guiding force of life stepped in to keep me from taking that course in life which would have left me feeling regretful, depressed, and unfulfilled: I was in high school. One of my part-time jobs was working at the Hudson's Bay Company. I worked after school and Saturdays. The stores weren't open on Sunday then. I worked in the grocery department stocking shelves and bagging and carrying out groceries for customers.

The store manager saw potential in me. His plan was to train me in the clothing department in the hope that I would make a career with the Hudson's Bay Company. It was a wonderful opportunity, so I began working Saturdays in men's clothing. I was going to be trained by the department manager and I was looking forward to my new position. But then a very strange thing happened to me: my arithmetic skills abandoned me!

I was a very affable young man with all the charm and personality a salesman could possibly want, and I was pretty good at selling clothes; but when it came to adding up the sales receipt for my customers my mind went strange on me, and for the life of me I could not figure out what was happening. The department manager had to step in every time to make out my sale receipt. This was disappointing, and before long I was back in the grocery department stocking shelves and packing groceries.

What happened to me? I wasn't mathematically challenged. I could add. Why did my arithmetic skill abandon me every time I made a sale?

I wasn't to find an answer to this question until just a few years ago when I was reflecting on my high school days and my job with the Hudson's Bay Company. My blood rushed to my face and I flushed red with embarrassment as I thought of the times the department manager had to step in to make out a new sales receipt for my customers. I could not believe it. How could I be so stupid?

I tried to laugh it off, but my humiliation wouldn't go away. I could not believe how I blew my chance with the Hudson's Bay

Company by being so stupid. But I wasn't stupid. I can remember as though I was right there doing it again how my mind went funny on me and I just could not add up the numbers correctly. It was bizarre.

After I calmed down I wondered what my life would have been like if I had not blown my chance to be weaned by the Hudson's Bay Company; and a few days later, perhaps a week, I got my answer by way of a dream:

I'm the manager of a Hudson's Bay store in a small community in Northern Manitoba. I am married with three children, and by all appearances I am a happily married man with a successful career, a pillar of the community and envy of my friends and neighbors; but the truth is that I am not happy. I have everything that a man could want: a beautiful wife, wonderful children, and a very good career. But I am dying inside.

I always wanted to be a writer, and I write stories now and then. My model was Ernest Hemingway, who was my hero in high school. I envied him the courage to pursue his dream of writing. I got swept away in my training with the Bay, moving from town to town to grow in the company until I was seasoned enough to have my own store and my dream of writing was reduced to a hobby that I dabbled in now and then.

I finally get my own store and am at that point in my life where I have everything that I have worked for, but I begin to feel regretful. I am moody and my wife cannot understand what is happening to me. Despite everything that I have, I feel empty and unfulfilled; and I hate myself for what I have done with my life.

But there is nothing I can do about it now. I write to escape my life, but it's too late for me. I am too responsible to do justice to writing, and I get more depressed. I wake up feeling like I took the wrong course in my life, and I am regretful.

That was the life I would have lived had the omniscient guiding force of life not stepped in to keep me from taking that course. I had no idea why my mind went funny whenever I wrote up a sale receipt for my customers, but I *know* now that it was divine intervention. I was meant to stay in Nipigon, which I did.

I ended up leasing a pool hall business at the age of twenty-one, which I expanded to include vending machines; and I was doing very well for myself until that godforsaken night when my archetypal shadow was awakened from the deep recesses of my unconscious and compelled me to do something that shocked my conscience awake and I could not live with myself, and I sold my business and fled to France.

When I came back from France I went to university to study philosophy, but in my third year I got "yanked" away from a life in academia (I wanted to become a professor of philosophy) by my discovery of Gurdjieff's teaching that called me to "work" on myself in the steam of everyday life; so I started my contract painting business, which was the perfect medium to practice the secret teachings of the Way according to Gurdjieff. But ten or twelve years later I wanted out, and the opportunity came up to buy a drive-in restaurant; and I had another dream that told me that contract painting was the course for me:

I'm with a group of four or five men. I know that I am on the Other Side, and that these wise men are counseling me on what course to take in my life. I know who they are when I am with them, but I don't remember who they are when I wake up. In my dream they tell me that I still have a lot to learn from my painting business, and they insist that I stay on that course; and I remember slipping back into my body feeling disappointed.

I don't know the date exactly, but an opportunity came up to buy the Nipigon Drive-In Restaurant not long after I had this dream. The husband and wife owners and I talked it over, and we shook hands on the deal; and I began looking into financing. But a few days later I got a call from them telling me that they had to back out.

It so happened that they met up with their close friends one evening and shared the good news with them; but for some strange reason their good friends offered to buy the drive-in from them. The friend who was going to run the drive-in because her husband was still working at the paper mill was my "flaky" cousin who had introduced me to the Way of the Eternal, but their offer put the owners in a moral bind and they called me that evening just to make sure I was still interested. But by some strange quirk of fate I got an invitation out of the blue to a friend's cottage that evening and wasn't home for the call, so they sealed the deal with a contract that very evening and I lost out.

I felt betrayed by my cousin and harbored resentment for years, but I continued with my painting business and learned all the lessons that I was meant to bring my karmic destiny into alignment with my spiritual destiny and realize the purpose of my parallel life; and unlike how I felt in my parallel dream lifetime as a Hudson's Bay store manager or my first real parallel lifetime as Orest Stocco, I can die right now with no regrets for the life that I have lived. And as much as I hate to say it, I'm thankful now for how the omniscient guiding force of life orchestrated the events that evening that kept me from buying the drive-in; because that would have taken me down an entirely different road in life which would probably have resulted in not achieving what I had come back to achieve.

15. *The Way of Being and Non-being*

Did I really live that life as a Hudson's Bay store manager, or did the Dream Weaver conjure up that life for me just to answer my question and confirm my belief that the omniscient guiding force of life intervenes to keep us on spiritual track?

I can't prove it, but I believe this is what happened: I would have lived that life had I gone that route; but the omniscient guiding force of life knew that I would not fulfill my spiritual purpose if I had gone that route, so Divine Spirit intervened.

I also know that I would not have fulfilled my spiritual purpose had I not sold my pool hall and vending machine business and gone to France. I would have become successful in Nipigon had I stayed in business; but I also had a dream where I was near the end of my life in Nipigon and I'm walking to the post office feeling that I have betrayed myself for not living the life I was supposed to live.

I felt unfulfilled and disappointed in myself, so the omniscient guiding force of life intervened once again and I sold my business and went to France to begin my quest for my true self, because when one is ready to enter the mesoteric stage of evolution all the forces in the universe conspire to assist him. I was ready, but I was also very stubborn.

The ancient Stoic poet Cleanthes wrote a poem that speaks to this peculiar situation that many souls like me find themselves in: "*Lead me Zeus, /and thou, o destiny, /the way I am bid by thee to go. /To follow I am willing, /for were I recusant /I do but make myself a slave, /and still must follow.*" I was recusant, and my destiny had to intervene; that's why I was possessed to do what I did that godforsaken night—because I had to reroute my life so that I could fulfill my destiny; which I did in my current parallel life.

This is very mysterious, and I'm still trying to wrap my mind around this whole concept of parallel worlds; but the more I explore this, the more comfortable I am with the idea that we live all of our lives simultaneously in parallel worlds. But we don't all live the same life over again in a parallel world, as I am doing. This is what puzzles me.

My daemonic poem *Noman* revealed that God had condemned me to the "fourth corner of the abyss" to find His "fish's scale" (my lost soul), and I would continue to be reborn until I found it; but how was I to do that? That was the purpose of my parallel life.

St. Padre Pio told me that the first time I lived my life as Orest Stocco I had not achieved the outcome that I was supposed to achieve, so I chose to be reborn into my same life to achieve a different outcome. He told me that in my first life I was not open-minded to that "other religion" (my current spiritual path), but this time I am; and I have achieved the outcome that I came to achieve—which was to find the lost soul of God.

I wrote a novel called *The Seeker, Quest for the Lost Soul of God*; and it tells the story of my secret life of the Way. My poem *Noman*, which I wrote in high school decades before I wrote *The Seeker*, speaks to the mystery of the lost soul of God.

Noman is our false self. It is the archetypal shadow self of all the shadow selves of our past lives, and at some point in one's life it can take over one's personality. How this happens is a mystery, but I *know* that it happened to me when I wrote my poem *Noman*. My false self erupted in one daemonic burst of consciousness, and from that day on my personality began to be imbued with the consciousness of my archetypal shadow self; and for the life of me I could not understand why I now had an impulse to falseness! I couldn't help myself, and I had to fight myself just to be honest and truthful!

A number of years ago I had a curious dream of two very successful Hollywood movie directors. They were good friends professionally, but personally they were complete opposites and couldn't stand each other. One was centered in his *non-being* (his archetypal shadow self), and the other was centered in his *being* (his authentic self), and they revealed their type by their character; their interests, manners, speech, and behavior.

One was miserable and impossible to please. Nothing was ever good enough for him, and he made life very difficult for everyone on his set; but he made great movies. The other was no less demanding, but in a completely different way. He was kind, understanding, and very generous with everyone on his set; and he also made great movies.

I had no idea what this dream meant at first; but then I remembered something that I read in *The Teachers of Gurdjieff* by Rafael Lefort. Gurdjieff was an enigma. He never revealed the source of his teaching, and Rafael Lefort went on a quest to find Gurdjieff's teachers. This story is probably allegory, because as J. G. Bennettt surmised in his book *Gurdjieff: Making a New World* he doubted that any of Gurdjieff's teachers were still alive when Lefort went on his quest. Nonetheless, one Sufi Master who taught Gurdjieff told him that there were two paths in life: one by way of *being*, and the other by way of *non-being*. This resonated with me, because I knew that mine was the path of *non-being*.

This was confirmed for me when I hit a brick wall with Gurdjieff's teaching and the omniscient guiding force of life intervened to get me back on spiritual track. I was sitting in my bedroom wallowing in self-pity because I could not make headway with Gurdjieff's teaching. I had taken the Work as far as I could go, and I came to a screeching halt; and I was so lonely and miserable that I wanted to cry. I put on Beethoven's Ninth Symphony to cheer me up. The Ode to Joy always lifted my spirits. Then I heard a voice in my mind that set be back on the right course: *"Why do you lie?"*

The voice startled me. I waited for more, but that was all I needed to hear; because that question was so powerful it jolted me out of myself and I was forced to look at myself from an entirely different angle—from the perspective of my false self. And I began to scrutinize my every thought, word, and deed; and

I was amazed to learn just how false I really was. That's when Gurdjieff's teaching finally made sense to me, especially the comment he made to his students in one of his private talks:

"To speak the truth is the most difficult thing in the world; and one must study a great deal and for a long time in order to be able to speak the truth. The wish alone is not enough. *To speak the truth one must know what the truth is and what a lie is, and first of all in oneself.* And this nobody wants to know." (*In Search of the Miraculous, Fragments of an Unknown Teaching,* by P. D. Ouspensky, p. 22)

The Inner Master's question *"why do you lie?"* forced me to look at myself in an entirely different way. I had to first acknowledge that I lied, and then I had to solve the mystery of why I lied; and that became the path to my true self!

I spent years observing myself with Gurdjieffian discipline, and I could not believe how subtle my false self was. It was only by virtue of my pathological commitment to authenticate my life that I managed to catch my false self in action, and then I either had to own up to my falseness (which became my alchemical process of self-transformation), or justify my false self—which I did more often than I care to mention.

But eventually I justified my false self less and less, because I began to master the art of not putting myself in a position where I might have to justify myself; that's how I began to see my shadow self, and the shadow self of others. And eventually my inner sight became so acute that I actually saw the Archetypal Shadow—meaning, the Evil One, or the Devil; but that's too personal to talk about and I will leave it for my fiction.

So I've had many experiences of the omniscient guiding force of life intervening in my life to help me stay on spiritual track; but what is this spiritual track, anyway?

We are all on the same spiritual track insomuch that we are all sparks of God divinely encoded to become our true self (like the thirty birds in *The Conference of the Birds*), but not all of us are aware that we are on this spiritual track; only those souls that have evolved enough through the First Circle of Life and are ready for the Second Circle.

When Jesus said *"many are called but few are chosen,"* he was speaking about those souls in the First Circle of Life that are ready to "put their hand to the plow" and live the Way consciously in the Second Circle. Nature has evolved them as far as she can, and now they have to take evolution into their own hands to complete what nature left unfinished; but why can't nature complete the process and take us all the way to our true self?

Gurdjieff explained this by way of analogy. He said that life is like a prison, but we don't know that we are in prison. And when we do realize that we are in a prison we try to escape; and many people do escape. But sadly, they have not escaped out of prison; they only think they have escaped. They have escaped into a much larger part of the prison which they think is outside the prison, but it is not. To escape from the prison, Gurdjieff said one needs the help of someone who has actually escaped—just as the prisoner's in Plato's cave needed someone who had escaped from the illusory reality of shadows to help them escape to the true reality outside the cave.

Our prison is the First Circle of Life, the exoteric first stage of evolution. The First Circle of Life is so vast, so immense, and so seductively real—it includes all planes of consciousness below the Soul plane; which are the physical, astral, causal, and mental planes—that very few souls ever escape without help of someone who has escaped to the Soul plane of consciousness. Many great souls believe they have escaped, and they go to great lengths to help other souls escape; but they only prolong the journey to one's true self. But God is merciful, and if we don't get it right in this life we will just keep coming back until we do. That's why I came back to my same life, because I did not get it right the first time I lived my life as Orest Stocco; but this time I did.

A few years ago I had a dream experience where I tried to get this point across to a student of Gurdjieff's teaching:

In my dream I'm on the Other Side. I don't know which plane of consciousness I'm on, but I believe it's the astral plane; and I'm walking down a busy street in a midsized city (several hundred thousand people). As I'm walking I spot a white cube delivery truck. Written in large black letters on the white panel is the word GURDJIEFF. *I can see three people in the cab; two men and one woman. The woman has her window open with her arm resting on the door panel. I shout out to her, "Hey, are you students of Gurdjieff?"*

She looks around and spots me. "Yes!" she replies.

"Can we talk?" I shout back.

She talks to the driver and he pulls over. She gets out, tells the others that she will catch up with them later, and walks over to where I'm standing on the sidewalk.

"Are you a student of Gurdjieff?" she asks me.

"I was for many years," I reply.

"Oh. What are you now?" she asks.

"Why don't we find a restaurant and talk over a cup of coffee?" I said; and we crossed the street and walked half a block to a restaurant she was familiar with.

Over coffee I ask her how she came by Gurdjieff's teaching, and how long she has been in the Work. She's in her late thirties, with blond hair and fine features; but her eyes attract me most. Beautiful clear blue eyes alive with the energy of the Work.

"I found Gurdjieff by accident," she tells me. "I was at a low point in my life. I tried all kinds of teachings, but they didn't do anything for me. Then someone told me that there was a talk scheduled on Gurdjieff's teaching. I had never heard of him, but I went to the talk not expecting anything; but I got the surprise of my life. Everything the speaker said made sense to me. That was about ten years ago. What about you? How long have you been doing the Work? And why did you leave the Work? That's what I want to know."

"I did the Work for years, but I outgrew it."

"You outgrew it? You can't outgrow the Work!"

"All paths lead to the Way, and when you find the Way you no longer need the path and move on," I explained, feeling that she needed to know. "I found the Way and moved on. Gurdjieff's Work led me to the Way of the Eternal, and the Way of the Eternal awakened me to the Way of Soul, which is an individual path home to God. You too will one day outgrow the Work and find the Way—"

"No way!" she exploded, with horror in her eyes. "I will never leave the Work! The Work is my life! I will never leave it!"

Realizing what I had done, I backed off. "I'm sorry. I didn't mean to upset you. I know how much the Work means to you. It meant as much to me. The Work is your path, and as long as it satisfies your spiritual need that's all that matters. All I meant was that the Work could do no more for me, and I had to move on."

"But the Work is the only way to go," she replied, with a puzzled look.

I smiled, knowing that I would never break through to her; she still had many years of the Work left in her, and after a few more minutes of small talk I paid for the coffee and we amicably parted company; and I woke up from my dream experience.

This dream reminded me of my dream with Dr. Maurice Nicoll when I was having strong nostalgic feelings about the Work. I missed the Work. I missed the intense struggle of the Work, the unbelievable demands it made of me; and I missed all the excited expectations of the new Gurdjieff books that I ordered every month from *Samuel Weiser* in New York City. I did not know anyone who belonged to the Work. I was all alone in the Work, and I dared not mention Gurdjieff to anyone. He was too much for most people, especially the people of my hometown. Even at university I didn't meet anyone who had even heard of Gurdjieff, including my philosophy professors.

Dr. Nicoll had outgrown the Work also, and he was now a High Initiate of the Way of the Eternal. He found the Way of the Eternal on the Other Side, and he encouraged me to stay on this path because it was the path for me. He told me that he also missed the Work, but it had served its purpose and he had to move on. "When the student is ready, the teacher appears," he said to me, with a warm smile; and I understood.

The vibrant blue-eyed woman that I met on the Other Side wasn't ready yet for the Way of the Eternal, and I had to ease off; but I enjoyed talking with her. She made me realize that **all paths serve their purpose**; and I brought this point home in *Jesus Wears Dockers* that I wrote years later when Penny and I moved to Georgian Bay.

But how does one know that they have outgrown their path? I didn't know I had outgrown the Work. Being an eclectic seeker, I was forever incorporating other teachings into my path. In fact I overlapped two other teachings with the Work. I was an initiate of the Way of the Eternal, and I was also a member of that offshoot Christian solar cult teaching that damaged my eyes. I dropped the solar cult teaching like a hot potato when I shook hands with the spiritual leader of that cult, but the damage had already been done; and I didn't drop the Work until I had a disconcerting dream with Gurdjieff.

I had met Gurdjieff in my dreams many times, and he was always full of tough love and kindness, and I loved him; but this time he was dressed in black with a menacing black moustache and dark, impersonal eyes. And when I woke up from this dream I knew that it was time to move on from the Work; which left me with only the Way of the Eternal until my dreams a few months ago that told me I had outgrown the outer teachings of the Way of the Eternal but not the inner teachings.

I dropped the solar cult teaching before I went to the ophthalmologist to have the burning sensation in my eyes checked out. When I shook hands with the solar cult teacher in Reno, Nevada I knew that I was in the presence of evil. He had deceived me from afar with his books and promises, but his personal energy could not deceive me.

I was an initiate of the Way of the Eternal when I shook his hand, so I had the Inner Master's protective presence; and the instant our hands touched I felt the solar cult master's energy withdraw into his body with such a swoosh that it felt like it had been sucked by a giant vacuum cleaner; and the look on his face startled me: it was fear.

I paid a dear price to learn my lesson with this cult teaching, but I had past-life karma with this man. He was my Sufi teacher in my lifetime as Salaam in ancient Persia, and he had such a psychic hold on me that I could not break free. But I did in this life, and despite the cost to my eyes I'm glad to be rid of him and all false teachings of Light.

16. *The Synchronistic Principle*

The omniscient guiding force of life is Jung's "synchronistic principle." It is also the Inner Master and the Dream Weaver. It is also the language of life, which in my spiritual path is called "the Golden-tongued Wisdom." But how can one prove this?

This was Jung's dilemma. He had to squeeze his spiritual experiences into a scientific paradigm, and he did an extraordinary job of it. This is why to the end of his life he never publically admitted that he was a Gnostic. And yet he wore a self-styled Gnostic ring till the day he died. And he tells us in *The Red Book* that he had a spiritual guide called Philemon, a Gnostic Master whom he later said was an aspect of his higher self. But I don't have that dilemma, because I don't have a reputation to safeguard. I'm just a seeker who found his way out of Plato's cave and am now obligated by spiritual law to share my gnosis.

Jung came as close as he possibly could to linking his synchronistic principle with the omniscient guiding force of life in *Synchronicity, An Acausal Connecting Principle*. He wrote: "The synchronistic principle possesses properties that may help to clear up the body-soul problem. Above all it is the fact of causeless order, or rather, of meaningful orderliness that may throw light on psychophysical parallelism. The 'absolute knowledge' which is characteristic of synchronistic phenomena, a knowledge not mediated by the sense organs, supports the hypothesis of a self-subsistent meaning, or even expresses its existence. *Such a form of existence can only be transcendental* (italics mine), since, as the knowledge of future or spatially distant events shows, it is contained in a psychically relative space and time, that is to say in an irrepresentable space-time continuum" (p. 90).

The omniscient guiding force of life has "absolute knowledge," and it knew that if I had gone the Hudson's Bay store route I would have ended up unfulfilled and regretful; that's why the synchronistic principle intervened to keep me on the right course (which I also believe intervened to keep me from buying the drive-in restaurant).

Obviously there was nothing wrong with my adding skills since I went into business for myself; but for reasons which boggled my teenage mind at the time, I just could not write up my sales receipts correctly and I blew my chances with the Bay.

But how many times have we heard people say that getting fired from their job was the best thing that ever happened to them? And how many times have we heard people say that getting cancer was the best thing that ever happened to them? Why? Because what happened to them set them back on their spiritual course, and they began to grow in spirit once more. They had come to a spiritual standstill in their life, and the synchronistic principle of life intervened to reconnect them with their life story that had become stuck. This was Jungian analyst Marion Woodman's experience:

"Because death is an essential part of life, to be fully alive is to be prepared for it. Cancer had prepared me. And that makes me grateful for my life, present to it and in it to a degree that life before cancer never attained. The gift of cancer is the gift of Now, a sense of all time precariously lodged within it. Living with death is a more abundant life." (Forward to BONE, *A Journal of Wisdom, Strength, and Healing,* by Marion Woodman)

Like me, these people were recalcitrant. They were ready to move on but could not extricate themselves from their dead-end path, and so the synchronistic principle of life had to intervene. When I came back from France I went to university to study philosophy because that's where I thought I would get answers to the questions *who am I?* and *why am I?* But in my second year I began to feel like I was cast adrift in a sea of endless speculation, and I began to dread that I was going to drown and I craved to be back on *terra firma;* that's when the synchronistic principle stepped in to set me on the right course.

A fellow student was going to Toronto for the Christmas break. He told me he was going to go to his favorite little used book store while there, and I asked him to bring me back a book that he felt might interest me. He came back with P. D. Ouspensky's *In Search of the Miraculous, Fragments of an Unknown Teaching.* I asked him why he chose that book, and he couldn't explain it. It didn't interest him, but he felt it was right for me.

Little did he know that that book would change the course of my entire life; but that was not the only time a book "fell into my lap" to assist me on my spiritual journey to my true self. I cannot count the number of times that a book "came" to me at just the right time, especially when I was writing *Healing with Padre Pio.* In fact one book, *The Only Planet of Choice*, by Phyllis V. Schelmmer, was brought right to my front door precisely when I needed it to complete the chapter I was working on in *Healing with Padre Pio!*

I illustrate how the synchronistic principle played a part in *Healing with Padre Pio,* so suffice to say now that the synchronistic principle of life is always working to keep us on the right course. But what is the right course for one person may not be the right course for another; it all depends upon one's karmic destiny. And this was the mystery that burst the damn that kept the waters of eternal life from flowing freely in my life.

Not until I had seven past-life regressions did I learn that we have two destinies: one spiritual and one karmic. When I was brought back to where all souls come from in the Body of God and learned that I had Soul consciousness but no self-consciousness, I solved one of the greatest mysteries of life—*the mystery of where we come from.*

I knew that I was an atom of God in the Body of God, so that answered the question *what am I?* My regression to the Body of God let me experience what I was and where I came from, but not until I was regressed to my first primordial human life did I piece the puzzle together and answer the question *who am I?*

But I had to take evolution into my own hands and "work" on myself with Gurdjieff's teaching, my *Royal Dictum,* and the sayings of Jesus to answer the question *why am I?*As an atom of God I was a spark of divine consciousness, a soul without self-consciousness; and then the Inner Master brought me back to my first primordial human life where I experienced the dawning of my reflective self-consciousness so I could piece out the puzzle of our purpose in life, which is to evolve in self-consciousness until we become conscious of our divine nature, like the thirty birds in *The Conference of the Birds.*

I experienced the birth of my reflective self-consciousness in my primordial life as a higher primate, and I continued to grow and evolve in self-consciousness through the natural process of karma and reincarnation until I was ready to take evolution into my own hands and complete what nature could not finish; that's why the synchronistic principle of life introduced the Way according to Gurdjieff into my life, and after years of living the Way consciously I gave birth to my Soul self in my mother's kitchen.

I grew in the First Circle of Life as far as nature could take me, and then I began to suffer the same anguish that gave birth to Jean Paul Sartre's angst-ridden philosophy of *being* and *becoming.* "I am what I am not, and I am not what I am," concluded Sartre; but this was only because he could not extricate himself from the First Circle of Life. Like most people, Sartre could not find the "strait gate" to the mesoteric second stage of evolution; and so concluded with seductively brilliant logic that life was contingent, meaningless and absurd, and that man was a "useless passion."

The exoteric First Circle of Life is all about growing and evolving in our existential human self-consciousness. We grow in our human self by the choices we make. Our choices create karma, and karma determines our personal destiny. This is why freedom was central to Sartre's existentialism and why he said,

"Man is condemned to be free." But man is only condemned to be free if he is stuck in the First Circle of Life.

Because man creates karma with every choice he makes, the truth is just the opposite of what Sartre philosophized: **man is free to be condemned, not condemned to be free.** And until he realizes that he is the author of his own karmic destiny he will always be condemned to be free; and he will just keep coming back until he gets it right.

Because we are all free to be condemned by our own karma, no two people have the same karmic destiny. One person becomes a musical genius like Mozart, and another becomes a megalomaniacal madman like Hitler; another becomes a surgeon, and another a poet—it all depends upon our karmic history what we become. But despite what our karmic destiny is, we are all spiritually destined to realize our divine nature. We are all Soul seeds divinely encoded to grow into our Soul self, which we can only do through our own karmic destiny; but not until we step into the Second Circle of Life can we complete nature's objective and free ourselves from our own karma. It's a hard truth to swallow, but **the only way out of life is through life.** There are no shortcuts to our true self.

As I "worked" on myself I took evolution into my own hands and entered the "strait gate" of the Second Circle of Life and extricated myself from the First Circle and brought my karmic destiny into alignment with my spiritual destiny and gave birth to my spiritual self in my mother's kitchen; this was how I brought closure to Sartre's incomplete philosophy and wrote: **I am what I am not, and I am not what I am; I am both, but neither: I am Soul.** I completed what nature left unfinished.

The Second Circle of Life is all about reconciling the consciousness of our karmic outer self with our spiritual inner self; and to do that we have to bring our karmic destiny into agreement with our pre-scripted spiritual destiny. Because we have free choice, our karmic destiny can stray too far off course from our spiritual destiny; and that's when the synchronistic principle of life steps in to get us back on course.

But how can we be sure that our personal destiny is aligned with our spiritual destiny? Or, to put it simply: how can we be sure that we are on the right course?

This question haunted me when I was living Gurdjieff's teaching. How could I be certain that I was on the right course in my life? I puzzled over this for a long time, and then one day—true to my nature of going to the extremes to find my true self—I got an insight that gave me the answer I was looking for: *I decided to let go and let God!*

Since I was responsible for my personal destiny by the choices I made, I decided to let God decide for me; this way I would be certain that I was on the right spiritual course to my true self. But how could I be sure that God would decide for me? That's when I got the brilliant idea to flip a coin and let God decide what I should do. And so began another chapter of my life (which lasted about six months) that incontrovertibly proved to me how the synchronistic principle of life works to keep us on the right course.

I did not flip the coin for every decision I made; only the big decisions. I flipped the coin and said: "Heads I do, tails I don't." But this is easier said than done. The trick to this unbelievably bold technique of letting go and letting God was to be true to the flip. If the coin said yes and I did the opposite, that nullified the whole purpose of letting go and letting God. I had to be true to the flip for my technique to work. I had to trust God!

And I was true to the flip. So true that something strange began to happen. I lost out on a possible romance with a woman I had feelings for because of the flip. But then, according to the logic of the flip, God did not think she was right for me or the coin would have given me permission to pursue her. Nonetheless, I began to notice a strange anomaly whenever I let go and let God. I began to notice that whenever I had to make a difficult decision and in my gut I felt I should do it, the coin agreed with my gut feeling; and whenever I had a gut feeling that I should not do it, the coin agreed with me. This happened so often that it went way beyond random chance. So much beyond random chance that I finally realized what was happening: *God was guiding me through the intuitive power of my gut feelings and confirmed it with the synchronistic principle in the coin's approval!*

Once I realized this I stopped doing the technique. It had served its purpose—just as Carl Jung stopped doing the divination technique of the *I Ching* when he had honed his intuitive skills enough to trust his own insights!

By letting God decide for me through the flip of the coin I learned that the omniscient guiding force of life speaks to us through our own intuition. But it wasn't as simple as all of that, though. I had to wrestle with some very tough decisions. In the wrestling I had to be true to myself. And the only way I could be true to myself was to ask myself the question: is this the best way to for everyone concerned?

To help me wrestle with my decision I had to be true to my personal ethic: is this the right-good-honest-just thing to do? So it wasn't merely a feeling in my gut. My gut simply confirmed the decision that I had to put through the wringer of my personal ethic; only then did the coin agree with me—*which only went to prove that we are our own higher self and the synchronistic principle of life!*

This was an extremely bold and reckless thing to do, and I cannot do this experience justice in passing; that's why I decided to explore this whole dynamic in a novel. My working title is *The Flip,* and although I'm only part way into the novel it has already revealed things about *letting go and letting God* that I did not know while I was in the throes of my experience, and I can't wait to find out how it ends.

17. *The I Am Principle of Life*

Near the end of his full and productive life Carl Jung summed up his feelings about life in his memoir *Memories, Dreams, Reflections*. In the closing section of the book titled "Retrospect," he concludes on a characteristic Jungian note of measured honesty:

"The world into which we are born is brutal and cruel, and at the same time of divine beauty. Which element we think outweighs the other, whether meaninglessness or meaning, is a matter of temperament. If meaninglessness were absolutely predominant, the meaningfulness of life would vanish to an increasing degree with each step in our development. But that is—or seems to me—not the case. Probably, as in all metaphysical questions, both are true: Life is—or has—meaning and meaninglessness. I cherish the hope that meaning will predominate and win the battle" (p. 359).

As I said, I took the way of *non-being* to find my true self; which was revealed to me in high school with my daemonic poem *Noman*. And the Inner Master confirmed this for me in my late twenties when he asked me the question in my mind *"why do you lie?"*

Of course I did not know it was the Inner Master who had asked that question; I wasn't to realize this until many years later when I became an initiate of the Way of the Eternal. But like Jung, who called his spiritual guide Philemon an aspect of his higher self, so too have I come to see the Inner Master as an aspect of my higher self. In fact, I would say that the Inner Master *is* my higher self. He is the personified consciousness of Soul, and although I know that I *am* Soul now, which was confirmed for me by the dream I had a few months ago where the Dictionary of Life defined Orest Stocco as Soul, I still have a long way to go before I coincide completely with the consciousness of Soul, as Jesus did. *"I and my Father are one,"* said Jesus, and his whole message was to show us how we could become one with our Father in heaven.

This is the premise of my novel *Jesus Wears Dockers*. I wanted to decode the cryptic sayings of Jesus, and I made Jesus central to my novel for dramatic effect. The point that I wanted to make with *Jesus Wears Dockers* is that one has to take evolution into his own hands to enter the "strait gate" of the Second Circle of Life and realize their Soul self.

Carl Jung found the "strait gate," but he took the way of *being* to find his true self; which was also confirmed for him in a dream late in his life when he saw high up on a hill a boulder lit up by the full sun with the carved words, "Take this as a sign of the wholeness you have achieved and the singleness you have become."

There's a sweet certainty to Jung's dream. The creative unconscious spoke to him in the symbolism of his achievement being *"carved in stone."* When we say that something is carved in stone, we take it to mean that it is for real and everlasting, and Jung's dream revealed to him that after all his years of individuating his outer self with his inner self (his conscious personality with his unconscious self) that the wholeness and singleness he had achieved was real and everlasting—i. e., carved in stone; which is to say that Jung had finally realized his Soul self. But how can we be sure that Jung took the way of *being* to achieve the wholeness and singleness of his Soul self?

Unbeknown to him, Jung revealed this in a BBC "Face to Face" interview that he had late in his life. John Freeman asked Jung, "Do you remember the occasion when you first felt consciousness of your own individual self?"

Jung replied, "That was in my eleventh year. There I certainly, on my way to school, I stepped out of a mist. It was just as if I had been in a mist, walking in a mist, and I stepped out of it, and I knew I am; I am what I am. And then I thought, but what have

I been before? And then I found that I was, that I had been in a mist, not knowing to differentiate myself from things. I was just one thing about many things."

Jung experienced the consciousness of his own individual *being* in his eleventh year, and his journey was to individuate his *non-being* with his *being*—to *differentiate* himself from everything else in life, as he put it. And the difference in our paths was that he was centered in his *being* and had to individuate his *non-being*, and I was centered in my *non-being* and had to individuate my *being*; and, fortunately, we both ended up realizing our Soul self. That's why I love the man. He's one of the thirty birds that looked into the Face of God, which Jung confirmed when Freeman asked him if he believed in God and Jung replied, "I know. I don't need to believe; I know."

Jung was accused of being a "mystic Gnostic" for saying this, as if being a Gnostic somehow invalidated his knowledge of God; but Jung was merely speaking gnostically—meaning, he had experienced God, because gnostic knowledge is born of one's experience and not one's mind. Knowing in the gnostic sense is seeing with one's inner sight; it is a spiritual realization. To knowing something with one's mind is to comprehend it, but to know something experientially is to apprehend it; it becomes yours, and Jung's experience with God was his apprehension of God. So, ironically, he was a "mystic Gnostic." But true to his nature, Jung had to explain in an open letter to the public what he meant by his God comment, because he had to safeguard his scientific reputation.

So Jung came to me in a dream then to talk about my book *The Way of Soul* because he saw in me the same dynamic that had driven him his whole life, the dynamic that he came to call the "individuation process." I called it the Work at first, because I was living the Gurdjieffian principles of self-realization; and when the Work awakened the Word in me I simply called it the Way. But it doesn't matter what we call this dynamic, it is the same in all paths in life; and the heart of this dynamic is the *I Am Principle of Life*.

When Moses asked God his name, God replied *"I Am that I Am."* When I asked St. Padre Pio in one of my spiritual healing sessions if only some people are born with an immortal soul and not others, he replied that we are all a part of the divine Whole and therefore we are all immortal; but we have to grow and evolve through life to realize our divine nature. This is the essential meaning of the *I Am Principle of Life* and the mystery that Jung wanted to talk to me about; not because I had reasoned it out philosophically, but because I had experienced it through my own path.

Jung recognized by my book *The Way of Soul* that I had gnostic knowledge of the Way, and he was anxious to learn how I had managed to wrest the answer of the alpha and omega of the self out of life. He admitted as much in the closing pages of *Memories, Dreams, Reflections* that for all of his seeking he was still in doubt:

"I am astonished, disappointed, pleased with myself. I am distressed, depressed, rapturous. I am all these things at once, and cannot add up the sum. I am incapable of determining ultimate worth or worthlessness; I have no judgment about myself and my life. There is nothing I am quite sure about. I have no definite convictions—not about anything, really. I know only that I was born and exist, and it seems to me that I have been carried along. I exist on the foundation of something I do not know. In spite of all uncertainties, I feel a solidity underlying all existence and a continuity in my mode of being" (p. 358).

I had given "birth" to my immortal Soul self, thereby confirming Christ's teaching of spiritual rebirth; so I had the gnostic knowledge of Christ's teaching. I had lived his sayings with pathological commitment, and I realized the validity of his teaching; but I also had other experiences that helped me piece together the Divine Plan of God, and that took all the mystery out of the individuation process. That's why Jung came to me in my dream.

But I have explored my dream relationship with Jung in my novel *The Waking Dream*, so I won't go into detail here. Suffice it to provide the experiences that address the *I Am Principle of Life*, because without them I would not have that gnostic certainty of the alpha and omega of the self that has haunted mankind since the dawn of time.

I Am is the self-definition of the Absolute, the divine Whole and foundation upon which everything rests. This was revealed to Moses when he faced God in the burning bush. *I Am* is the first cause principle, which I experienced when I was sitting in my back yard of our family home warming my face in the spring sun. I relaxed my mind and travelled back through time to the primordial past when the Earth was totally barren of life and the gases of the Earth rose up and blended with the gases of the sky to form the first building blocks of life in the amino acids, and I entered the amino acids and initiated the life process.

I initiated the life process, thereby telling me that I am the first cause principle; which made me the *I Am Principle of Life*. But as exciting and mind-boggling as this experience was, it would take the next forty years of my life to decode it—and only because I had my past-life regression to the Body of God and my first primordial human life.

These were the two missing pieces that I needed to piece together the puzzle of the alpha and omega of the self; and even then I had to fall upon the creative process to connect all the dots. That's why I was daimonically driven to write ten books in two years while holding down my demanding day job of drywall taping and painting. As I abandoned to the creative process, I connected one dot to another until finally I began to make sense of my unbelievable experience of initiating the life process in these lower worlds.

For years I puzzled over how I could be responsible for the genesis of life on Earth, but I could not deny what I experienced. I felt myself slipping into the amino acids of the blended gases, and the moment I entered the first building blocks of life I *experienced* the inception of the life process. But how could this be? Only when I had my past-life regression to the Body of God and experienced myself as an atom of God did I connect the dots and realized that the "I" that entered the first building blocks of life was my un-realized Soul self. And only when the Inner Master took me back to my first primordial human life where I experienced the dawning of my reflective self-consciousness did I connect the dots and realize that we begin life as un-self-realized atoms of God and that we have to evolve through the natural process of evolution until we give birth to our reflective self, as I did in my primordial human lifetime; and I say "human" only because the moment I gave birth to my reflective self I ceased to be a higher primate and became a self-conscious human.

So when I went back through time and experienced the genesis of life in these lower worlds I was a self-realized Soul; but I didn't make the connection that when I initiated the life process in these lower worlds I was an atom of God with Soul consciousness but no reflective self-consciousness; that's why my experience boggled my mind and gave me the inflated feeling that I was more than what I really was—a feeling that I kept to myself until my past-life regressions when I connected the dots with my writing.

I breathed a sigh of relief when I connected the dots and realized that **it was the consciousness of Soul that had initiated the life process**, not me personally; and the experience of me entering into the first building blocks of life and jump-starting the life process was really a regression of myself to the origins of my existence in the lower worlds as an atom of God beginning my journey through the life process as the un-self-realized *I Am Principle of God*—hence, the essential dynamic of life being *I Am* THAT *I Am!*

THAT is the operative word. THAT is a transitive verb, and THAT *I Am* is the dynamic of the life process, because the "I" of God (the un-self-realized Soul) evolves through life to become aware of itself. This is why God said to Moses, *"I Am* THAT *I Am."* God was telling Moses that God was God forever becoming God.

And this is why Paul Twitchell wrote that man is as important to God as God is to man!

Through man, God becomes more God; which, interestingly enough, is the same conclusion that Jung arrived at with his understanding of the individuation process. The unconscious archetypal self of man evolves by individuating the *being* and *non-being* outer self of man until one achieves wholeness and singleness of self; and what Jung found fascinating about my book *The Way of Soul* was how I had learned to speed up the process of individuation by mastering the art of living the Way consciously.

But I have Gurdjieff to thank, because his teaching awakened me to the Way, which is everywhere to be found if one has eyes to see. I didn't have to go all over the world looking for my spiritual path; it always came to me when I was ready for the next stage of my journey through life. And one day, God willing, I will go to the cemetery in Avon near Fontainebleau, France and lay a yellow rose on Gurdjieff's grave; and then I will visit Jung's gravesite and house on Lake Zurich in Kusnacht with the words carved in stone above his front door: *Called or not called, God is present,* because I owe an inestimable debt of gratitude to these incomparable pioneers of the soul.

18. *Unconscious Dream Therapy*

I woke up this morning, Monday, February 4, 2013 from another dream of my hometown of Nipigon. Once again, my hometown dream disturbed me:

I was at our family home. Only my mother lives in the family home now. My father is long dead and all the children are out on their own. I am not sure if I am living at home or not. I am walking into the driveway and find a key on the driveway and wonder if it's the key to the house. My mother and another woman are changing the lock on the door. I give them a hand. The scene changes and I'm in a restaurant in Nipigon. I know the men sitting at the counter. There is some banter going on, a little hostility between two men. I inquire about my car. I used to have a little black Pontiac Fiero sports car, but someone came to my house and took it away. I'm told that one of the garage owners took it away. He's the same person who got my first little black Pontiac Fiero for nothing. The transmission went on it and it would have cost too much to fix it, so Penny gave it to him without my permission. This happened in real life. In my dream he came and got my second little black Fiero, and I don't know why. This really bothers me. The scene changes. I'm at my mother's home again. She's cooking for some men who are working at the house. That same lady is helping her. I tell my mother I don't have a key for the house. My mother does not show motherly emotion for me. This bothers me very much. I'm not sure that I am welcome at home anymore. The scene changes again. I'm at the family home and I see that my Fiero is not in the garage and I am informed that some man came and took it away. I want to go and find out and I get into my van. Two men want to join me, but my van is full of my work stuff and there's no room for the men; so I ask them

*where they have taken my Fiero and I drive over to find out why
they have taken my car without my permission.*

*This whole dream disturbs me. I don't have a key to our family
home, and someone has taken my car without my permission. I
wake up feeling alone and very insecure.*

I've had more dreams than I care to remember about my
family home and my mother and siblings, and I would love to
move on; but it seems that something keeps me dreaming about
my family and family home and hometown, and I sat on the edge
of my bed this morning trying to figure out what these dreams
could possibly mean.

At 4 A. M. I got dressed and booted my computer and sat
down in my reading chair trying to get my mind off my dream by
reading. I picked up *The Undiscovered Self* by Jung and turned to
"Symbols and the Interpretation of Dreams."

I glossed over the pages reading my highlights, but nothing
seemed to click; and then I remembered something that I read in
Edgar Cayce On Dreams, by Harmon H. Bro, Ph.D. (under the
editorship of Hugh Lynn Cayce) and picked it up and found the
highlighted passage that had come to mind. Cayce said dreams
work to accomplish two things: **They work to solve the
problems of the dreamer's conscious, waking life. And they
work to quicken in the dreamer new potentials which are
his to claim."**

I pondered Cayce's comment. Then I remembered two other
Nipigon dreams that I had in the last couple of weeks that spoke
to my disturbed state of mind, and **I got the insight that my
dreams had translated my disturbed state of mind into
symbolic images to alleviate the fear of insecurity that I
was experiencing.**

"Maybe that's what last night's dream was all about also," I
said to myself, and sat back to reflect on the healing function of
dreams; but as I reflected I remembered another scene in my
dream that spoke to my relationship with the people of my
hometown of Nipigon, but I don't know which parallel life:

145

Our family home is on Newton Street, and I am walking up the street past G. R.'s house. He was at teacher at the elementary Catholic School in Nipigon, but he's retired now and a deacon of the Church. He makes a sly remark about me not being as physically active as I should be, and his wife tells him to watch what he says to me because she's afraid of what I might write about them. I don't remember any more of the dream.

Now, the fact is (or so St. Padre Pio has led me to believe) that I have lived my life already in Nipigon, and I died there; but now I'm living my same life over again, and I'm having difficulty determining which life I'm dreaming of. Or are my dreams a blend of both lives at once? I don't know. It's all so strange that I can't make heads or tails of it; and I sit and ponder some more. Why do I feel so insecure in my hometown dreams?

My insecurity is both emotional and financial, and I wake up disturbed like I did this morning; so what problem was my dream trying to help me with? What frame of mind was I in last night when I went to bed? I reflected on this...

I went to bed feeling sorry for myself. As always, I felt that if only I had poured more energy into my contracting business and less into writing we would be much better off today. I poured so much energy into my questing and writing that I could have been financially very secure today had I poured even half of that energy into my business instead; but I didn't, and I feel sorry for myself because as satisfying as writing has been for my soul, it has not been financially rewarding.

Not yet, anyway. But we're not getting any younger, and I feel bad that I have not been able to give Penny enough security to ease her anxiety. I didn't expect to have bypass surgery, which meant that I had to retire sooner that I wanted to; but that's life.

Not that we're in bad shape financially. We're managing, and my fears may very well be false fears. Our beautiful home in Georgian Bay is mortgage free. We still have an eighty-seven thousand dollar mortgage on our triplex in Nipigon, but all three apartments are rented out. This covers the mortgage, insurance, and upkeep; but we're on a tight budget, and there is always financial anxiety. And this bothers me because I know I could have done a lot better had I been less preoccupied with writing. If people only knew how much time and energy goes into writing just one book they would have a little more respect for writers; but that's only deflecting the problem.

The problem is my sense of insecurity, which my dreams are addressing by translating my fears into images of my family and hometown; and the more I wonder why I keep having these dreams of my life in Nipigon, the more convinced I am that they really have nothing to do with my insecurity as such, because it's a false fear.

I think my creative unconscious is translating my insecurity into dream images that play out my fears on the screen of my life in Nipigon. When I see my insecurity played out in a movie-like story in my dreams I also get a mild cathartic feeling after I get over the shock of my insecurity, like the good feeling I had yesterday afternoon when Penny and I came out of the theater in Barrie where we went to see the movie *Lincoln*.

It was a wonderful movie, and it left me feeling full of pride for President Lincoln, whom I have always admired. Daniel Day Lewis played such a moving role as President Lincoln that he left an indelible impression upon my mind of the honesty, integrity, and courage that President Lincoln had to have to abolish slavery.

It touched my heart. The goodness the movie left me with was like a healing balm, and that's what I began to feel about my dream last night. I was emotionally and financially insecure in my dream, as if life was working against me; but the more I thought about it, the more I compared it to the movie Penny and I had just seen: and I could feel the healing balm of my dream working on my feelings of insecurity.

I believe I may have taken my hometown dreams much too literally because of how I felt when I woke up. I always woke up disturbed. I believe now that they are symbolic dreams. My creative unconscious is translating the problems of my daily life into dream images that are drawn from my life in Nipigon, and creating a story for me to live out in my dreams. This story of our family home (which I dream of often, many dreams having to do with water and our family home), my siblings, my vehicles (I've had a number of dreams with my vehicles; all disturbing), and the people of my hometown (a number of people keep recurring in my dreams), this story of my life in Nipigon is my unconscious way of alleviating my fears, my doubts, anxieties, and insecurities by playing them out dramatically in my dreams. In effect, I believe **I'm having these dreams to dissipate the energy of my fears so they will have less power over me.**

I'm beginning to see these dreams as some kind of unconscious therapy. My creative unconscious is healing my conscious personality. My unconscious is my Soul self, and dreams are one way that my creative unconscious helps me deal with the problems of my conscious daily life. And if this is so—which I am strongly inclined to believe—then I may have found the solution to why I keep dreaming of my hometown.

After all, my unconscious has to work with what it has; so it takes my experiences in Nipigon and writes a new script for me to play out in my dreams—*which is a completely symbolic world!* And for what purpose if not to solve the problems of my daily life and quicken the new potentials which are mine to claim?

This shifts my perspective on my hometown dreams, which as I've said probably once too often, have been bothering me for years. But I'm trying to make sense of my parallel life, and all I have is my dreams to work with; so it's quite possible that I have made a breakthrough with this new insight on dreams.

Among other things, **our dreams function as a form of unconscious therapy by translating the contents of our life into dream stories for us to play out the problems of our life in a completely symbolic context that addresses the issues of our fears that we cannot come to terms with consciously.**

As humorous as this may sound, it's like the ostrich sticking its head in the sand to avoid what it does not want to see. In like manner, I have a tendency to stick my head in the sand to avoid acknowledging my fears and insecurities. Actually, in all honesty, I have a rabid fear of confronting my fears, which is why it took me years before I went to an optometrist to have my eyes checked out again; and I was really beginning to worry about my eyesight. In fact two people with psychic gifts told me to have my eyes checked, but I still refused to go because I didn't want to face the humiliation of telling my optometrist about how I had damaged my eyes. I finally went last summer, and what a relief it was to confront that fear. It was like I had gotten rid of a ball and chain! **So what we refuse to face consciously our unconscious has to deal with**; that's why I'm having these dreams.

The symbols in my dream then are telling me something about myself that I am not willing to face consciously. The symbols that jump out at me are: family home, my mother, key, my vehicle, and my hometown of Nipigon. But what do these symbols mean?

House for me has always symbolized one's state of consciousness. One's house is one's home, and so is one's consciousness; and not having a key to my family home symbolizes that I have been locked out of my family consciousness, which is another way of saying that I have outgrown my family consciousness and should move on.

I had a dream a number of years ago that confirms this: *In my dream I met Paul Twitchell, the modern day founder of the Way of the Eternal. I had just become an initiate of this spiritual path, and it was a real privilege to meet Paul Twitchell in my dream. He gave me the most penetrating gaze that I have ever received from anyone. His eyes sized up everything about me, like I was measured and weighed by his glance; and then he said, "Your name and you don't fit." I woke up puzzled, but curiously comforted.* Now I'm certain that this dream means that I have outgrown my family consciousness.

And the symbolic message of my mother locking me out of the family home reinforces that I have outgrown my family consciousness. My vehicles have always been a symbol of mobility, and my dream is telling me that I have outgrown that old mode of mobility. My unconscious took my little sports car from me without my permission, because I refused to give it up on my own. I didn't need it. It belonged to my past, and I had outgrown my past. In fact, I had outgrown my whole life; and as to the people of my hometown with whom I no longer resonated, my dream was telling me that I'm in a different state of consciousness—*eureka! My parallel life!*

This explains the dream I had about six years ago: *I'm walking down the Main Street of my hometown of Nipigon. I'm on the sidewalk just in front of where I used to have my pool hall business. I meet people walking, but something's not right. I'm walking at my normal walking pace, but everyone else is walking in slow motion!*

I've always taken this dream to mean that because I lived the Way consciously I raised the level of my vibrations, which explained why everyone that I met on the sidewalk was walking in slow motion—because they were in lower frequency. I still believe this; but now I also believe that this speaks to my parallel life.

I came back to relive my same life again so I could find the Way, which I did; and I have achieved the outcome that I came to realize—to give birth to my spiritual self, which I did in my mother's kitchen. That's why the people in my hometown and I do not resonate, and possibly why I keep going back there in my dreams, because the Dream Weaver is trying to tell me that I am living my same life in a parallel world!

I began this book with the chapter "The Key to My Dreams is My Dreams," and I remember now that in my dream last night I found a key in the driveway of my family home and wondered if it was the key to the house; but my mother and another woman were changing the lock, which I helped them do. This tells me that as much as I want to have a key to our family home (consciousness), I cannot enter because I no longer belong there. I have outgrown that exoteric state of consciousness, and my dream confirmed it.

This means that I am visiting my first life as Orest Stocco in my dreams in the body of my second life as Orest Stocco, and **the two lives do not fit because of their different states of consciousness.** In my first life I was stuck in the exoteric First Circle of Life, but in my second life I'm in the esoteric Third Circle of Life (I worked my way through the mesoteric Second Circle and was initiated into the third circle of the Soul plane of consciousness), so as disturbing as the dream made me feel when I woke up this morning, **the dream was merely telling me that I am now living my parallel life**; and this changes the whole dynamic of my family and hometown dreams!

Among other things then, the Dream Weaver, who is my creative unconscious, is also my therapist; so I'm going to pay closer attention to my family and hometown dreams, because knowing why I am having them now they're going to start telling me a different story; *which hopefully will quicken the new potentials that are mine to claim!*

19. *The Ground of All Being*

As I said, I would not have connected the dots had I not had those three phenomenal experiences—travelling back through time to experience the genesis of life on Earth; my regression to the Body of God; and my regression to my first primordial human life where I experienced the dawning of my reflective self-consciousness. These experiences allowed me to solve the mystery of our purpose in life; but there was one more dot that I had to connect before I could see the big picture of life—consciousness.

What part does consciousness play in life? Hard science believes that consciousness is an epiphenomenon of the brain. But then, hard science does not believe in the soul; so it's only natural that science would posit the brain to be the creator of consciousness. And when the body dies, science would have us believe that the energy that made up the body goes back into nature; but what happens to one's individuated consciousness? Does that die also when the brain dies? Or does one's mind live on somehow?

I used to be concerned with these questions, and I read a lot of books to find answers; but then I decided to build my life upon my own experiences, and slowly the questions began to resolve themselves. One by one all of my questions about life and death were answered, including the puzzling question of consciousness which was resolved when I unexpectedly and miraculously experienced the genesis of life on Earth.

When I slipped into the amino acids that had blended from the Earth and sky gases to form the first building blocks of life, I *knew* that I was responsible for the inception of life on Earth; and although I was not yet a self-realized Soul (because I went back to that point in time, I knew that it was me that had slipped into the amino acids), I would learn many years later that Soul was the first cause principle of life because Soul is the I-consciousness of God. This was the last dot that I had to connect to see the big picture of life.

Strangely enough, the brilliant pioneer of science and spirituality Dr. Amit Goswami came to the same conclusion—but he did so through quantum physics. In *The Self-Aware Universe* he proposes a new scientific paradigm and "shows how we develop a science that embraces the religions of the world, working in concert with them to understand the whole human condition. The centerpiece of this new paradigm is the recognition that modern science validates an ancient idea—the idea that consciousness, not matter, is the ground of all being" (Part 1: *The Integration of Science and Spirituality*).

I knew this because I had experienced it, and after I connected the dots and caught a glimpse of the Divine Plan of God the mystery of man's purpose in life dissolved like the morning fog in the warm rays of the rising sun; but there was one little issue left to clear up—the distinction between Divine Spirit and Soul.

I *knew* that in the beginning I was an atom of God in the Body of God, and that I had Soul consciousness but no self-consciousness, and I *knew* that I was sent into the lower worlds to acquire my own identity through natural evolution; but I had no corroborating evidence to validate my experience. But I trusted the omniscient guiding force of life, which always answered my questions in the fullness of time; and eventually I found supporting proof in John Keats, Rumi, and the Epistles of St. Paul who all reflected the Divine Plan of God according to their own experience. And that left me with one more loose end to tie up: what was the distinction between Divine Spirit and Soul?

I got my answer in the literature of the Way of the Eternal which posits that individual souls are made of Divine Spirit. I grasped this distinction, and all I had to do now was connect the dots to see that Soul is the consciousness of Divine Spirit; and I did that with my creative writing which finally revealed to me that I grew in Soul consciousness by learning how to catch the energy of Divine Spirit.

It's written in the holy scriptures of the Way of the Eternal that "Spirit cannot be taught; it must be caught." As I "worked" on myself with Gurdjieff's teaching, my *Royal Dictum*, and the sayings of Jesus I learned how to catch the "vital life force," and I grew in spiritual consciousness enough to give birth to my spiritual self; so it was only a matter of time before I realized that the "vital life force" that I had learned to catch by living the Way consciously and Divine Spirit were one and the same energy. But it would take a few more years before I came to the simple realization that the consciousness of my immortal self and Soul were one and the same—*which made Soul the consciousness of Divine Spirit!*

And with further creative writing, the creative life force (Divine Spirit, which I simply call my Muse) revealed to me that the consciousness of Soul is the "I" of God; that's why when I entered into the first building blocks of life and experienced the genesis of life in these lower worlds I made the connection and realized that it was the "I" of God—the *I Am* first cause principle—that had entered into the first building blocks of life to initiate the life process on Planet Earth; and I had to evolve through life to become a fully spiritually self-realized, God conscious Soul. *And that constituted the Divine Plan of God!*

I now realized that Divine Spirit was the Body of God and ground of all being, and that Soul was the consciousness of Divine Spirit; which meant that Soul was the consciousness of God. But all the holy books that I studied told me that God was Love; ergo, the Body of God and ground of all being had to be Love!

This logical deduction was confirmed by Jesus in Glenda Green's book *Love without End, Jesus Speaks*. Jesus appeared to Glenda so she could paint his portrait, and while she painted his portrait he expounded upon the mysteries of life. One of the mysteries that he resolved for me was the mystery of reincarnation, which implied the Divine Plan of God; and in his revelation he also confirmed my deduction that Love is the ground of all being—that one unifying energy and first cause principle. Jesus speaks:

"There was a time before which you were, but there will never be a time after which you are not. There was a time when you were one and complete within the Source of Love (which I experienced as an atom of God in the Body of God!). *Love, however, decided to give you immortality as yourself and to grant you an identity of your own* (which I experienced when I was sent into the lower worlds and evolved through life and experienced the birth of my reflective self-consciousness in my lifetime as a higher primate). *It was a great and glorious gift that you were given, full of promise, opportunity, and responsibility* (which I experienced as I evolved from lifetime to lifetime until I took evolution into my own hands with Gurdjieff's teaching and gave birth to my spiritual self in my mother's kitchen). *But the children of God, having no point of reference other than the simplicity of a common light, experienced it as a shock and interpreted the gift as separation. Many wounded themselves by viewing it as rejection"* (p. 78).

All souls in the exoteric First Circle of Life feel this separation from God, because they are not yet conscious of their Soul self; which is why Jesus died on the cross to bridge man's separation from God with his teaching of self-sacrifice. Jesus promised that whoever found the correct interpretation of his sayings would have eternal life; and with Gurdjieff's teaching of "work on oneself" that awakened me to the Word, I "heard" the Word behind the words of Jesus and found the correct interpretation of his sayings—which, in the simplest words possible boils down to this: **as you live the sayings of Jesus, they reveal their meaning to you.** This is how you arrive at the correct interpretation.

Jesus brought his own personalized teaching of the Way to the world to bridge man's separation from God with his symbolic death upon the cross. When I experienced my spiritual rebirth in my mother's kitchen I *knew* that I was immortal and would never die. I had bridged my separation from God by transforming the consciousness of my exoteric self (my *being* and *non-being*) and realized my Soul self; that's why I could write in my journal: **I am what I am not, and I am not what I am. I am both, but neither; I am Soul**.

Resolving the paradox of man's *being* and *non-being* was at the heart of Christ's teaching, which I expound upon in my novel *Jesus Wears Dockers;* and the way to resolve this paradox according to Jesus was to "die" to our life—which he symbolized with his death upon the cross.

"Dying" to our life is the mystery of Christ's teaching, which I discussed with the Ascended Master in my novel *Healing with Padre Pio* because he was a living Christ. Padre Pio suffered the holy wounds of Jesus for fifty years, and he knew the way of self-sacrifice better than anyone. He had died to his lower self to realize his higher self, and from his place of all knowing and all seeing he confirmed what I had come to realize about Christ's teaching; that's why he said to me, "We are very much alike."

Self-sacrifice is the way of suffering, which Jesus confirmed to Carl Jung at the end of *The Red Book*. Jung writes: "It was noon on a hot summer's day and I was taking a stroll in my garden; when I reached the shade of the high trees, I met Philemon strolling in the fragrant grass. But when I sought to approach him, a blue shade (Christ) came from the other side, and when Philemon saw him, he said, 'I find you in the garden, beloved. The sins of the world have conferred beauty on your countenance.'"

They converse for a while, and then Philemon says to Jesus, "I know only one thing, that whoever hosts the worm also needs his brother. What do you bring me, my beautiful guest? Lamentations and abominations were the gift of the worm. What will you give us?"

And Jesus replies, "I bring you the beauty of suffering. That is what is needed by whoever hosts the worm" (*The Red Book*, pp. 551-553).

Jesus gave us his teaching of self-sacrifice to transform the "worm"—the lower self of man, which is the *being* and *non-being* aspect of our nature. By living Christ's sayings consciously—or as Jesus said, *'he who doeth these sayings of mine shall build his house upon a rock'*—one will transform the consciousness of his *being* and *non-being* and give birth to his spiritual self. This is what it means to live the Way consciously. This is what Gurdjieff called "conscious suffering" and Jesus called "the beauty of suffering."

Every initiate of the Way knows this. What they may not know is that there is beauty in unconscious suffering as well, because through karmic suffering the consciousness of one's *being* and *non-being* is transformed also.

This is how one grows spiritually in the exoteric First Circle of Life. And when he has grown enough to take evolution into his own hands he will learn the art of conscious suffering, which will take the meaninglessness out of suffering and give one incentive to "die" to his life to "save" his life—which will be the theme of the book that I hope to write one day soon: *The Beauty of Suffering, Reflections on Jung's Red Book.*

20. *The Dual Self of Man*

It was such a simple realization, but one which completed my understanding of the duel self of man: **we do not have two selves, one lower and one higher (or one inner and one outer, as the case may be); we have only one self which is dual in consciousness.** St Paul called it the "selfsame thing," and his gospel was all about making one out of our two selves, which he called a "new creature."

It is a fundamental tenet of the Way of the Eternal that we are Soul; and the premise of this path is that we only have to realize it. I am Soul, you are Soul, and everyone is Soul; and realizing that we are Soul is what this path is all about. But the journey to Soul-realization consciousness is easier said than done; that's why there are so many spiritual paths in the world to accommodate Soul's individual journey.

All paths lead to God, but not all paths are the same. The Christian who believes that our immortal soul is created at the moment of human conception and that we only live one life that Jesus died on the cross to save does not live his life as the Buddhist who believes that we do not have an individual self and must save ourselves from the illusions and transitoriness of life. And the Sufi lives an entirely different life. He seeks to transform the consciousness of his lower self to realize his higher self.

These are all different paths that speak to different levels of human consciousness. I was born Roman Catholic, but I felt stifled by my Christian faith and became a seeker so I could breathe freely; but it was not easy letting go of my Christian faith, because there was something about being a Christian that had a pernicious hold upon my psyche.

The hold that Christianity had upon me was its core belief that Jesus Christ is the way, the truth, and the life; and only through Jesus can we be saved. I had a customer in my hometown who was a devout Christian because of this core belief; and yet she was miserable in her faith because it no longer nourished her soul.

I painted for her every few years, and every time I painted her house we would sit in her small kitchen over tea and talk about religion, life and death, karma and reincarnation, and whatever—including that "kooky Shirley MacLaine," as she called her.

I loved Shirley MacLaine and thought she was very brave to put herself out there with her belief in reincarnation that threatened the Judeo-Christian status quo of the western world, and I stuck up for her with my customer who had outgrown her Christian faith but didn't have the courage to pursue another path more suited to her consciousness.

But why would my customer refuse to let go of her Christian faith that she had obviously outgrown? I was stumped by this question until I found C. G. Jung and learned about the shadow self—that aspect of our personality that keeps us trapped in a state of unresolved karmic consciousness; and not until we confront our false self will we be free to find our true self. It was easier for my customer to believe that Jesus died for her sins than to accept responsibility for her own karma; that's why she could not let go of her Christian faith. The responsibility of karmic accountability terrified her.

Shirley MacLaine realized this. She tells us as much in her latest (and my favorite) memoir, *I'm Over All That.* She writes: "The truth is that no matter where I went, I was always looking for myself. That journey into myself as I evaluated my beliefs and values, whether living at home or in far-flung corners of the world, has been the most important journey of all"—because **all journeys bring us back to ourselves!**

St. Padre Pio told me that life is a journey of the self, and Shirley MacLaine was on her own personal journey; that's what made her "kooky" to the world—because it takes an inordinate amount of courage to break free of the status quo and live our own life.

This is why I love C. G. Jung. The courage that it took him to severe his relationship with Sigmund Freud to pursue his own path in life was soul-wrenching; and it drove him into a state of depression that almost destroyed him. But he pulled himself out because he was called by his destiny to realize his true self.

By the age of forty Jung had "achieved honor, power, wealth, knowledge, and every human happiness," yet somehow managed to lose his soul. "My soul, my soul, where are you," Jung writes in his Black Book series which became *The Red Book;* and so began one of the greatest spiritual quests ever to be recorded in human history.

"The knowledge of death came to me that night..." Jung writes in *The Red Book.* "I went into the inner death and saw that outer dying is better than inner dying. And I decided to die outside and live within...I turned away and sought the place of the inner life" (*Carl Jung, Wounded Healer of the Soul,* by Claire Dunne, p. 11). Whether he knew it or not, Carl Jung had found the "strait gate" of the "narrow way," and he began to live the Way by "dying" to his outer life so he could "live within." As Jesus said, *"he that loseth his life for my sake shall find it"* (Math. 10: 39); "for my sake," being the Way, or what Jung came to call "the secret way of life."

Thus began Jung's confrontation with the unconscious. I began my confrontation with the unconscious when I stepped off the breakwater that connected the little island in the Nipigon River with the mainland. I had gone for a long walk to ponder my destiny. I was in my second year of philosophy studies at university, and I wasn't getting the answers that I expected. I was desperate, so I asked God what price I had to pay for truth; and to my surprise I was "given" my *Royal Dictum*—my "edict" of self-denial that I vowed to live for the rest of my life. And with my *Royal Dictum* I began to die the excruciating slow death of my outer life—just as every truth seeker who enters the "strait gate" and begins to live the "narrow" Way with conscious purpose!

This is the dilemma of the modern world: no one wants to die the slow death of the lower self. Gurdjieff's teaching was based upon the idea that man is asleep, and only by waking up to his true condition can he begin to "work" on himself and realize his potential that nature cannot fulfill; but waking up to life is not easy. People wake up momentarily and realize just how painful it is to be conscious of all the responsibility that comes with taking evolution into our own hands and they slip back into the great sleep of life and pray to God for their salvation instead; or else they resign themselves to that sate of conflicted consciousness that Henry David Thoreau called "quiet desperation."

But why do people prefer to stay asleep?

This question haunted me for years until I remembered how difficult it was to quit smoking. I tried for years to quit smoking, but not until I vowed to get to the source of my life with my *Royal Dictum* did I finally make sense of it.

My *Royal Dictum* was inspired by the Nipigon River which flowed past me while I pondered my fate and I recalled the words of *Ecclesiastes* about all the rivers flowing into the sea and returning to the place from whence they came: I felt that by denying myself the pleasures of my life I would be going against the currents of life and go back to the source of my life. This was the new path that I forged for myself to find my true self; and slowly, with each excruciating death of my personal pleasures, I began to see just how inextricably meshed our lower self is with our higher self and how difficult it was to set ourselves free.

"I deem that the true disciple of philosophy is likely to be misunderstood by other men," said Socrates in Plato's *Phaedo*; *"they do not perceive that he is ever pursuing death and dying."* And just what did Socrates mean by this?

The same thing that Jesus meant with his teaching of self-sacrifice. By sacrificing our lower self we realize our higher self. When we "die" to our lower self we purify the consciousness of our inner self, and the more pure the consciousness of our inner self is the more we realize that we are Soul. This is the logic of the Way, which Socrates couched in his philosophy. *"And what is purification but the separation of the soul from the body,"* he said in the *Phaedo*; *"the habit of the soul gathering and collecting herself into herself, out of all the courses of the body; the dwelling in her own place alone, as in another life, so also in this, as far as she can; the release of the soul from the chains of the body?"*

But who wants to be released from the chains of the body in today's world where every pleasure can be satisfied almost instantly? This is why I told my archetypal Jesus in my novel *Jesus Wears Dockers* that his teaching was for another time, and that it just does not work in today's self-indulgent world. His teaching needed new bottles.

However, as trapped as man may be by the consciousness of his lower self, when nature has evolved him as far as she possibly can he will have no choice but to seek a way to liberate himself, because he will not be able to stand the weight of his *non-being*. So burdensome will the consciousness of his false self be that out of desperation he will be forced to find a way out of himself; just as I had to do, and Carl Jung had to do, and every soul that is ready to begin the journey to their true self will have to do.

21. *Live, Love, and Enjoy Your Life*

My novel *The Waking Dream* was inspired by a water color artist who had come to an impasse in his art. He had lost his connection with the artist in himself, and how I helped him to reconnect with his inner self inspired my first "Soul talk" book *The Way of Soul,* which drew C. G. Jung into my gravitational field in a dream one night.

As I said, *The Way of Soul* wasn't published out here yet; so it was exciting to know that it was published on the Other Side and that Jung had read it and wanted to talk with me about what he called "the alpha and omega of the self." So I wouldn't have met Carl Jung in my dream if it hadn't been for Kevin Archer, the water color artist in my novel.

Kevin had come to a standstill in his art, not unlike the great Canadian artist Robert Bateman whose abstract art also brought him to a standstill. "Is that it?" he asked himself, as he studied his last piece of abstract art. "Is that all there is to art?"

Abstract art no longer nourished his soul, because the path of abstract art had taken him as far as he could go; and in its mercy the omniscient guiding force of life nudged him to take in a showing of the realist painter Andrew Wyeth's work in Buffalo, New York; and after studying Wyeth's work he exclaimed to himself, *"I found my way!"*

He called this "my road to Damascus." Wyeth's work reconnected him with his inner self, and he went on to become one of Canada's most successful nature artists; and, true to the inherently redemptive power of the Way when one taps into the water of everlasting life within, Bateman became an active environmentalist to help save our planet.

This is one of the great mysteries of the Way that no-one has ever explained. The Way is the Word, which is Divine Spirit, which is the ground of all being, which is Love; and Love has the power to reconcile the dual nature of man, which is why Jesus made love central to his teaching; and when one taps into the creative life stream he is tapping into the "I" of God—the first cause principle and omniscient guiding force of life that has the redemptive power to bring Soul back home to God.

This is how great artists become "saviors." They tap into the redemptive energy of God with their art. But unless they have some measure of balance between their lower self (ego) and their higher self (Soul) they inevitably become "fools" of God because ego will become intoxicated with the energy of Divine Spirit, not unlike the reformed alcoholic who attributes his salvation to Jesus Christ and goes out to save the world in the name of Jesus—little realizing that it wasn't Jesus that saved him but the redemptive power of Divine Spirit that his belief in Jesus connected him with.

Finding balance between my inner and outer self was very hard for me when I tapped into the stream of everlasting life, and had Gurdjieff not directed me to take a vow of silence about the Work I would have probably become a "fool" of God.

When Dr. George Sheehan said *"In running I found my salvation"* he as much as told me that he had tapped into the stream of everlasting life—that same water that Jesus was talking about to the woman at the well in the city of Sychar in Samaria: **"Whosoever drinketh of this water shall thirst again. But whosoever drinketh of the water that I shall give him shall never thirst again; but the water that I shall give him shall be in him a well springing up unto everlasting life"** (John 4: 13).

The water of everlasting life that Jesus is talking about is the Word of God, which is the Way. The Way is Divine Spirit, and Divine Spirit is the omniscient guiding force of life; and when one connects with his inner self he taps into the Word of God, the redemptive energy of the Way—or, in Christ's words, he drinks in the water of everlasting life.

Divine Spirit is the ground of all being, so it is everywhere to be found; which means that the water of everlasting life flows through all life. Jesus revealed to the woman at the well that she could drink the water of everlasting life if she followed him, which I proved for myself when I took the sayings of Jesus out into the marketplace and *lived* them with pathological commitment; but there is more than one way to tap into the water of everlasting life that flows within. In fact, there are as many ways as there are souls. This is the meaning behind St. Padre Pio's words **"life is a journey of the self."**

The Gnostics knew this, as did the Sufis; which is why they said that there are as many ways to God as there are souls of man; so if each person is their own way to God, how does one find their own path?

As strange as this may sound, not everyone is ready to take their own path back home to God. This is the meaning behind Christ's words ***"many are called but few are chosen."*** And what makes one ready is the season of their harvest. Everything in nature's garden has its own season of harvest, and man is no different; he must grow until he is ripe enough to be harvested. That's when he will be ready for his path. This is the meaning behind the saying, *"when the student is ready the teacher will appear."*

The teacher is the omniscient guiding force of life, and it may come in many forms. It may come as a man, a woman, a book, a new teaching, a new career, whatever; the teacher is one's connection with his inner self, because the inner self taps into the well of everlasting life that one needs to grow in spiritual consciousness to realize his true self.

When Kevin Archer tapped into the well of everlasting life within himself with the Word that flowed out of me every time we talked, he no longer needed me to help him stay connected with his inner self; and we parted ways. I haven't seen him since; but knowing how the Way works, I am certain that when he comes to another impasse in his life a new teacher will appear, because this is how life works.

Jesus puzzled the world with his teaching. Few people have found the correct interpretation of his sayings and solved the mystery of spiritual rebirth; but the secret to his teaching is to be found in the living of it, because the Way will only reveal itself as one *lives* the Way—regardless what path one is on. This was Gurdjieff's gift to me.

As I "worked" on myself with Gurdjieff's techniques of *non-identifying, intentional suffering, conscious effort, self-remembering,* and *non-self-justifying* I awakened to the Word (the language of life) and gravitated to the sayings of Jesus; and as I "worked" on myself with the sayings of Jesus, they revealed their secrets to me. That's how I found their correct interpretation. This was the inspiration for my novel *Jesus Wears Dockers, The Gospel Conspiracy Story*; but as comprehensive as my archetypal Jesus and I were in revealing the correct interpretation of his sayings, there is still much to say, and connecting with one's inner self is central to understanding how the Way works in life.

One can connect with one's inner self any which way. One can be a back yard mechanic and connect with his inner self; or a housewife with her garden; a writer with his poetry; a doctor devoted to his practice; a musician who sacrifices everything for his music; a carpenter who loves doing woodwork; or a runner who has to run every day to get his daily "fix." It doesn't matter what one does, **as long as one loves what he's doing he will connect with his inner self, because love is the connecting principle!**

Jesus has returned many times since he died on the cross, and he will continue to help the world awaken to the Word. This is his purpose as an Ascended Master. And every time he returns to the world he reveals a little more about the Way, and always according to the spiritual needs of the time and place; which is why I'm so thankful that St. Padre Pio suggested that I read Glenda Green's book *Love without End, Jesus Speaks*—because it satisfied my need to know everything about the Way that I needed to know. I *knew* that we have to connect with our inner self to tap into the water of everlasting life, but Jesus offers a much more complete understanding in Glenda's book. Jesus speaks:

*"Never underestimate the power of **your connection to life**— the center of self in contact with the Reality of God. It will humble you. It may also ennoble you, enlighten you, or bring you to tears. Aside from everything else, it surely will lift you above the problems which have been oppressing you.*

"A woman in childbirth could hardly endure the pain were it not for her connection with the miracle in progress. An athlete would not persist through the pain of a dislocated shoulder were it not for the collective spirit he shares with his team members.

***"Life is an adventure in connecting.** The connections you make affirm and strengthen your character. The ones you make in love are the ones you will hang your garlands on. All the rest are consumable experiences. They may entertain you or challenge you, but in the end they will leave you hungry and thirsty for the real meaning of life.*

"The soul is crying for a reality experience which only the physical life can give to it. The body is crying for an immortality experience which only the soul can give to it. As you permit this union to fulfill itself, you will directly know what it feels like to be the love that you are" (pp. 87-88).

This is why St. Padre Pio said to me in my letter to him when I opened up in that special way for him to speak to me: **"Live, love, and enjoy your life; and don't worry about tomorrow. Tomorrow never comes. There is only today."**

22. *The Fallacy of the Ego*

One of the most spiritually rewarding insights that I garnered on my journey through the mesoteric circle of life was that **ego is vital to our spiritual growth, and it is foolish to treat ego as the bane of our spiritual life.** This is why I got a chuckle when Jung travelled to India and let it be known to his Indian friends how foolish it was for them to try to extinguish the ego in their spiritual teachings, because it cannot be done.

Jung knew that ego is the conscious aspect of our inner unconscious self, and that the individuation of the unconscious self is what life is all about, which it can only do through the conscious personality; and the ego self cannot be extinguished because this would be like extinguishing life itself, which Jung found an absurd proposition.

The Buddhists believe that ego is illusory, and in many ways it is; but only when one fails to see the hidden, unconscious aspect of the self. When Jung was very young he felt that he had two personalities, which he called his No. 1 and No. 2. No. 1 was his outer personality, and No. 2 was his inner personality; and it was Jung's destiny to bring his two personalities into agreement, into one individuated self—which he did.

"A few days before his death Jung told of a dream he had, the last one he was able to communicate. He saw a round stone in a high place, a barren square, and on it were engraved the words: 'And this shall be a sign unto you of Wholeness and Oneness.' Then he saw many vessels to the right in an open square and a quadrangle of trees whose roots reached around the earth and enveloped him and among the roots golden threads were glittering" (*C. G. Jung, His Myth in Our Time*, Marie-Louise von Franz, p. 287).

Jung devoted his life to unraveling the mysteries of the individuation process; but just what did he mean by "individuation process"?

Since I began writing *The Summoning of Noman* I have read many more books on Jung and reread a number of Jung's works, and the more I read the more fascinated I was with his life and destined mission, which became painfully evident to me when I read *The Red Book* that chronicled what he called his "confrontation with the unconscious."

Penny and I saw the movie *Lincoln* the other weekend, and I was fascinated by Daniel Day Lewis's role as President Abraham Lincoln because he brilliantly captured what Lincoln felt was his destiny to emancipate the slaves of America. The weight of his destiny upon his shoulders was so poignantly portrayed by Daniel Day Lewis—who apparently stayed in character 24/7 until the movie was made—that I came out of the theatre with tears in my eyes and a lump in my throat.

In like manner, the more I read about Jung's life and his works the more I felt the weight of his destiny upon his shoulders; and many times I was brought to tears because I knew in my heart the price that he had to pay to realize his destiny. And what I love and admire most about Jung is that he chronicled his journey in *The Red Book* for the rest of us to witness and learn from on our own journey of self-individuation, which I began reading Christmas Day and on through to New Years Day, 2013 and which turned out to be the most satisfying Christmas present of my life.

Jung was a trailblazer, and he had to blaze a trail through the tangled forest of the human mind—both conscious and unconscious; and the end result of his trailblazing is a psychological understanding of how the self individuates through life.

If I did not have the experiences I had I would be totally mesmerized by Jung's psychology of individuation, as most people who read Jung are; and as much as *The Red Book* helps to break the code of Jung's personal journey of self-individuation, it is still a tangled web of esoteric concepts and mystifying images that continue to tax Jungian scholars. But need it be so confusing? Need the Way be so difficult to understand?

"God's kingdom is spread out upon the earth, and people do not see it," said Jesus; and by "God's kingdom" Jesus meant the Way. Although Jung does not spell it out exactly, because he had to safeguard his scientific reputation, he translated the arcane Gnostic and alchemical teachings of the Way into his psychology of individuation, and he was relieved to learn through Richard Wilhelm's translation of the *I Ching* and *The Secret of the Golden Flower* (for which he wrote a brilliant commentary) that he was not alone in his discovery of the secret of man's destiny to individuate the consciousness of God; but as thorough as he was in his efforts to take the mystery out of man's spiritual destiny, he went to the Other Side feeling that he had failed. A few months before he died he wrote to an English correspondent: *"I have failed in my foremost task to open people's eyes to the fact that man has a soul, that there is a buried treasure in the field."*

But he did not fail, because Jesus said that the Way was not for everyone; it is only for those that are ready to take evolution into their own hands. This is the meaning behind his disconcerting remark, *"Many are called but few are chosen."* And what makes one ready for the mesoteric second stage of evolution is life itself, because through the natural process of karmic growth one will reach a point where he will no longer be able to withstand the weight of his own ego and will be forced to find a way to liberate himself from himself—as Jung himself confessed in *The Red Book*. This is the lost key that unlocks the mystery of Jung's psychologically mystifying process of individuation.

Jung admitted that by the age of forty he had satisfied all of his No. 1 personality's egoic needs—"honor, power, wealth, knowledge and every human happiness"—but in the process he lost his soul. "My soul, my soul, where are you?" he asks; thus beginning the spiritual journey of integrating his outer self (ego) with his inner self (Soul).

Like every person whose ego becomes bloated with karmic experiences that weigh heavily upon one's soul, Jung had to get out from under because he was suffocating from the burdensome consciousness of his massive ego—and there is evidence that Jung's ego was something to contend with during the first forty years of his life; and that's when destiny called and he had no choice but to find a way out of his spiritual impasse.

As the poet Cleanthes implied with his poem, we either walk alongside our destiny or we're going to be dragged by it; and the world renowned young psychiatrist who had achieved all of his No. I personality's dreams decided to take destiny into his own hands and dive into the depths of his unconscious to look for his lost soul.

I knew this kind of commitment well, because I had done exactly the same thing at the age of twenty-three; I sold my pool hall and vending machine business and fled to France to look for my lost soul. Not that I had achieved everything that I wanted out of life, far from it; I just could not suffer the suffocating weight of my non-self—the shadow self of my Parisian past-life personality that was set free that godforsaken night.

I knew that whoever did what he did that night was me but not me, and I had to find out what had happened to me. Why did I do what I did? Who was that person that had taken over my personality? I knew it was me, but I also knew that it was not me; and this paradoxical self-consciousness fueled my quest until I "chanced" upon Gurdjieff's teaching whose fundamental premise was that "man has no permanent and unchangeable I."

I took Gurdjieff to heart and began my impossible quest for my permanent and unchangeable I that my poem *Noman* called God's "fish's scale." It took many years, but I finally broke the code of my poem and learned that God's "fish's scale" was my lost soul, and that my soul was lost in the consciousness of Noman—meaning, my non-self.

Just as Jung had lost his soul to the consciousness of his brilliant and accomplished ego self (his No. 1 personality), I had lost my soul to the consciousness of my insatiable shadow personality that was made up of all the egos of my past lives; that's why the mandala of my life was to do the impossible— because in extricating myself out of the consciousness of my non-self I would be extricating myself out of the consciousness of the *Archetypal Noman*, which was so difficult to do that one day out of sheer mental, emotional, and spiritual exhaustion I wrote in my journal, *"Satan, you are so crafty that I know not which is you and which is me!"*

But as I lived the Way with single-minded devotion (it would not be incorrect to call it pathological), I became more and more conscious of my elusive false self, until one day I could "see" the *Archetypal False One* in the shadow personality of everyone I met (Satan did say that his name was legion); and believe me, this was very hard on me because I had to completely readjust my behavior with people. And with some people I simply couldn't adjust, like the man who said to me when he saw me running in arctic freezing weather, "What the hell are you trying to prove out there, anyway?"

As I said though, had not the Inner Master intervened with the question *"why do you lie?"* when I came to a dead stop with Gurdjieff's teaching, I don't know what would have happened to me; because in my effort to answer this question I had to put myself under the microscope, and the more I studied my every thought, word, and deed the more I was able to discern my false self. But it wasn't enough to see my false self; I had to authenticate the consciousness of my false self, which put me through so much anguish and personal humiliation that I still blush at the memory. But after years of struggling with my false self I gave birth to my spiritual self, and my most powerful saying: **"The shortest way to God is through hell."** In a word, I had finally resolved the paradox of our ego self.

23. *The Fourth Corner of the Abyss*

When God condemned Noman to the "fourth corner of the abyss" to find His "fish's scale," God condemned me because I was Noman. I was a teenager in high school, and I had no idea what happened when I wrote my poem; but whatever happened, I knew that the person that God had summoned for a reckoning was me. It took many years to come to an understanding of the symbols of my poem, but the more I transformed the consciousness of my false self as I lived the Way consciously the clearer the poem became to me.

The three main symbols of my poem are: 1. Noman; 2. "fish's scale"; and 3. "fourth corner of the abyss." Noman symbolizes the archetypal non-self of Everyman. The non-self is the collective consciousness of one's past life shadow personalities.

Every time we are reborn into life we create a new personality. Each time we create a new personality we create a shadow personality. The shadow personality is the repressed side of our conscious personality. When we die, our personality does not die with the body; we take it with us to the Other Side in our Soul body.

Our Soul body is our immortal Soul self, which is reborn from life to life to fulfill its destiny of spiritual self-realization and God consciousness; and the identity of our Soul body is made up of all the personalities that we create in our physical lives. This is how our Soul self individuates from one life to the next until it is fully self-realized.

When we are reborn into a new life we don't remember our past-life personalities for a specific reason. If we were allowed to remember our past-life personalities they would interfere in our freedom to choose how we live our life; and it is only through freedom of choice that we can transcend ourselves and realize our spiritual destiny.

Our past lives however have a very strong unconscious influence upon our current life; as my lifetime as the *"le salaud de Paris"* affected me, for example. This was my sexually and morally depraved lifetime when I turned on the Holy Roman Catholic Church, on Jesus Christ, on God, and on love because my heart was fractured into a million pieces when the Cardinal of Paris forbade his niece from marrying me. I vowed to avenge the honor of my love for Claudine by stealing as many souls from the Church as I could.

I was sexually gifted, and I satisfied every woman in the noble courts of Paris—but only if they forfeited their soul to me. That was the moral debauchery that earned me the soubriquet *"le salaud de Paris."* And it was this morally and sexually debauched personality that erupted from my unconscious that godforsaken night when I did what I did that so shocked my conscience that it catapulted me into my quest for my true self.

So our past lives certainly do affect our current life, but they do so unconsciously; which means that we are always free to choose a new path that will transform the karmic hold that our past lives have over us—as I did by choosing to sell my business and go to France to search for my true self. But why France?

There is a back story to every decision we make, and it would take a whole novel to unpack everything that went into making my decision to go to France; suffice to say that I had karmic reasons for going to France to begin my quest for my true self.

The next symbol in my poem is "fish's scale." God asked me, "Noman, hast thou my fish's scale?" I had absolutely no idea what this meant when I wrote my poem, nor did I even begin to suspect what God meant until I began my quest for my true self and it finally dawned on me one day that "fish's scale" meant soul.

God was the Great Fish, and I was a "scale" on God's Body; but this only made sense to me after I had my past-life regression to the Body of God when I learned that I was an atom of God with Soul consciousness but no self-consciousness. I was then sent into the "abyss" of the lower worlds to create a new "I" of God, and as I evolved through the evolutionary chain of life I individuated the life force, which is the un-self-realized I-consciousness of God, until I gave birth to my reflective self-consciousness in my first primordial human life. And from lifetime to lifetime I continued to grow in self-consciousness until I was called by God for a reckoning of my life.

This is not allegory. This is what I experienced. God sent me into the lower worlds to create a new "I" of God, because this is how God grows in God-realization consciousness; and when I grew enough in self-realization consciousness to take evolution into my own hands so I could become spiritually self-realized and God-conscious, God called me home.

So when God shouted, "Noman, hast thou my fish's scale?" God wanted me to get off my butt and start the journey back home to the higher worlds of God, because I was ready to step into the Second Circle of Life and take evolution into my own hands; and the only way I could do that was to gather and collect myself into myself. *"And what is purification but the separation of the soul from the body, as I was saying before; the habit of the soul gathering and collecting herself into herself,"* said Socrates in Plato's *Phaedo*.

As an atom of God with Soul consciousness but no self-consciousness, I lived countless lives before I individuated enough life-consciousness to give birth to my reflective self in my lifetime as a higher primate; and I had to live many human lives before I was ready to take evolution into my own hands and realize my spiritual destiny.

But I had outgrown the First Circle of Life in my current life, and it was time to begin the second stage of evolution; that's why God called me for a reckoning. He wanted me to step into the next stage of evolution, but I did not want to go. I wanted to stay in the First Circle; and that's when Soul stepped in and dislodged *"le salaud de Paris"* from the depths of my unconscious which compelled me to do what I did that godforsaken night.

I confess however that as horrified as I was for doing what I did that night, I now know that God in its infinite mercy had to intervene for me to take evolution into my own hands so I could fulfill my spiritual destiny; that's why my debauched personality was dislodged from the depths of my unconscious to possess me that night. So that night wasn't godforsaken after all; on the contrary, it was divinely sanctioned.

The next symbol is the "fourth corner of the abyss." It took a while to decode this symbol, but it refers to the mental plane of consciousness. When I became an Initiate of the Way of the Eternal I learned of the planes of consciousness: the physical, astral, causal, mental, and Soul planes. And above the Soul plane are many more spiritual planes, but the atom of God begins its evolution in the physical plane; which in this case is Earth.

The physical is the first plane of consciousness; the astral is the second; the causal is the third; the mental is the fourth; and the Soul plane is the fifth. And the atom of God begins its evolution in the physical plane and evolves up through the astral, causal, and mental planes until it is ready to enter the Soul plane of consciousness.

So when God condemned me to the "fourth corner of the abyss" I was sent to the mental plane of consciousness to find my lost soul; but why the mental plane?

I would never have pieced this out had I not become an Initiate of the Way of the Eternal where I learned that we have a body for each plane of consciousness. We have a physical body for the physical plane; an astral body for the astral plane; a causal body for the causal plane; a mental body for the mental plane; and a Soul body for the Soul plane. But only our Soul body is real and everlasting; all of our other bodies are finite and temporary. They constitute our ephemeral self, as Buddhists believe.

As the atom of God evolves through the First Circle of Life it constellates the life force, which is the un-self-realized consciousness of God. When the atom of God has constellated enough life force to individuate a new "I" of God, as I experienced in my first primordial human lifetime, it grows and evolves in self-consciousness and begins to form a body for the astral, causal and mental planes of consciousness.

The atom of God is an un-self-realized Soul body, or a Soul seed if you will; and it evolves through these lower bodies to realize its spiritual destiny of God-realization consciousness. The astral body is our emotional body; the causal body is our karmic body; the mental body is our mind body; and as the atom of God evolves from one life to the next, it grows in the consciousness of each of its bodies.

So we have a physical or biological self; an emotional self; a causal self; and a mental self. And all these selves constitute our Soul self. And we will continue to evolve through natural evolution in the First Circle of Life until we are ready to take evolution into our own hands to grow in spiritual self-realization and God consciousness.

In effect then, we have to evolve through all the lower planes of consciousness to get to the Soul plane, the first of the spiritual worlds of God and our true home; but to evolve through these lower planes we have to resolve the karma that we have created in each of our lower bodies that keeps us bound to the lower planes.

So we have physical, astral, causal, and mental karma that has to be resolved to realize our Soul self; which is why Socrates called life a prison. *"There is a doctrine uttered in secret that man is a prisoner who has no right to open the door of his prison and run away; this is a great mystery, which I not quite understand,"* he said in the *Phaedo*; and neither did I understand until I gave birth to my spiritual self in my mother's kitchen and was initiated into the Soul plane of consciousness, the Third Circle of Life.

The Way began to reveal the secrets of the Divine Plan of God from the moment I stepped into the esoteric circle of life; but I was far from home free. I still had a lot of karma to resolve in my lower bodies, which I did as I lived the Way consciously; and then all I had to do to break my personal cycle of karma and reincarnation was to resolve the karma of my mental body—and that's why God condemned me to the "fourth corner of the abyss." I was stuck in the fourth, or mental plane of consciousness; and not until I broke the hold that my mental self had over me would I find my lost soul—meaning, God's "fish's scale."

This is why St. Padre Pio told me in one of my spiritual healing sessions that I had returned to live my same life over again to achieve a different outcome; *because in my first lifetime as Orest Stocco I could not escape from the prison of my own mind!*

24. *The Prison of My Mind*

One would think that the unconscious personality of my lifetime as *"le salaud de Paris"* was enough to contend with when it compelled me to do what I did that night, but it made a dramatic reappearance into my life many years later when Penny and I moved to Georgian Bay and I had seven past-life regressions, because my third regression brought me back to my lifetime in Paris and all hell broke loose in my life.

I would never have survived the onslaught of all my past life sexual consciousness that began to overwhelm me had I not invoked the Inner Master's help. For one thing, I had to know why in my lifetime as Riel Laforchette (this was the name I was given) I could satisfy any woman that I seduced; and he revealed to me that I could hold back my orgasm, which over time would only come when I went to greater and greater extremes in my depravity. Suffice to say then that my sex life began to take on a dimension of rapturous intensity that was both extremely gratifying and terrifying—because it was so damn easy to abandon to sex again as I did in my Sufi lifetime as Salaam in ancient Persia.

The average man would give almost anything for this kind of sexual pleasure, but I was not your average man; I was on a mission to return to the higher worlds, and one cannot do that if he remains stuck in his lower bodies. So despite the mind-blowing sexual experiences that one can have when they awaken the kundalini, which I had accidentally done when I lived in France, the peak experience of sexual orgasms cannot take one beyond the lower planes of consciousness, and it keeps one trapped in his lower self.

I know this for a fact, because I trapped myself in my Sufi lifetime as Salaam. I was a member of the secret Sufi Order of the White Tiger (whether there is such an Order or not, I honestly can't prove; but that's what came out in my regression), and I failed to pass my test of initiation because I could not master my "tiger of desire."

The spiritual premise of our Order was that we would be united with God when we mastered our "tiger of desire," and we were given techniques to do this; but try as I may, I always submitted to my "tiger of desire" and indulged in sensual pleasures; and the tension between my desire for God and my desire for pleasure drove me out of my mind.

I was torn apart by what I called my "two stallions of desire," my love for God and love for pleasure; and after failing to pass my third and final test of initiation I had to leave the Order and ended up becoming a fool of God wandering the streets begging for food and spouting verses from the Koran and Rumi and my own delusional verses to God.

I died of malnutrition lost in my own mind, and my Salaam personality came back to haunt me in my current life, many years before I was regressed to that life. I was living Gurdjieff's teaching, and I *non-identified* with sexual pleasure to "catch" the life force so that I could grow in spiritual consciousness; but because I had awakened the kundalini when I was in France I had to contend with such a powerful current of creative energy that it was next to impossible not to sublimate it through sexual pleasure, and inevitably I gave way to rich sexual fantasies—just as I had done as Salaam. This was my inner conflict.

But this was not the only inner conflict that I had to contend with. I was also pulled into my own mind by something that happened to me while living in France. I don't want to go into detail here, because one day I might have enough courage to write a novel on my disorienting experience in Annecy; suffice to say now that while playing around with a Ouija board one evening with some friends I opened myself up to psychic influences, and this began to play havoc with my mind when one evening alone and desperately lonely in my one room apartment I started to dabble in automatic writing.

It was unbelievably seductive, because I would ask questions and my hand would write out my answers; but the answers were so vague that I was never satisfied. And this drew me in deeper, and deeper, and deeper; until I began to play out scenarios with people in my mind as if they were psychic realities. And even though I tested many of these psychic realities and they never proved to be true, I continued to be seduced by the control I had in the world of my own mind, and before long I couldn't help myself and began talking to the people in my mind as if they were real. This was my private hell.

And this is how I lost myself in my lifetime as Salaam; I couldn't extricate myself out of the fantasy world of my own mind, and I died a babbling fool of God. I was not the only fool of God who wandered the city streets. There were many fools of God throughout the land of Persia, and we were treated as holy messengers of God and given food to eat for the mindless spiritual nonsense that we spouted for them.

After years of struggling with my irrepressible desire to escape into my own mind, I finally managed to ground myself in the real world; and I did that by pouring myself into my contract painting business and working seven days a week, and by practicing Gurdjieff's most difficult technique—*non-identifying* with the objects of my desire.

I broke the seductive spell of my own mind, and because I was intimately familiar with the fantasy world that we can slip into I began to recognize it in other people. In some people it was less obvious than others, and in some it had gotten out of control; these were the people that I saw in shopping malls or in some corner of a bar talking to themselves.

There was one young man in my home town a few years younger than me who was married and into drugs and who slipped into his own mind and talked to his fantasy people just as I used to do, but believing that no-one noticed. He could be in the middle of a group of friends in one of the hotel bars and carry on a conversation and then slip into his fantasy world without anyone noticing but me. His eyes always gave him away. And then one day as I was driving by the Nipigon Café on my way to give a painting estimate I saw him standing on the sidewalk in the rain talking to himself. His lips weren't moving, but I knew that he was lost in conversation with the people of his own mind.

It was still raining and he was still standing in front of the café when I returned from my estimate an hour later and I pulled over and opened the passenger door of my little Camero and shouted, "Get in the car, Brent; I want to talk with you!"

Startled, he looked at me, and I repeated: "Get in, Brent. I have something I want to tell you. Come on, get out of the rain!"

He got in and I took him for a long drive down Highway Eleven where I went for my daily run and I spared him no punches: "Brent, I know what you're doing. You're talking to yourself. You've created a fantasy world, and you can't help yourself. You get pulled into your own mind because you believe there's something psychic going on; but it's not real. It's all a fantasy world..." And I went on, shocking him. He didn't deny what he was doing, and that opened the door for me to tell him to get professional help. He said he would, but he didn't; and a few weeks later he was found dead of a drug overdose.

I knew another person who showed signs of the same affliction, a very bright math graduate from Waterloo University that I went to high school with whose mother died of Alzheimer's and who was terrified of becoming like her mother. She had come home after she graduated and her mother died and she stayed home for her father's sake, and she went for long daily walks by herself and I would pick her up and take her for coffee and we talked and became good friends; and I told her what I felt was going on with her.

She was amazed that I could see into her mind and wondered if I was psychic; but I told her that I had been where she was headed, and I was just giving her a heads up. Finally her father bought her a car so she could drive to Calgary where her only sibling lived and look for a job; and she left. But we corresponded regularly, and she revealed to me in one letter how she was in the office typing when she left her body and was watching herself working and wanted to know if she was going out of her mind. I replied that she wasn't, because out-of-body experiences were not that uncommon; and I recommend books by Doctor Raymond Moody, who had coined the term out-of-body experience. She replied and thanked me and took my advice to get herself a pet dog; and when she and her big Labrador came home to visit her father a few years later she was very well grounded.

So when I discovered Blavatsky's little theosophical work *The Voice of Silence* in my never-ending quest for new ways to "catch" the life force and learned that the Mind is the great slayer of the Real and that the disciple of Truth must slay the Slayer, I knew exactly what she was talking about because many lonely people fall prey to this mental aberration that I knew so well; but what about the strong minded people who erect monumental edifices of brilliant thought, people like the author of the infamous "God is dead" pronouncement, Frederick Nietzsche, and Bertrand Russell, Jean Paul Sartre, Albert Camus, Schopenhauer, and scientists like Richard Dawkins—all brilliant atheists? Did these great thinkers get lost in the world of their own mind also?

I dropped out of university in my third year because I felt myself getting lost in the endless worlds of philosophical thought. I needed a strong dose of reality, and with Gurdjieff's teaching under my arm I left and got a job for Abitibi in a bush camp as a skidder operator; and shortly after I started my own contract painting business.

"The mind is its own place and in itself can make a Heaven of Hell, a Hell of Heaven," said John Milton in *Paradise Lost*; and as true as this may be, it is still the mental plane of consciousness, and one cannot realize his true self if he gets stuck on the mental plane. The sad truth is that one's true self cannot be found on the mental plane, but on the Soul plane of consciousness; and the only way to get to the Soul plane is through the mental plane. This was Jung's gift to the world with his *Red Book*.

Everyone gets stuck on the mental plane. There are no exceptions. And it takes many lifetimes to break the hold that the mind has over us. This is why I was so moved by my waking dream experience of shattering the smoked glass top of our coffee table which inspired my novel *The Waking Dream*; because this waking dream experience spoke to how I had shattered the "glass darkly" of the mental plane of consciousness.

I explain how I did this in my novel, so suffice to say now that I shattered the "glass darkly" of the mental plane by mastering the art of the selfless self—because only by transforming the consciousness of our selfish ego will we be pure enough to burst through the mental plane of consciousness and enter into the Soul plane of our true self.

I shattered the glass plate of our coffee table that day because I was so replete with Soul energy from dictating into my mini recorder the final chapter of my "Soul talk" book *The Soul of Happiness*, which dealt with the theme of transforming the consciousness of our ego self, that when I rested my feet on the coffee table my energy poured out of my energy field into the brass rim of our coffee table until it was powerful enough to make contact with the brass eagle in the center of our coffee table which became so charged with Soul energy that the glass plate imploded and shattered into half a dozen pieces.

"Oh, Orest; what have you done now?" Penny said to me, after she got over the shock; but I was innocent. My energy had shattered the glass plate.

Carl Jung kept the pieces of the kitchen knife that shattered in his mother's house with no apparent explanation, but I never kept any pieces of the shattered glass; I didn't need to. I had figured out why it shattered, and I poured it all into my novel *The Waking Dream* that tells the back story of how I raised my consciousness enough to vibrate at a frequency that shattered the glass plate of our coffee table; and the back story is the story of how I broke out of the prison of my own mind to realize my Soul self.

This is why in my dream a few months ago the Dictionary of Life defined Orest Stocco as Soul, and why St. Padre Pio said to me in my last spiritual healing session that I had transcended my own voice and the voice of my spiritual community; because I had achieved what I had been reborn into my parallel life to achieve.

25. *Many Are Called but Few Are Chosen*

Soul is who we are, but Soul has to evolve through the First Circle of Life to acquire a personal identity, or what in the letter to his brother "The Vale of Soul Making" John Keats called "a bliss peculiar to each one by individual existence," and it most certainly is a bliss, because Soul has just given birth to a new "I" of God.

Soul acquires a personal identity through natural evolution in the first stage of evolution, and when the process of unconscious karmic growth has evolved the new "I" of God as far as it can be evolved in the First Circle of Life, Soul will have to step into the Second Circle and take evolution into its own hands for the next stage of conscious evolution to total self-realization consciousness. To do this, Soul has to find the Way.

The Way is not hidden from the world. The Way is not hermetically sealed in arcane Gnostic teachings, alchemical texts, or ancient shamanic rituals; the Way is everywhere to be found, because the Way just *is*. Which means that the Way is omnipresent. But as Jesus said, one must have eyes to see and ears to hear; and this is where it gets tricky.

Thanks to Gurdjieff's teaching of "work on oneself," the most important discovery that I made about the Way is that it resolves the paradoxes of life—but only when one has resolved the mystery of the Way first, which is that **the Way will only reveal itself as one lives the Way**; otherwise one will remain blind to the Way.

And this is the mystery that few people resolve and why so many Souls get stuck on the mental plane of consciousness—because they cannot transcend the paradoxical realities of the mind. "I am what I am not, and I am not what I am," concluded Sartre after a lifetime of trying to make sense of man's existence in the First Circle of Life.

But just because he could not resolve the paradoxical nature of his *being* and *non-being* does that make man a "useless passion"? And is man "condemned to be free" in the paradoxical reality of *being* and *becoming* because he cannot transcend himself, or is man only "condemned to be free" because he does not know how to transcend himself?

This was Sartre's dilemma. He was blind to the Way. The irony of the Way is that man is always free to condemn himself by his own karma, because it is one's own karma that keeps one from transcending the paradoxical reality of *being* and *non-being*; and I know this to be true, because when I gave birth to my spiritual self in my mother's kitchen that glorious day I transcended myself and wrote in my journal: "**I am what I am not, and I am not what I am; I am both, but neither: I am Soul.**"

Paul Twitchell, the modern day founder of the Way of the Eternal, said that some Souls seek the Way, and other Souls are sought out by the Way. One seeks the Way when he is ready for the Way, and I knew that I was a seeker in high school when I read Somerset Maugham's novel *The Razor's Edge*. Larry Darrel, Maugham's hero in the novel, had a life-changing experience as a pilot in WW II that inspired him to become a seeker. Larry Darrel sparked the flame in me, and I became a seeker too.

I wish I could remember if I wrote my poem *Noman* after I read *The Razor's Edge,* or before; but I can't remember. I would like to believe that I wrote my poem after, because it makes more sense that *The Razor's Edge* sparked the flame in me first and then combusted in my daemonic poem *Noman* after reading about Larry Darrel's quest for the meaning and purpose of life. Either way, I knew that I was a seeker; that's why the omniscient guiding force of life assisted me in my quest for my true self.

On the other hand, there are many Souls that are ready to take the next step in their evolution through life but for one reason or another can't take the initiative; and so the Way must come to them. This often happens by way of a new book, or one may meet someone who introduces them to a new teaching; however it happens, when one is ready the Way will find them because this is how life works. Even so, when the Way finds them they still have to choose the Way because the Way is a conscious spiritual path.

Eric Stanford was ready for the Way. Eric (not his real name) was a retired RCMP officer in my hometown. I didn't know him personally, but I often saw him walking to the post office every morning on my way to work. Summer and winter, he would walk down to the post office for his mail; but early one summer I sensed something wasn't right with Eric. I sensed that he was going through the dark night of the Soul.

This went on for several weeks, and each time I saw him he seemed to be more lost in his dark night; and my heart went out to him. Then I got a phone call from him. He wanted a painting estimate. I drove up to his house and worked out an estimate for painting his back entrance stairwell, kitchen, and living room. He hired me, and I painted his house.

This was unusual, because Eric always did his own painting. He was in his early seventies, and in good health; so I asked him and he said he just didn't feel like doing it any more. Up close I could sense his energy, and I was right; he was going through the dark night of the Soul, and so I steered our conversation in that direction.

Eric fascinated me; not just because he was lost in his dark night of unknowing, which I knew only too well; but because he had called me to paint his house. I knew that I was called for a reason, which was to introduce him to the Way; and within one hour of working at his house the subject of reincarnation came up.

Eric was a lifelong member of the United Church. His wife continued to attend Church regularly, but Eric couldn't see the point anymore; so he stopped going. His minister talked with him, but Eric got no consolation; and he began to explore other paths. "Have you read Edgar Cayce?" he asked me, opening the door for me; and we talked non-stop all day long, and the next two days that it took me to paint his house.

I didn't introduce him to the Way of the Eternal, because I never let anyone in town know what spiritual path I was on. The most I would tell anyone was that I was an eclectic and drew the best from all paths; but I brought him some books to read.

One book was on the Way of the Eternal, by the Spiritual Leader of my path, and several other books on different paths; and I left it to him to decide which path spoke to him. He thanked me, and told me that he enjoyed our conversations very much; and then a week or so later I had a dream that spoke directly to his dark night of the Soul:

I'm driving up the Main Street in my work van on my way to work one morning, and as I make the turn to cross the CP railway crossing I spot a wallet in the middle of the road. I pull over and pick it up. I open the wallet to see who it belongs to, but there is nothing in the wallet to identity the owner. The wallet contains three things: a large amount of money, all in bills; a watch; and a compass. And then for whatever reason I suddenly know that the wallet belongs to Eric Stanford; so I drive up to his house and knock on his back door. A small boy about ten years old answers the door. He was visiting with his parents. They were from Ireland. He calls Eric and I tell him I found his wallet downtown. He's surprised to get it back, and he thanks me. He gives me a five dollar bill to show his appreciation, but I tell him it's not necessary. I was just glad he got his wallet back, and I woke up.

After work that day I drove to Eric's house to share my dream with him. His wife was a bit uncomfortable with me, not really knowing what to make of me; but I was used to people behaving that way around me. Eric was a retired intelligence officer, and he was fascinated by me; so he asked his wife to make us a cup of tea. "What do you think it means?" he asked me; and I told him what I thought.

The symbols were his wallet, which had no identification; money; a watch; and a compass. No identification meant that he did not know his true self; the compass meant that he could find his true self; the watch meant that he still had time in his current life to find his true self; and the money meant that he had the wherewithal to go on a quest for his true self, and after I interpreted the dream I broke into a chuckle.

Mystified, Eric stared at me. His wife had a look of horror on her face. She could not believe that I had read her husband's situation so clearly. The Dream Weaver had taken weeks, perhaps months and years of his spiritual doubts and confusion and translated them into a dream story for me to interpret that made perfect sense of his worrisome state; but I had to share my laughter with them.

"Eric, what's the Mountie's motto?" I asked.

"The Mountie always gets his man," he replied, not making the connection.

"My dream augurs well for you, then," I said, with an ironic chuckle.

Eric thought for a moment, made the connection, and smiled. We talked a while longer, and when I left he thanked me for sharing my dream. "It's a wake-up call," he said, shaking my hand in gratitude.

Several weeks later I bumped into him at the post office and he asked if we could go for coffee; he had a couple of dreams he wanted to run by me. He rode with me in my van and we had coffee at the Texaco Restaurant and he shared his dreams.

In one dream he was fishing on the bank of a river. As he cast his line it got caught on an overhead hydro power line. He couldn't make sense of this dream. And his second dream had to do with a donkey, and he couldn't make sense of that one either.

I smiled at the irony. The Way is the Holy Current of God that runs through life. He was fishing for another spiritual path and he snagged the Way; but he didn't know that he had snagged the Way in one of the books that I had given him and in our long conversations while I painted his house, because as we talked the Way just poured out of me.

And his second dream spoke to his stubborn nature ("stubborn jackass," as the phase goes), which told me why he resisted taking up what claimed to be the most direct path to God in the Way of the Eternal, because rumor had it in town that it was a cult teaching and he couldn't risk the stigma of being associated with it.

The compass points true north, and the Way of the Eternal pointed to his true self; but for the sake of propriety he started going back to Church, and although we never spoke again I could tell whenever I saw him walking downtown that like so many people in the world he had painfully resigned himself to a life of quiet desperation.

Adrienne Rich defined poetry as an act of the imagination that transforms reality into a deeper perception of what is. I wrote a poem inspired by my experience with the retired RCMP officer who got lost in his dark night of the Soul. I called my poem, *Many Are Called but Few Are Chosen:*

From deep within the holy seed sprouted,
the desire to be more; but the path he walked
had grown empty, and he prayed to God
for guidance. In a dream one night he saw a sign
when his fishing hook snagged a power line;
but afraid of what people might say,
he refused to walk the Way. True to his nature
he played it safe, because it takes courage to
believe; the fear of ridicule mocked his spirit,
and stopped his seed from growing. Desperate,
he returned to Jesus Christ, savior of the
status quo; but the emptiness within could not
be filled, and he refused to see why.
He looked for answers in all the wrong places,
because it kept him far away from home; but alone
at night he saw his life's lie, and he broke down

and cried. Again he prayed to God for guidance,
and in a dream one night he saw the sign of an ass;
but his obdurate mind objected, and now he lives his
lonely life waiting in fear to die.

I also wrote a short story on my experience with Eric, calling it "The Mountie's Last Case," but I haven't done anything with it yet. I'm sorry that Eric didn't follow up on the message that the Dream Weaver gave him through our dreams, but this only goes to show that it takes a lot of courage to break free of the status quo and take evolution into our own hands. Perhaps in his next life; or, maybe, his parallel life?

26. *When All Is Said and Done*

Every book that I write is a new journey into the far country of Soul, and *The Summoning of Noman* is no different. Because I started to record my dreams for this book, I have had doors open to other disciplines that could take one or two more lifetimes to study and understand; like the dream I had last night, for example.

The dream is vague, but I remember distinctly what the Dream Weaver wanted to impress upon my conscious mind. *I'm working outdoors with a man called Ed from my hometown, and a bird swoops down in a menacing manner which told me to pay attention because I knew the language of life was trying to tell me something;* but the whole point of the dream was for me to remember what I said to Ed. *"See that bird, Ed? It's a harbinger. It's telling us to be careful." Ed didn't know what harbinger meant, so I defined it as an omen; a warning sign of something to come. He wanted to know how I knew this, and I told him that I had learned this from reading Greek mythology.* And then I woke up.

I reflected on my dream for a moment to impress it upon my mind so I would recall it for my dream journal, and then I rolled over to go back to sleep because it was too early to get up; but as I tried to go back to sleep the name Patricia Garfield popped into my mind, and when I got up the first order of business was to look her up on the Internet.

Patricia Garfield is a clinical psychologist and an internationally recognized authority on dreams. She's the author of *Creative Dreaming*, which I read the first time I became interested in dreams because of my immersion into Carl Jung's writing. I had forgotten about her book, but I knew it was in one of my many boxes of books in the basement which I suspect the Inner Master wanted me to read again; but I did have another Garfield book in my writing den that I had picked up at a book fair at the Bayfield Mall in Barrie last summer—*The Dream Messenger,* which I read; but why was I reminded of her?

I Googled Patricia Garfield and reacquainted myself with *Creative Dreaming* (I'll dig up my copy later today) and looked into her other books, and then I checked out another book that came up in my search, *Conscious Dreaming* by Robert Moss.

This book caught my immediate attention, so I checked it out on Amazon and then did some research on Robert Moss; and then I went to his blog and read something that I knew was meant for me to find. In fact, I believe the whole point of Patricia Garfield popping into my mind was the Inner Master's way of getting me to find my way to Robert Moss's blog so I could read something he wrote that corroborates what I feel *The Summoning of Noman* is leading up to—the "Holy Now," as Jesus calls it in Glenda Green's book *Love without End, Jesus Speaks*. In short, the Inner Master wanted to confirm my intuition that when all is said and done it all comes down to NOW.

We can read and study other teachings and paths until the cows come home, because there is no end to knowledge; it is a never-ending reality play that keeps re-inventing itself in the mental plane of consciousness, an infinite source of endless truths woven into new and exciting pathways of the mind, and Soul can wander in the mental worlds of knowledge until the end of time; but one day (and that day is NOW for me) one will have to step up and say: *fascinating, but so what?* Which reminds me of one of Gurdjieff's favorite sayings about the mind: "It's all a pouring from the empty into the void."

I will order Robert Moss's book *Conscious Dreaming,* and probably all of his other books as well because I checked them out and they fascinate me. I'm sure they will satisfy my intellectual need to know and offer me a refreshing perspective on dreaming that will give me hours of reading pleasure, but as to the spiritual efficacy of liberating Soul from the mental plane of consciousness I suspect they will leave me wanting—because there is only one way out of the mental plane on one's journey to one's true self on the Soul plane, and that is to master the Holy

Now by finding the "strait gate" of the Way. Ironically this is what Robert Moss is slowly coming to realize, as he intimates on his blog.

His entry is titled "In the Treasure Cave," and it deals with a new writing project that he's working on: "I am writing about certain passages in my life—in which I learned about essential things about the nature of the multiverse and how to operate within it," he writes; and he concludes his entry with the following insight, which I believe was the reason I was intuitively guided by the Inner Master to find:

"I feel sympathy and compassion as I monitor how younger Roberts tried to make sense of all this while lacking any really helpful mentor in this reality, and how they struggled to keep body and soul together on the roads of this world. I wonder, as I consider how "past" and "future" aspects of myself looked in on each other and sent each other mental texts, whether my present acts of observation are changing things in, say, 1987-1988. That thought quickens my interest in these journals that are not really old; *they confirm the idea that the only time is always Now and that all our pasts and futures and probable reality are accessible in the moment of Now, and can be re-visioned and revised for the better*" (mossdreams.com, Feb. 7, 2013; italics mine).

That's exactly what my Muse has awakened in me with *The Summoning of Noman*— that all of our past and future and parallel lives can be re-visioned for the better in the Holy Now; and by "better" I mean specifically the divinely ordained imperative to realize our Soul self, which can only be done when we learn how to "get it right."

"If you don't get it right in this life, you will just keep coming back until you do," said Paul Twitchell in one of his talks; and I came back into my same life as Orest Stocco to get it right, because I failed to get it right the first time I lived my life.

I know that I came into my life to break the cycle of karma and reincarnation, but the first time I lived my life I made choices that did not align my karmic destiny with my spiritual destiny, and I strayed too far before I realized what I had done. That's why I had a dream of myself late in my life walking up to the post office in my hometown feeling like I had betrayed myself. I had not achieved what I was born to achieve, and I died with a pain in my heart for not getting it right. So I returned to my same life to try again, and I did get it right this time around; but just how did I get it right?

The simple answer is that I transcended my life, which means that I worked my way through the lower worlds and realized my true self on the Soul plane of consciousness; and I did this because I found the "strait gate" and initiated myself into the inherently self-transcending mysteries of the Way. That's what I failed to do the first time I lived my life as Orest Stocco. Like most Souls, I got stuck on the mental plane and karmically destined myself to return to try again, which I did; but l had absolutely no idea that I had returned to my same life to try again until St. Padre Pio revealed this information to me.

I read the sample chapters on Amazon of Robert Moss's books, and I'm fascinated by how dreams have played the role they have on his journey to his true self; but without reading his books in their entirety, I can safely say from what I have rendered from his fascinating journey through life that on a personal level DREAMS FUNCTION TO BRING OUR KARMIC DESTINY INTO ALIGNMENT WITH OUR SPIRITUAL DESTINY; and it doesn't matter what manner, shape, or form our dreams take they are all messages from Soul to help us bring our lower self into agreement with our Soul self—which we can only do in the Holy Now of the life that we are currently living.

This is why I said to Padre Pio in my last spiritual healing session that reincarnation was moot in Christ's teaching of the Way, because the Way just *is*—meaning the Way is always NOW! But one has to find the Way to live the Way, and that's what the Way of the Dream is all about—to help us become conscious of the Way. Which makes Christ's teaching relevant throughout time and in all worlds, because the Way just *is*.

Jesus was a Way-shower who introduced the world to the Way with his death upon the cross. The central premise of Christ' teaching is self-sacrifice *("He that loveth his life shall lose it; and he that hateth his life in this world shall keep it unto life eternal,"* John 12: 25), and Jesus sacrificed his life on the cross to symbolize his message of self-transcendence through the death of the lower self, which can only be done by taking evolution into our own hands and transforming the consciousness of our lower self. This is the premise of my novel *Jesus Wears Dockers, The Gospel Conspiracy Story.*

The irony of Christ's teaching however is that it's not for everybody, as such; it is only for those Souls that are ready to "put their hand to the plow," to use Christ's metaphor for taking evolution into one's own hands; everyone else will have to evolve through the natural process of karmic growth in the First Circle of Life until they are ready. As Jesus said, *"many are called but few are chosen."*

The Three Circles of Life are distinct, separate states of consciousness; but they merge into each other constantly. Or, to put it differently, they co-exist one within the other; and one is always influenced by the consciousness of each state. And what defines the consciousness of each state is the level of spiritual awareness.

The First Circle of Life is the exoteric first stage of evolution; and it is primarily defined by unconscious karmic experience. Through trial and error, experience after experience after experience, we learn our karmic lessons and eventually wake up to the simple fact that we are the authors of our own karmic destiny.

Through the hard knocks of life we all learn to make more discerning choices. This is how we get it right in the First Circle of Life. But we are not alone. We are always guided by the omniscient guiding force of life, especially in our dreams; like I was when I had my past life recollection dreams in my youth that helped break the hold my Roman Catholic faith had upon me so I could explore other teachings. That's how I gravitated to Gurdjieff's teaching of "work on oneself" that awakened me to the Way in life.

Gurdjieff taught me how to live the Way consciously; and the more conscious I became of the Way, the more I transcended the First Circle of Life and initiated myself into the mesoteric second stage of evolution where I learned how to gather and collect Soul into herself, until one day I reached critical mass and experienced my immortal self in my mother's kitchen while she was kneading bread dough on the kitchen table.

When I gave birth to my spiritual self I shifted my center of gravity from my lower self to my higher self; from the First Circle of Life to the Second Circle, and I began to gravitate to the Third Circle of Life and deeper mysteries of the Way of Soul.

Soul is who we are, and Soul is pre-destined to realize its divine nature; but because we are free to create our own karmic destiny we are often at variance with our spiritual destiny. This is why we dream. **Dreams are Soul's path home to God. Dreams bring our lower self into agreement with our Soul self, and the more aligned our karmic destiny is with our pre-scripted spiritual destiny the easier our path will be.**

But how exactly can we bring our karmic destiny into alignment with our divinely ordained spiritual destiny? We have to live the Way consciously, to be sure; but how can one live the Way consciously if one does not know what the Way is?

This mystery left thousands of birds stranded by the wayside in the Sufi allegory *Conference of the Birds*, because they did not know where to go next to continue their quest for God. But we are never stranded, because Soul is forever guiding us by way of dreams; like I was when I was told in my dream that I had to stay in the contract painting business because I still had lessons to learn. I wasn't ready to move on yet.

In effect, we cannot be initiated into the deeper mysteries of the Way until we earn the karmic right to be initiated; that's how I deduced that to find my true self I had to exile myself out of the kingdom of my own senses with my *Royal Dictum*. I asked

God what price I had to pay for truth, and I paid the price with my inspired edict of self-denial; that's how I earned the karmic right to be initiated into the mysteries of the Way.

Without realizing that I was living the Way consciously with my *Royal Dictum*, I initiated myself deeper into the mysteries of the Way; and day by day the Way revealed itself to me. This is how I broke the code of Christ's cryptic sayings and the Gnostic secret of spiritual self-realization and God consciousness. And as abstract and metaphysical as this may sound, it all comes down to a question of values—which I clearly spell out in my little book *Why Bother? The Riddle of the Good Samaritan*.

Jesus was asked by a cynical lawyer what he had to do to inherit eternal life, and Jesus replied with the Parable of the Good Samaritan, which sums up Christ's whole teaching of the Way. But one has to have ears to hear the Word behind the words of Jesus; so, true to my creative instinct, I abandoned to my Muse to transform the reality of my experience with the virtue of goodness into a deeper perception of goodness in the hope that my reader would hear the Word behind the words of the parable; that's why I wrote *Why Bother? The Riddle of the Good Samaritan*.

27. Dream Ending to a Beautiful Mind

It doesn't matter how many lives we live, as long as we live them in the lower worlds—parallel worlds or not—we will never realize our Soul self until we transcend the lower worlds and enter the Soul plane of our true self.

Our Soul self is a spark of divine consciousness that comes into the world from the Body of God as an un-self-realized atom of God, or Soul seed; and it evolves through life to realize its own identity, "a bliss peculiar to each one by individual existence," as John Keats intuited, and as I was privileged to experience with my past life regressions.

Being Soul seeds, we are all made of God's DNA; and we are divinely encoded to become God-realized. This is our pre-scripted spiritual destiny. And we can only realize our spiritual destiny through the evolution of our personal self in the lower worlds of God—the physical, astral, causal, and mental planes of consciousness. Jung also intuited that the unconscious self can only be realized through the conscious personality.

Above the lower planes of consciousness is the Soul plane, the first of the higher worlds of God and the essential nature of our Soul self; but our Soul self is not conscious of itself. It has to evolve through the lower planes to become spiritually self-realized and God-conscious. This is the purpose of life. "Unconscious wholeness therefore seems to be the true *spiritus rector* of all biological and psychic events," wrote Jung in *Memories, Dreams, Reflections*. "Here is a principle which strives for total realization—which in man's case signifies the attainment of total consciousness. Attainment of consciousness is culture in the broadest sense, and self-knowledge is therefore the heart and essence of this process" (p. 324)—meaning, total self-realization consciousness.

We evolve through life until we give birth to a reflective self, as I experienced in my primordial lifetime as a higher primate; and because we now have a personal self we create personal karma, which is responsible for our changeable karmic destiny.

As we evolve through life we create a separate body for the astral, causal, and mental planes, and our Soul self evolves through our lower bodies; which means that we have to evolve through all the lower planes of consciousness to realize our Soul self.

As we experience life we create karma for our physical, astral, causal, and mental bodies; this is how we grow in self-realization consciousness. Karma is individuated life energy, which I know from my experience of the genesis of life on Planet Earth to be Soul consciousness; so **the more we experience life, the more we grow in our Soul self**. This is why some people hunger for life; they hunger to be who they are!

Karma is the life force that we individuate with every experience we have, and we cannot grow in self-realization consciousness without karma; but the natural process of evolution cannot take us to the Soul plane of consciousness where we realize our Soul self—our individuated whole self if you will, as Jung realized in a dream late in life.

The natural process of karmic evolution takes us through the physical, astral, causal, and mental planes of consciousness; but unfortunately Soul gets stuck on the mental plane, and some Souls get so lost on the mental plane that they become unbalanced, like the brilliant mathematician and Nobel Laureate in Economics, Professor John Nash.

Sylvia Nasar wrote a book on John Nash's life called *A Beautiful Mind,* which was made into a movie starring Russell Crowe. This book had special meaning for me, because while I was having open heart surgery several years ago I dreamt that I rewrote the ending to *A Beautiful Mind.* I also had an out-of-body experience and saw my surgeon and his team operating on me. And the day after surgery I had another paranormal experience that speaks to Soul's historical journey through these lower worlds and getting stuck in them; but I relate all of this in my novel *The Sweet Breath of Life*.

Unfortunately, I cannot remember the ending that I wrote in my dream to *A Beautiful Mind*; but I know intuitively that my ending had to do with how John Nash could escape from the prison of his hallucinating, schizophrenic mind—which, ironically, Nash himself intimated in his Nobel Prize address to be the "mysterious equations of love."

Nash was not asked to give a speech for his Nobel Prize acceptance in December, 1994; but he did say a few words that were put together into a fictional speech for the movie: "I've always believed in numbers. In the equations and logics that lead to reason; but after a lifetime of such pursuits I ask, what truly is logic? Who decides reason? My quest has taken me through the physical, the metaphysical, the delusional and back, and I have made the most important discovery of my career...the most important discovery of my life. It is only in the mysterious equations of love that any logical reasons can be found."

It was his wife's love that kept John Nash "balanced" enough to live the rest of his life without medication for his schizophrenia. He continued to hear voices in his mind (as opposed to seeing people as he did in the movie), but he made enormous efforts of will to not relate with them as he did before being diagnosed schizophrenic, which always lured him into hallucinations that derailed his sanity; and had it not been for his wife's love he would have been pulled so deeply into his own mind that he would have lost himself completely and made it that much more difficult to "get it right" in his next life.

As often happens whenever I'm working on a new book, the synchronistic principle kicked in a few hours after I began writing this chapter. The idea for this chapter was given birth by the previous chapter which called to mind the dream I had during open-heart surgery, and I jotted the title ("Dream Ending to A Beautiful Mind") and the opening sentence that came to me; and the next morning I began writing my new chapter.

The central idea of this chapter has to do with liberating oneself from the mental plane of consciousness, but I needed a context for the idea to play out; so I proceeded to provide the context, which I did; and then I stopped writing for the day.

It was Family Day, and a federal holiday. Penny didn't have to work, so we decided to drive into Midland and do some grocery shopping; but all the grocery stores were closed and we came home and Penny went for her trail walk and I turned on the TV, put on a nice cozy fire, and started preparing a spaghetti and meatball sauce for dinner. And as I was making the sauce I heard something on TV that arrested my attention. I took a look and recognized the movie that had just started playing—*A Beautiful Mind!*

I smiled at the remarkable coincidence. I enjoyed the movie when it came out a few years ago, but now I had a vested literary interest in the story; so I made my sauce, put it on simmer, and sat down to watch John Nash's journey into the hallucinatory dimensions of his mind that I was familiar with from my own experiences of talking with imaginary people. The only difference between John Nash and me was that he heard voices in his mind, and I didn't; I imagined my fantasy people as I imagined them for a novel, only they played out in my mind instead of the context of my fictional stories. In other words, my characters spoke to me; but they spoke in silence, not audibly as they did in John Nash's mind.

I've had years to ponder this mystery, and not until I gained a deeper insight into Jung's theory of archetypes did I begin to make sense of my experience; and the conclusion that I came to is that our mind has an enormous capacity to imagine its own reality and people it with archetypes conjured up from the collective unconscious.

This is the mystery of creative writing that no one has been able to explain; but I think Jung came very close to solving this mystery with his theory of archetypes. Novelists know that characters can pop into their story from the deep regions of their mind (the collective unconscious, no doubt), and play their part in the story; and some writers create their characters first and then wait for them to be ensouled by an archetype.

That's how I write my novels. I create a composite character, and when my character is ready to be ensouled by an archetype, it comes to life; and from that moment on I have no more control over my character's life. This was especially true of my character Cassie O'Shaunessy in my novel *My Unborn Child*; and also in my last novel *Jesus Wears Dockers*. I conjured up the best Jesus that I could from all my reading about his life and many years of *living* his sayings, and then an archetypal Jesus took over. And the moment my composite Jesus was ensouled by an archetypal Jesus he had his own life; and I just went along for the ride, as it were.

Because I was a novelist I knew something about how the mind creates its own reality, so I saw a very strong distinction between the world of my own mind and the world out there; that's why I could never get lost in my own mind. I just couldn't, regardless how much I wanted to some days. (That's why novelists hate it when their story comes to an end; they miss their characters.) Besides, I had pre-conscious past-life memories of what it was to be lost in my own mind. I got so lost in my own mind in my lifetime as Salaam the Sufi that I died of starvation babbling messianic nonsense; and I had a moral obligation to not be seduced by the fantasies that I could so easily conjure up in my mind.

It was a long struggle to liberate myself from the seductions of my own mind, and I made the final breakthrough when I dictated the last chapter of my "Soul talk" book *The Soul of Happiness*, called "The Ontology of Happiness." And what convinced me that I had broken through the mental plane of consciousness was my experience of shattering the smoked glass plate of our coffee table less than an hour after I dictated my chapter.

Shattering the *smoked glass* of the coffee table simply by resting my feet on the brass edge of our coffee table told me that the energy of my last chapter was strong enough to shatter the *"glass darkly"* of the mental plane of consciousness that keeps us blind to the Soul plane of consciousness; and the reason my chapter "The Ontology of Happiness" was so powerful was because it revealed the secret knowledge of how to transform the consciousness of our selfish ego (mental self) and realize our Soul self. This was the secret that John Nash intimated with his "mysterious equations of love."

"Love is who you are," Jesus told Glenda Green in her book *Love without End, Jesus Speaks*; and the leader of my spiritual path has said this from the moment he became the Outer and Inner Master of the Way of the Eternal; but it's one thing to know it intellectually, and quite another to experience it. This has been my path my whole life—to *experience* what I know intellectually; and believe me, I earned my gnostic knowledge.

The single most important discovery that I made about the Way as I "worked" on myself was that we do not have two selves, one lower and one higher—or one inner and one outer; we have only one self. In short, I do not have a soul; Soul is who I am, and realizing this is what the journey through life is all about. And as much as it pains me to say this, everyone—*and I mean everyone!*—gets stuck on the mental plane of consciousness on their way to realizing their true self on the Soul plane of consciousness.

Because we are all teleologically driven to realize our Soul self, we will all suffer unbearable anguish when we get stuck in one of the lower planes of consciousness, most especially the mental plane which is next to impossible to transcend. If one can imagine tender grass shoots suffering as they struggle to break through asphalt to take in the life-giving nourishment of the sun's rays, that's the kind of suffering that Soul has to endure as it tries to break through the spiritual impasses of its lower bodies in its inherent drive to realize total self-realization consciousness. It can break one's spirit.

"Life is a tale told by an idiot full of sound and fury signifying nothing," we shout, in hopeless dismay; but there is a way out of our spiritual impasses. And the way out can always be found in one of the "mysterious equations of love," because love is inherently self-transcending.

28. *The Mysterious Equations of Love*

"To everything there is a season, and a time to every purpose under the heaven," said the Preacher in *Ecclesiastes,* and I knew that the season of my *Royal Dictum* had come to an end; so I went out to one of the local hotel bars for a drink, picked up a young lady, brought her home with me and we made love, thus ending my sexual abstinence.

I had vowed to live my *Royal Dictum* for the rest of my life, because that was the price I was willing to pay for truth; so what happened that I should break my vow of self-denial after only three and a half years?

The short answer is that I simply *knew* that it was time. I simply *knew* that my *Royal Dictum* had served its purpose, and it was time for me to move on. But I was not without conflict. I *knew* that it was time to move on, but I had made a promise to myself to live my *Royal Dictum* for the rest of my life; so what prompted me to break my vow?

Ironically, it was the same inspiration that brought forth my *Royal Dictum* that would bring my *Royal Dictum* to an end—the Preacher's words in *Ecclesiastes.*

My *Royal Dictum* was inspired by the Preacher's words: *"Vanity of vanities, all is vanity. What profit had a man of all his labors which he taketh under the sun? One generation passeth away, and another generation cometh; but the earth abideth forever...all the rivers run into the sea; yet the sea is not full; unto the place from whence the rivers come, thither they return again"* (Eccl. 1: 2-7).

I was standing on the breakwater watching the Nipigon River flowing swiftly past me when the Preacher's words came to mind. I knew that the river had its source, and I intuited that to get to my true self I would have to go to the source of my life;

and after quoting the Preacher's words out loud Sophocles' play *Oedipus Rex* came to mind.

King Oedipus banished himself out of his kingdom of Thebes when he learned that he was the cause of the plague that blighted his kingdom for murdering his father and defiling his mother's bed, and by some transcendental leap of logic I reasoned that if I banished myself out of the kingdom of my own senses I would purify myself enough to get to the source of my life and become aware of my true self; that's how my *Royal Dictum* came to be: *I am like Oedipus Rex. I have exiled myself out of my own kingdom. I embrace my becoming blindly, and I leave all of my sins behind me. I am going to go against the natural course of evolution; and each obstacle that I encounter I will consume.* And the moment I stepped onto the mainland I began my life of self-denial, which lasted until that night three and a half years later when I made love with Debby.

I was sitting in my separate apartment in my parents' home feeling very listless, and for some reason I picked up my Bible and opened it at random to *Ecclesiastes*; and I read the Preacher's words carefully, fully appreciating his wisdom which spoke to me now on a different level. And for some providential reason the Golden-tongued Wisdom spoke to me when the Preacher brought his discourse on man's purpose in life to closure with the following words: *"And further, by these, my son, be admonished: of making many books, there is no end; and much study is a weariness of the flesh. Let us hear the conclusion of the whole matter: Fear God, and keep his commandments; for this is the whole duty of man. For God shall bring every work into judgment, with every secret thing, whether it be good, or whether it be evil"* (Eccl. 12: 12-14).

When I read those words I *knew* that my *Royal Dictum* had been brought to judgment, and it was time to let it go; and with all doubt cast out of my mind I went to the Nipigon Inn Hotel for a drink. I met Debby there with a couple of friends, asked if I could join them, and after a few drinks asked if I could take her home; but we went to my place instead. And we continued to date, thus killing the rumors in town that I was gay.

The way to one's true self can take any number of turns, and will; but it takes courage to let go of the old and embrace the new. This is why I wrote in my *Royal Dictum* that I embraced my becoming blindly—because I had no idea where my new path was going to take me; but I knew that I had to take it. I had been summoned by God to find my lost soul, and I had no choice; I had to find my true self at any cost.

When I'm called by Soul to do something, I have to do it; like the time I was called to go to France. I wrote in my journal: "I'm going to go away to find something that I know lies in my own back yard, but I have to go." And when I came back from France to study philosophy at university I went for that memorable walk down the CN railroad tracks at the back of our house (my back yard) and on to the breakwater where I created my *Royal Dictum* which initiated me into the Gurdjieffian teaching of "work on oneself" that awakened me to the Word behind the words of Jesus, and when I had grown enough in spiritual consciousness I gave birth to my spiritual self in my mother's kitchen one fine day while she was kneading bread dough on the kitchen table; so I understood exactly what Robert Frost meant with his iconic poem *The Road Not Taken*.

I came to so many crossroads in my life that I often wonder how I managed to survive. That's why I liken life unto war that we have all been drafted into, but not all of us survive intact; which is why I have made it my mission in life now to point the Way to every Soul that has been called to their true self. And with *The Summoning of Noman* my intended purpose is to shed some light on the process of self-realization consciousness.

This is why I enjoyed my spiritual healing sessions with Ascended Master St. Padre Pio, because we saw eye to eye on the question of the self, and which I dwelt on specifically in Chapter 13 of my novel *Healing with Padre Pio*.

Called "The Selfless Self," the theme of this chapter posits that the individuation of the self through life ultimately leads to the realization of the selfless self, which St. Padre Pio knew only too well after fifty years of living *la via di sofferenza*, and which I was intimately familiar with through my own path of "dying" to my life to "find" my life.

But as I said to the Good Saint, the way of self-sacrifice that Jesus taught is so extreme that few people will sacrifice their life to save it (*"For whosoever will save his life shall lose it; and whosoever will lose his life for my sake shall find it"* Math. 16: 25); that's why we agreed on the concept of the spiritually balanced life.

But even that in today's world is next to impossible to do, because all of life conspires to satisfy our insatiable ego self; and that's the conflict that lies in the heart of man—because we are all driven by an *a priori* imperative to realize our Soul self, and if we don't take destiny into our own hands we're going to be dragged by it. *"For were I recusant, I do but make myself a slave and still must follow."* said Cleanthes.

I refused to take destiny into my own hands in my first life as Orest Stocco, which is why I died feeling regretful and unfulfilled; but in my parallel life I made an agreement with Soul to find the "strait gate" of the Way and find my true self. That's why Soul intervened in my life with my daemonic poem *Noman*, and why I became possessed one night by the archetypal personality of my *"salaud de Paris"* past life that compelled me to do something that shocked my conscience awake and catapult me into my quest for my true self. I was severed from my life many times, the last and probably most traumatic time with the publication of my two novel memoirs that so disturbed the shadow personality of my hometown that Penny and I had to relocate for peace of mind.

Each time that I was severed from my life I suffered unbearable anguish, but when I realized that we have no choice but to rise up and clasp the hand of God when we are called all of my suffering made sense; that's why I understood Jesus when he brought Jung's *Red Book* to closure with the words, "I bring you the beauty of suffering. That is what is needed by whoever hosts the worm."

The worm is the archetypal Noman, the unresolved karmic self of Everyman; and there are only two ways to resolve the consciousness of our worm: *unconscious suffering*, through natural evolution (kicking and dragging our feet); and *conscious suffering*, by taking evolution into our own hands and living the Way consciously.

Unfortunately the unconscious way of evolution will not resolve the worm enough to realize our true self, because it cannot take us beyond the First Circle of Life; that's why Jesus gave us the gift of conscious evolution with his teaching of self-sacrifice. But only when one lives the Way consciously can one appreciate why Jesus called it "the beauty of suffering," because there is only self-initiation into the mysteries of the Way.

I understand what Jesus meant because I lived the Way consciously; and curiously enough, John Nash intimated this secret with his insightful comment on "the mysterious equations of love." To understand this however, one has to understand the secret logic of spiritual growth; and the only way to understand the logic of the Way is to be initiated into the secret ways of love that Nash intimates with "the mysterious equations of love."

Nash admitted that it was his wife's love that brought him back from his world of delusion; so what is the power of love that can "save" someone's life? We've all see love in action in great literature and movies, and some of us have been blessed to experience it firsthand; but what is this mysterious power of love?

Does love have a face that we can see? It's not enough to say, like my spiritual community loves to say as if it is the magic panacea to all of life's problems, "I am love." Given the logic of the Way, it is true that we are all love because love is the ground of our being; but saying "I am love" does not grant one the grace to solve the problems of life. One has to DO love in Christ's sense of DOING his sayings to see the face of love; and, sad to say, in my experience more people talk about love than DO love.

The single most important lesson that Gurdjieff's teaching of "work on oneself" taught me was that to find my true self I had to BECOME my true self; and this was next to impossible to do because I was unconsciously centered in my *non-being* and had to authenticate my false self to find my true self—which took me through the bowels of hell. Indirectly then, Gurdjieff taught me that **to BE love we have to BECOME love;** and the only way to do that is to walk the talk, as the saying goes. And this gave birth to another one of my favorite sayings: **to get love you have to give love.**

Now, just what is at the root of Nash's "mysterious equations of love"? Nash was a brilliant mathematician and code breaker, so he knew the logic of the mind well; but what did he mean by the "mysterious equations of love"?

He couldn't penetrate this mystery, but he experienced it in his wife's love. What is the logic of love? If we could understand that we would solve the mystery of life; which, strangely enough, some people do. Mystics like St. Teresa of Avila solved the mystery of love, which she revealed to the world in her book *The Way of Perfection,* a theme taken up by the contemporary mystic Carolyn Myss (*Entering the Castle, Finding the Inner Path to God and Your Soul's Purpose*); and St. John of the Cross, the author of *Dark Night of the Soul;* and St. Padre Pio, who suffered the stigmata for fifty years.

Had it not been for St. Padre Pio's love I would never have been healed of my anger and deep-seated vanity that kept me from transcending myself; so when I "chanced" upon the book *In the Spirit of Happiness,* by the Monks of New Skete in a second hand book store in Barrie one day and came upon the chapter "What Does Love Look Like?" my heart leapt with joy—because finally someone had given a face to love!

"Love is peaceful," Father Laurence said to the Seeker. *"It is able to resist the temptation to tear others down with gossip, envy, and resentment. It is never threatened or defensive; it shows self-possession; it always delights in the goodness of another...Love admits and understands its own imperfections, that*

we're all together in this human condition, and thus it seeks to look compassionately on the faults of others. Such self-disciplined love lets go of past hurts—forgiving from the heart...Isn't it wonderful when we encounter a person who appreciates us for who we are, instead of as a threat to their self-esteem? Love desires to do this for others....Love?...love looks like generosity. It spends itself willingly (and wisely) for others, be it with time, attention, money, or simply concern...A generous love is expansive. It is willing to be flexible and inclusive, not rigid...Love is not so presumptuous or proud as to suppose that it can do without the love of others; and so it appreciates even the smallest expression of concern from another. Love gives and receives freely, without expectation or demand. It recognizes that no price could ever be attached to it, that there can be no life without it. It shows appreciation...Love looks like friendliness. It gives to others the benefit of the doubt in favor of goodness, rather than suspiciously presuming hidden agendas...It sincerely intends and evokes the good in others" (*In the Spirit of Happiness*, pp. 254-6).

THAT IS THE FACE OF LOVE. And we all recognize it when we see it; so it is not enough to simply say, "I am love" and expect God's grace to flow upon you. To get love we have to give love, and **giving love is what living the Way consciously is all about**. But again, what is this magical power of love that can change one's life?

It took many years to connect the dots that allowed me to see the magical power of love, and once again I have to thank Gurdjieff's teaching of "work on oneself" which awakened my primal survival instincts and initiated me into the mysterious "way of the sly man"—the secret knowledge of how to contain and collect the vital life force.

The more I "worked" on myself the more I awakened to man's primal nature; and gradually I began to discern how man appropriates the vital life force from his fellow man. This was confirmed years later when I had my past life regression to my primordial lifetime as "Grunt" when I appropriated the life force from my clan members by the power of my grunts alone. So

213

terrified were they that they forfeited their will to me; and I realized that their will was the life force that they were individuating for their own self-realization.

When a domineering husband browbeats his wife to do his bidding, he appropriates her will-to-be and robs her of her identity; which is why many browbeaten, submissive housewives say, "I don't know who I am anymore." People in positions of power have honed their primal skills for appropriating a person's will-to-be, and the more one forfeits their will-to-be the less they grow in their own identity; and one day they will lose their sense of self altogether and wonder who they are.

This is how the self grows and evolves in the First Circle of Life. It is primal, brutal, and merciless—a jungle and dog-eat-dog world. Man has to be selfish to survive. This is just the way it is out there. Everyone knows this, and we have to be on guard all the time for fear of being "screwed" by life. This is why I called life an old whore that likes to screw us of our virtue in my book *Old Whore Life, Exploring the Shadow Side of Karma*—because I had awakened to man's primal nature and wanted to paint a picture of "old whore life" for the world to see. But this is only the first stage of evolution.

We all came into this world as Soul seeds, and we are all hard-wired to realize our divine nature; but we can only do that by individuating the vital life force, which is Soul consciousness (as I confirmed when I experienced the genesis of life on Earth). So the self of the First Circle of life is going to be selfish, because it has to be to survive; this is why it is next to impossible to sacrifice one's life to save one's life, as Jesus taught—*because it goes against our primal nature to sacrifice our life!*

What was Jesus up to, then? Surely he must have known about man's selfish primal nature; so what is the logic behind his teaching of self-sacrifice? What did he know about the individuation of Soul through life that allowed him to sacrifice his life upon the cross to impress his teaching of self-sacrifice upon the world?

Why would Jesus die for us? That's the question that has stumped the Jesus Society and all rational thinking people; but that's only because we cannot see beyond the veil of the First Circle of Life. To understand Christ's motive for dying on the cross for us we have to see the logic of the Way, which is the logic of self-transcendence.

The logic of the Way is inherently paradoxical, which is why many of Christ's sayings don't make rational sense. How can one save his life by dying to his life? That doesn't make sense. Or cutting off one's hand or casting out one's eye to be made whole? What madness is that? And how can one be born again? Nichodemus didn't know. It didn't make sense to him. How can I go back to my mother's womb? he asked Jesus. And what about the rich young man who asked Jesus how to obtain eternal life and was told to give away all his riches and he would be granted eternal life? Was Jesus crazy?

No, he wasn't crazy; he was speaking from a higher level of consciousness, from the esoteric Third Circle of Life where the logic of the Way is pure redemptive love. Soul cannot realize its divine nature in the First Circle of Life, because the Soul self of the First Circle is not pure enough to become aware of its divine nature; so Jesus showed man with his sacrifice on the cross how to purify the self so that Soul could transcend itself.

Jesus was speaking in the paradoxical language of the Way, which can only be understood when one lives the Way consciously. I lived the Way with such pathological commitment that I gave birth to my spiritual self in my mother's kitchen; which is why I could write in my journal: **the more you give of yourself, the more of yourself you will have to give; and the less you give of yourself, the less of yourself you will have to give.**

I understood the spiritual logic of love, and I knew that to grow in spiritual self-realization consciousness we have to transform the consciousness of our selfish primal nature; because that's the only way we can realize our spiritual destiny. And the simplest, most effective way to transform our selfish

215

nature is by mastering the art of giving love; because the more love we give—*"be it with time, attention, money, or simply concern"*—the more we grow in the love that we are. That's the paradox of the Way that Professor Nash caught a glimpse of with his "mysterious equations of love."

29. *The Paradoxical Mystery of Love*

The mind can't handle paradox. It throws the mind into confusion. This is why the brilliant mathematician could not escape the prison of his own mind and why I rewrote the ending to *A Beautiful Mind* in my dream while undergoing open-heart surgery.

I wish I could remember exactly how I rewrote the ending, and perhaps someday I will retrieve that memory (Robert Moss tells us on his dream blog that this is possible); but I do know with gnostic certainty that there is only one way out of the mental plane where John Nash was trapped, and that's by mastering the art of giving love.

The mental plane is the last plane in the lower worlds that we have to transcend to realize our individuated self on the Soul plane of consciousness. The mental plane includes the subconscious plane, which is called the etheric plane; and the other planes are, in descending order, the causal, astral, and physical planes.

Because we have a body for each of these planes of consciousness, we exist on all of these planes simultaneously in parallel worlds; and we have a self for each of our bodies. Or, to be precise: we only have one self, which is our Soul self, but it expresses itself accordingly on each plane. So we have a physical (biological) self; an astral (emotional) self; a causal (karmic) self; a mental (thinking) self; and an etheric (subconscious) self. And as we experience life we grow in the self-realization consciousness of all our bodies.

The self of all our bodies is our conscious personality; and ego is the "I" of our conscious personality. Our Soul self is not conscious of itself, which is why it has to individuate through our conscious personality. Ego then is vital to our spiritual growth. This is why Carl Jung found it ludicrous that one would try to extinguish his ego to achieve spiritual enlightenment. This went against nature and the purpose of life, which is to expand the consciousness of God through the evolution of the atoms of God.

Ego cannot be extinguished, because ego is our Soul self not-yet-realized; and the only way to achieve enlightenment is to spiritualize the consciousness of our ego self, which can only be done with the "mysterious equations of love."

When Jesus said that we have to "die" to our life to "save" our life, he meant that we have to spiritualize the consciousness of our lower, or ego self. But ego will not be spiritualized for the asking, because ego is the individuating consciousness of our selfish primal nature; which is why man is always in conflict with himself. In effect, **the more ego-centered we are, the more we resist our spiritual destiny**. This is why ego has always gotten a bad rap from the spiritual teachings of the world.

When I awakened to the spiritual purpose of ego I had a radical shift in attitude towards people with big egos. I used to find them insufferable (I was projecting); but now I smile in admiration, because I know that they are highly evolved Souls stuck in one of their lower bodies; and my heart goes out to them because I know what lies ahead. That's why I want to bring some spiritual clarity to the individuation process to help ease the burden of the journey to one's true self, which I can do by explaining the paradox of love.

Again, I have to thank Gurdjieff for bringing this to my attention; not because I learned about the redemptive power of love from his teaching, just the opposite. The more I "worked" on myself with his teaching, the more I grew in self-realization consciousness; but it wasn't enough. That's when I gravitated to the paradoxical sayings of Jesus that introduced me to the inherently self-transcending power of love.

"But when thou doest alms, let not thy left hand know what thy right hand is doing," said Jesus. *"That thine alms may be in secret; and thy Father which seeth in secret himself shall reward thee openly"* (Math. 6: 3-4). And having

learned from Gurdjieff that there is only self-initiation into the mysteries of the Way, I began to practice the discipline (and believe me, it is a discipline!) of doing good and *non-identifying* with the good that I did—because *non-identifying* was Gurdjieff's technique for what Jesus called storing our treasures in heaven.

According to Gurdjieff, not everyone is born with an immortal soul; and his whole teaching was founded upon the principle that one must create his own soul. This struck fear into the heart of his students. And although Gurdjieff was a very compassionate man (which I experienced in my dreams with him), his teaching was shrouded in fear; and many of his students went away broken hearted, and some even committed suicide.

Gurdjieff's teaching opened up to me when I began living my *Royal Dictum;* but even then I came to a dead end, and the Inner Master had to intervene with the question *"why do you lie?"* which gave me the inspiration to continue on my journey to my true self; but it was the paradoxical sayings of Jesus that brought me home.

Once I began to master the discipline of doing good I began to grow in spirit exponentially, and I went out of my way to do good; that's why every summer for seven years I volunteered my time and labor to Habitat for Humanity (which became the basis of my novel *On the Wings of Habitat*), and I picked up hitchhikers (often giving them meal money), and I picked wild blueberries for some of my elderly painting customers, and so on until I was initiated into the paradoxical mystery of the Way and realized that **the more you give of yourself, the more of yourself you will have to give!**

This is the paradoxical mystery of love: by giving love you get love. In effect, you grow in the love that you are (your Soul self) when you give love—but only if you don't vaunt the love that you give, because this only feeds the ego.

As Jesus said: ***"Take heed that ye do not do your alms before men, to be seen of them; otherwise ye have no reward of your Father which is in heaven. Therefore when doest*** *thine alms, do not sound a trumpet before thee, as the hypocrites do in the synagogues and in the streets, that they may have their glory of men. Verily I say unto you, They have their reward"* (Math. 6: 1-2).

This was Gurdjieff's gift to me. By mastering the discipline of *non-identifying* with the love that I gave in my good deeds, I bypassed ego and stored my treasure in heaven—meaning, I grew in spiritual self-realization consciousness; and I grew so much that one fine day I shifted my center of gravity from my ego self to my spiritual self in my mother's kitchen while she was kneading bread dough and I gave birth to my Soul self!

But I wasn't home free by any means. This was just the beginning of my journey into the esoteric Third Circle of Life, because now I had to learn the hard lessons of adjusting my newly realized state of spiritual consciousness with the raw, primal energies of life; and it took all the intelligence that I had to negotiate my way through life.

I suffered many devastating humiliations along the way; that's why I was forever reading. I had to learn from those that had walked the Way before me. I needed their wisdom to help me survive spiritually in a grossly materialistic, sexually obsessed world; and I'm still learning. In fact, doing research for this book has brought me to new levels of humility that I did not think possible after St. Padre Pio slew the spirit of my vanity a couple of years ago. It seems that regardless whether one has shifted his center of gravity from ego to Soul, one still has to contend with the consciousness of their ego self.

Ego doesn't go away because one has given birth to their spiritual self. On the contrary; ego becomes so subtle, nuanced and mercurial that it becomes almost impossible to discern. That's why it shocked the hell out of me when St. Padre Pio held up a mirror so clear and polished that it was impossible for me not to see my deep-seated vanity, and I wanted to throw up because I was so repulsed by what I saw. This is what gave birth to my new saying, **"life is a journey through vanity to humility."**

But to be humbled again so soon after my spiritual healing experience with the Ascended Master took me by surprise. It crept up on me this time as I read book after book in my research for *The Summoning of Noman*; and when I "chanced" upon dream teacher Robert Moss and all the books he has written on the dynamics of dreaming and his dream blog I wanted to go to the back of the class and put a dunce cap on my head.

For the life of me, I could not figure out why I never came across his books before (once again confirming my belief that our whole life is choreographed), and I mopped in my wounded conceit for days. Then I picked myself up and dove right in as I always do whenever I discover someone that has something to teach me; and what a pleasant surprise I got, because Moss is a gifted explorer of the mystical dimensions of dreaming. But what fascinated me most about him was that he's an incorrigible reader always on the lookout for new books (as I have been my whole life) that will expand his spiritual horizons; like his "discovery" of the Seth books by Jane Roberts, for example.

If I'm not mistaken, I have a Seth book in one of my boxes of books that I have yet to unpack from our move to Georgian Bay, and I may have read it years ago; but I didn't pursue that thread of knowledge because my path pulled me elsewhere. This has happened to me dozens of times in my spiritual quest; but now it seems that I'm much more amenable to the Seth material, which was brought home to me when Moss quoted Seth on his dream blog: *"There is one God, but within that God are many. There is one self, but within that self are many. There is one body, in one time, but the self has other bodies in other times. All "times" exist at once."* (mossdreams.com December 24, 2012)

Seth is an "energy personality essence," or a higher entity if you will, channeled by Jane Roberts; and I was no less impressed by the information that Seth revealed in this one quotation than Robert Moss was. "I am thrilled by the simplicity and vital importance of his key statements," said Moss about Seth, adding that the above quotation "goes to the heart of what it means to be a conscious citizen of the multiverse."

This Seth quotation confirmed what I had spent years working out about the nature of God and the self; that's why I felt wounded by my "chance" discovery of Robert Moss—because it always annoys me to no end when I have to learn something the hard way only to find out that that trail has already been well-blazed by someone else.

Maybe that's why Robert Moss reads so much. He knows this secret; and he tries to head himself off at the pass, as it were, and avoid all the pitfalls. And why not? After all, he does believe that we can influence our past and future lives from our current life.

But this is too metaphysical. As St. Padre Pio would say, suffice to say that I have been brought to a new place of understanding; and I have to just go with it to see what lies ahead. Which reminds me of a dream I had while I was having my spiritual healing sessions with the Ascended Master: *Penny and I are in a theater-like setting, and on the screen we see a river very much like the Nipigon River where I created my Royal Dictum. The movie screen is life itself, but it's a river flowing gently. The river takes many turns, and we watch it flowing on its way to Lake Superior. The river represents our life, and we see the river flowing, and we're flowing with it and watch many repeats of the river flowing; and then a new image appears on the screen. It's the same river, but now there's a new bend in the river, and on the screen the words NEW CORNERS appear.* The dream ends.

The Summoning of Noman has brought me to a new bend in the river of my life, and I *know* that my new research into the dreaming process is going to expand my spiritual horizons beyond my expectations (new corners). In fact, it's already having an effect on my dreams; because I'm beginning to see that my dreams of my hometown (which I seem to have almost every night) are dreams of my first parallel life.

It seems like I'm visiting the parallel world of my first lifetime as Orest Stocco in my Soul body; and my suspicion is that I'm doing what in my spiritual path is called "vahana work" by bringing a message of the Way to the lost Souls of my hometown—*myself included!* Is it possible? Am I visiting my first life in my dreams from my second life in a parallel world to help myself find my lost Soul in the "fourth corner of the abyss" where God had condemned me? Is this why I keep dreaming of my hometown?

I honestly don't know; but I'd sure like to find out...

30. *Creating the Right Kind of Personality*

In principle, Gurdjieff was wrong to believe that not everyone is born with an immortal soul, because we are all a spark of divine consciousness; but in practice his teaching precipitated the process of spiritual self-realization consciousness, and for this I will be eternally grateful despite how difficult it was to practice.

The same can be said about Jesus Christ's teaching of self-sacrifice. It is almost impossible to practice, because it goes against our primal nature to "die" to our life to "save" our life; that's why I had to confront St. Padre Pio on this issue.

I had an incredible opportunity to speak with an Ascended Spiritual Master who spent most of his life as a Capuchin monk suffering the holy wounds of Jesus Christ (they only disappeared a day or so before his transition to the Other Side), and I wanted to know that if from his place of all knowing and all seeing he still held onto his Roman Catholic beliefs that he embraced when he was alive; and, I'm happy to say, he had transcended them—which is why we saw eye to eye on the question of spiritual self-realization consciousness and came to the understanding that the best life to live is a spiritually balanced life.

If I'm not mistaken, this is going to be the theme of my next book with St. Padre Pio; but for now I want to start bringing *The Summoning of Noman* to closure, because I can hear my Muse calling it home; and although I'm not quite there yet, I have to bring to resolution what I've expounded upon so far about my parallel life as Orest Stocco.

In my first parallel life as Orest Stocco (I distinguish between my parallel lives as Orest Stocco, because according to St. Padre Pio I have lived my same life over again three separate times), I failed to achieve what I was born to achieve; and I believe I was born to achieve liberation from the recurring cycle of karma and reincarnation.

I got stuck on the mental plane of consciousness in my first life as Orest Stocco, and it was my intended purpose to liberate myself from the hold that my mental self had over me in my second life as Orest Stocco, which I have done; and when I distill what I learned on my journey to spiritual self-realization consciousness I can break it down into essentially three categories of thought: 1. Gurdjieff's teaching of "work on oneself"; 2. Christ's teaching of self-sacrifice; and 3. Jung's psychology of individuation. And when I put all three categories together they add up to creating the right kind of personality. And just what is the right kind of personality that will break the cycle of karma and reincarnation?

In one of my spiritual healing sessions St. Padre Pio surprised me by telling me that there are people in the world today that live a karma-free life; but when I pleaded with him to tell me how this was possible, he refused to tell me. He said that I would work this out on my own; and, believe it or not, I think I'm on the cusp of understanding how one can live a karma-free life in this karma-making dualistic universe.

The Good Saint said that it has to do with a higher state of spiritual consciousness, which I had no problem understanding; but what I wanted to know was how to precipitate this higher state of spiritual consciousness, which he wouldn't tell me because, as he implied, we have to earn the privilege of this esoteric knowledge.

But in his offhanded manner he did let me know that to realize the fruits of the spiritual life we have to live the spiritual life; and this is what I intend to illustrate with what I learned about my own spiritual self-realization process. In effect, one has to learn how to live the spiritual life first before he can realize the fruits of the spiritual life.

Jesus revealed the sum of his teaching of self-sacrifice in his imperative, *"Be ye therefore perfect as your Father which is in heaven is perfect"* (Math. 5: 48). Jesus said this as a summation of his gospel on how to live his teaching of self-sacrifice; and when all is said and done, his teaching comes down to creating the right kind of personality.

So the question that Christ's teaching begs, as does Gurdjieff's teaching and Jung's understanding of the individuation process is this: just what is the right kind of personality that will allow our unconscious Soul self to become aware of itself?

In a word, **the right kind of personality that will liberate Soul from the recurring cycle of karma and reincarnation is an inherently self-transcending personality**; which means that one has to live by values that "gather and collect" Soul into herself, as Socrates tells us in Plato's *Phaedo*. And according to Socrates these values are the noble virtues, of which Goodness is the highest and noblest. This is why I summed up the philosophy of my own life with the saying, **"the purpose of life is to simply be a good person."**

But what makes the noble virtues inherently self-transcending? In other words, as so many people want to know in today's confusing world of values, why be good? Essentially this is the question that the Preacher asked in *Ecclesiastes*: *"what profit hath a man of all his labor which he taketh under the sun?"*—and which I answered in my little book *Why Bother? The Riddle of the Good Samaritan.*

I'm reading Robert Moss' dream blog, and in one entry (July 26, 2010, "On a state of indescribable busyness") he reveals just how busy his day is—writing for his two dream blogs, working on several new books of fiction, editing his book about to be published, reading several books at once, putting together a book of poetry, preparing for his dream workshops in various parts of the world, journaling, doing online research, answering emails, tending to his physical needs like buying groceries and paying bills, walking his dog, making travel arrangements—a whole list of things that brought back memories of when I scrambled to fit as much life as I could into the day, and I had to chuckle as the Preacher's words popped into my mind: *"Of making many books there is no end, and much study is a weariness of the flesh. Let us hear the conclusion of the whole matter: Fear God, and keep his commandments; for this is the whole duty of man"* (Eccl. 12: 12-13). And then St. Padre Pio's words came to me: "Live, love, and enjoy your life; and don't worry about tomorrow. Tomorrow never comes. There is only today."

This is certainly not to pass judgment on Robert Moss (if one were so inclined, one could almost envy such talent and industry), because life is an individual journey; I'm just making the point that this is HIS way. This is HIS individuation process. As St. Padre Pio told me in a spiritual healing session, "There is no one way." In fact, he created an image of a river for me to get the point, which I relate in *Healing with Padre Pio*.

But I knew this, because I had come to the realization that the Way just *is*; and what I want to make clear is that **until one finds the Way one is still on their own path to the Way, both in one's physical life and one's dream life**, and until one awakens to the Way one will always be living the Way unconsciously, regardless how much life one packs into one's day. In effect, **one lives the Way unconsciously until the Way makes him ready to live the Way consciously**; and this is the "profit of all his labor which he taketh under the sun." In short, everything that we do in life prepares us to live the Way consciously.

That's the difference between the first and second stage of evolution; but, sadly, one can never become conscious of the Way until one enters the "strait gate" of the Way, which one can only do with the noble virtues. Then slowly, without really noticing, one comes to the simple realization that his own life *is* the Way, and that the Way just *is*; and then one's life, however busy or routine, takes on a completely new meaning—because one is now conscious of the inherently self-transcending power of the life of virtue.

I saw this natural process of karmic reconciliation at work when I volunteered my time with Habitat for Humanity. I wanted to write a novel on my experience, so I asked some of the men and women on the job site why they volunteered their time to Habitat, and they all said that they wanted to give something back to life.

This was love in action, and although they did not know that they were waking up to the Way by giving back to life they nonetheless realized the spiritual benefits of their charity; which is why they all told me that it felt good to give back to life. The "good" that they felt was their "treasure" in heaven; which is why I made *doing good* central to my personal ethic—because I wanted to precipitate my spiritual growth.

I believed in the Law of Karma implicitly; so it followed logically that the more good I did, the more goodness ("treasure in heaven") I would store. In effect, I was living the Way consciously; and the more I lived the Way consciously, the more conscious I became of the Way. That's how I initiated myself into the mysteries of the Way. And one very deep mystery that revealed itself to me was the mystery of our two destinies.

Our spiritual destiny is fixed, because it's in our spiritual DNA to realize our divine nature; but we can only realize our divine nature through our karmic destiny, which we can change because we are blessed with the gift of free choice. This is the source of all our conflict—because **our karmic destiny is forever at odds with our spiritual destiny**.

We create karma with every life we live; karma that will have to be resolved in our current life or future lives. Karma cannot be absolved by prayer or forgiveness. Karma is our debt with life, and life will exact that debt whether we like it or not. This is our karmic destiny, and we will be dragged by our destiny until we pay our debt to life.

But after enough suffering and cursing and shaking our fist at God (some of us get so angry that we even deny the existence of God), we eventually wake up and realize that we are the authors of our own circumstances, and we begin to make more discerning choices in how to live our life. In effect, we're taking destiny into our own hands; and by doing this we make ourselves ready for the second stage of evolution.

It's a long, slow process to the second stage of evolution; because it takes a lot of life experience to come to the simple realization that life is all about give and take. This is where expressions like **"what goes around comes around"** and **"you get back what you put out"** come from. As a wise grandmother once said, "There are two kinds of people in the world: givers and takers. The takers eat well, and the givers sleep well."

This is the slow dawning of karmic awareness. But not everyone can make the causal connection between doing good and storing one's treasure in heaven, like the flower shop lady in Nipigon who said to me one summer day, "Are you crazy?"

I had volunteered six weeks of my busy summer to help paint the interior and exterior of the St. Sylvester Historic Mission Church on the shores of Lake Helen in my hometown of Nipigon. St. Sylvester's was the reservation church, but it needed some restoration; and while I was working inside with several native volunteers (I may have been applying a coat of polystucco on the front wall where Jesus hung on his big wooden cross) the lady who owned the flower shop in Nipigon had seen me working there for several weeks came into the church one day to check up on the progress and said to me, "I hope you're getting paid for all the work you're doing here."

"No; it's all volunteer work," I said.

"What? Are you crazy?" she said, unable to fathom my motive.

"No, I'm not crazy. I love my work, and I'm sure they'll appreciate it," I replied.

That's how I learned to create the right kind of personality that would align my karmic destiny with my spiritual destiny. And that's why it was vital to keep silent about my charity; because too much charity can threaten people, as it did the flower shop lady whose whole value system was thrown into disarray by my goodness—which gave birth to another one of my sayings: **you can only be so good before society turns on you.**

This is why mystery schools practice the Law of Silence, to protect the student from the raw, negative forces of life. Ego is threatened by the good that people do, because ego is the "I" of our primal, selfish nature; and it takes a lot of wisdom to negotiate one's way through life when one lives the Way consciously, because ego loves the status quo.

At the risk of breaking the Law of Silence, then; when I asked St. Padre Pio if Jesus had actually died on the cross, he wouldn't tell me. He said I wasn't ready to understand the mystery of his crucifixion. But he did tell me something that I had never heard before, but which I have to reveal for this book; he said that **Jesus came from the future.**

By this time in my relationship with the Ascendant Master I trusted him implicitly, so I didn't question this new fact about Jesus; but I did ask him to tell me where the world was headed before Jesus introduced the Way to the world.

Again, he wouldn't tell me. It had to do with the inner workings of the universe, and there was much that I needed to understand first; but I suspect that I was on the right track to believe that the world soul was headed for a spiritual cull de sac, and Jesus came back from the future to show man a way out with his teaching of the Way.

In effect, Jesus gave man a choice to change his karmic destiny with the way of self-sacrifice, which he symbolized with his death upon the cross; but what intrigued me about Jesus coming from the future was that he must have had a reincarnational history. So I asked the all-knowing Saint if that was so, and he said yes; which implied that the Jesus who died on the cross was the second, parallel Jesus Christ!

I don't know if this is true or not, and short of Soul travelling to the time of Jesus and asking him in person I don't know of any other way of proving it; but what difference does it make? As Jesus said to Glenda Green: *"All too often people who look to the subject of reincarnation for answers are actually trying to find themselves. This is a misdirection. There is* **no other** *time or place to find yourself.* **Now** *is your only context. The past is gone. Only the ego would cling to an identity out of context...The source of your identity does not lie in any kind of linear path. The source of your identity lies only in your love"* (*Love without End, Jesus Speaks*, p. 77); which is why the first words that Jesus spoke to Glenda when he manifested to her for his portrait were, "*Glenda, love is who you are.*"

And how else can one be brought to this realization other than by creating the right kind of personality that will allow one to see that love is who we are?

So it doesn't matter what path one is on, until one learns how to create the right kind of personality they will never find their true self; and they will just keep coming back until they get it right. This is why I came back to live my same life over again; I had an incredible opportunity to get it right this time around!

31. *My Agreement with St. Padre Pio*

I'm not one to get depressed, so whenever I fall prey to this state of consciousness—which I believe to be a disconnect from the creative life force of one's inner self—I let it linger for a time just to let it have its way with me and satisfy that part of me that induced this state, and then my spiritual survival instincts kick in and I look for a way out.

That happened this week. I was dreaming of my hometown again, or some version of my hometown in a parallel reality, and I woke up from one dream the other morning that affected my mood all day long because in my dream I felt trapped by my Nipigon life.

I didn't fight it. I lived in it all day long just to experience this dismal, lifeless, and hope-killing state of consciousness that so many people fall prey to when they are possessed by their shadow self (which I've been exploring again with books like *Meeting the Shadow, The Hidden Power of the Dark Side of Human Nature*); and when I felt I had enough, my spiritual survival instincts kicked in and I was nudged to go downstairs and dig up my Seth book because Robert Moss had ignited my curiosity about Seth.

I have four or five thousand books, most still in boxes; but I have five or six rows of books already stacked on a temporary bookshelf that I had made of leftover bricks from our new house and shelving that I picked up at the hardware store, so I decided to go through the books on the shelves first, and for some reason my eye fell upon *When You See the Emu in the Sky, My Journey of Self-discovery in the Outback,* by Elizabeth Fuller; so my inner guiding principle insisted that I read it again. And then I "chanced" upon *A Primer of Jungian Psychology,* which I had looked for three or four times already, and this excited me very much because I knew that my guiding principle was on high alert; and then I spotted it on the top shelf—*Seth Speaks, The Eternal Validity of the Soul,* by Jane Roberts.

I took it down and put it with my other two books and continued to look because I wanted to see what other books my guiding principle wanted me to read, and it didn't surprise me in the least when I zeroed in like a tractor laser beam on *Undiscovered Country, In Search of Gurdjieff,* by Kathryn Hulme, a student of Gurdjieff and author of *The Nun's Story* which was made into one of my favorite movies starring Audrey Hepburn, one of my favorite actresses who also starred in *Roman Holiday* with Gregory Peck, probably my favorite actor who starred in my favorite movie *The Man in the Gray Flannel Suit*; and I added *Undiscovered Country* to the other three books to bring upstairs.

I began to feel better already, because these books awakened memories of my seeker days when I was so hot on the trail for my true self that nothing else mattered; so I continued to let my instincts guide me to other books that would enforce this wonderful feeling of being alive with the consciousness of my seeker self. And I zeroed in on *The Tao of Zen*, by Ray Grigg, which reawakened my excitement for the Way in the oriental traditions; and *Close Range, Wyoming Stories* by Annie Proulx, which contained the story "Brokeback Mountain" that was made into the critically acclaimed movie by the same name which I had seen and loved for its portrayal of the repressed shadow side of human nature (it's a story about two cowboys who fall in love); and *John Updike, More Matter, Essays and Criticism*, which excited my literary spirit because Updike's writing intimidates the hell out of me and I have to read him every now and then just to keep myself humble.

I started reading *Undiscovered Country* first, because my Gurdjieff days were the most exciting days of my life. I was so hot on the trail for my true self when I put Gurdjieff's teaching of "work on oneself" to practice that I couldn't wait for my next shipment of Gurdjieff books to come in from *Samuel Weiser Publisher* in New York City because I lived my life through the stories told by Gurdjieff's students; and one hundred pages into the book gave me enough of a Gurdjieff fix to dive into *When You See the Emu in the Sky*, which I enjoyed the first time I read it but was much more taken by the story now that I was reading Robert Moss's dream blog. Moss is an Australian, and he awakened my interest in Aborigine Dreamtime; and I read the book in one sitting, which took me the rest of the day. And this book inspired me to re-read *Mutant Message Down Under*, by Marlo Morgan, which I devoured the next day and enjoyed much more this time because it spoke to me on a different level. In fact, something that Dream Healer, one of the Real People tribal elders said to Morgan gave me a clue on how to live a karma-free life.

Two days after my dark mood brought on by the dream of my hometown possessed me, it was all but gone by reconnecting myself with my creative inner self with the books that awakened memories of my seeker self; but I got a pleasant surprise when I started reading the Seth book, because I found a sales slip inside with the date of my purchase: THUNDER BAY BOOKSHOP CO-OP INC. & RECORD CENTRE, Seth Speaks, October 10, 1974, $3.95— *thirty-nine years ago!* God, what a journey it's been...

If one hasn't been called to the Way, he will never understand what it means to be driven to find the Way; that's why I'm enjoying reading Robert Moss's dream blog, and I'm looking forward to reading his books when I order them from Amazon.

Every soul will be called to the Way when it is ready to find the Way, and every soul will seek the Way according to its own karmic destiny; so one soul can be called to find the Way through Sufism, another through Taoism, or Buddhism, Jungian psychology, art, music, poetry or whatever; it all depends upon one's karmic resonance with the Way.

Robert Moss was called to the Way through his dreams. A successful foreign correspondent and best selling mystery writer, his life made him ready for the Way and he was called to leave his hectic life and explore the Way of the Dream (just as Marlo

Morgan was called to the Way of Aborigine Dreamtime when she was ready); and today Robert Moss is one of the world's foremost shamanic dream teachers who gives workshops and seminars all over the world, keeping his readers abreast of his research on the Way of the Dream through his two dream blogs and phone-in radio show "Way of the Dreamer."

I was called to the Way of Soul. The Way of Soul is the Way of all ways; that's why my seeker life was like that of a honey bee going from flower to flower to gather the sweet nectar of the Way. This was both good and bad. It was good because it satisfied my spiritual craving, and it was bad because it always left me wanting more; which is why I had to be unbelievably innovative to satisfy my insatiable longing for my true self.

That's how I developed an instinct for extracting exactly what I needed from each teaching that I was drawn to and not linger around to devour the whole teaching as most seekers do. I was a Hound of Heaven, and I had to go where the scent took me; and I dread the memories of what I had to go through to find my true self.

That's why I hate my Nipigon dreams. They take me back to my first parallel life as Orest Stocco, and they always leave me with a feeling like I failed to live up to my expectations—which I did, or I wouldn't be living my same life over again.

But all the reading and online research that I am doing for this book has expanded my horizons, and I can now look at my Nipigon dreams as parallel realities that I can change anytime. As Jesus said to Glenda Green, *"**Now** is your only context. The past is gone. Only the ego would cling to an identity out of context...The source of your identity does not lie in any kind of linear path. The source of your identity lies only in your love."* WOW!

After years of writing, I've come to realize that every book I write gives birth to its own truth; and I believe *The Summoning of Noman* has just given birth to the truth that I set out to find—the solution to my Nipigon dream life! But as St. Padre Pio told me in one of my spiritual healing sessions, one has to be ready before they come to a new understanding; so what made me ready to see the truth of my dream life?

But first, what is the truth of my dream life? Thanks to what Jesus said in Glenda's book, I now believe **the truth of my dream life is that I am clinging to "an identity out of context."** I am going back to my Nipigon life in my dreams because I am still fixating on my parallel ego-personality that failed to live up to my expectations; and speaking from my higher self, I can very easily say now, "Get over yourself, please!"

So you were "less than perfect," as St. Padre Pio would say; so what? Not all dress rehearsals are perfect, and every life we live is just another dress rehearsal in the drama of our multidimensional life; so there's no need to play it over and over in my mind, or in my dreams. And what made me ready for this understanding were my sessions with St. Padre Pio, because his love slew the vanity that kept me from transcending myself.

Marlo Morgan was living in Australia for a few years because of a health project that she was involved in, and one day she went to a science museum. The tour guide wanted to chat with Marlo about the United States, so they made arrangements for a lunch date in a quaint tearoom in the heart of the city that advertised fortune-tellers.

Closing time approached, and her new friend hadn't shown up; so Marlo bent over to pick up her purse to leave when a young man walked up to her table. "I have time to give your reading now," he said, in a quiet voice.

"Oh, I was waiting for a friend. But it doesn't seem she was able to make it today. I'll be back," Marlo replied.

"Sometimes that works out for the best," he commented as he pulled out the chair across from me at the small round table for two. He sat down and took my hand in his. Turning it palm up, he began his reading. He didn't look in my hand; his eyes remained fixed looking into mine.

"The reason you have come to this place, not this tea-room, but this continent, is destiny. There is someone here you have agreed to meet for your mutual benefit. The agreement was made before either of you were born. In fact, you chose to be born at the same instant, one on the top of the world and the other here, Down Under. The pact you made was on the highest level of your eternal self. You agreed not to seek one another until fifty years had passed. It is now time. When you meet, there will be instant recognition on the soul level. That is all I can tell you," he told her, and stood up and walked away. (*Mutant Message Down Under*, pp.33-4)

Marlo's friend phoned that evening to apologize and explain why she could not make it to their luncheon, but she became very excited when Marlo explained what happened and her friend vowed the next day to seek the reader and get information about her own future; but when she phoned the next day she said to Marlo, "The tearoom has no male readers. They have a different person each day, but all are women. On Tuesday it was Rose, and she doesn't read palms. She reads cards. Are you sure you went to the right place?"

Marlo had gone to exactly the right place, because her life was choreographed; and the young fortune teller was probably a Spiritual Master who had come to tell her that it was time for her to connect with the Way through Aborigine Dreamtime as her higher self had agreed to do because she was ready now. And thus began her spiritual journey with the Real People of the Outback that connected her with the Way.

St. Padre Pio and I also made an agreement on the highest level of our eternal self before I was reborn into my same life, which he revealed to me in one of my spiritual healing sessions; that's why I had to ask him if we would be working on another book together after I finished writing *Healing with Padre Pio*.

He said yes, that our work was not yet done; and I asked him if this work was to help introduce the Way to the world with my books. Yes, he said; that was our purpose, and he would help by "planting seeds" for my writing, like telling me that I have lived my same life over again three separate times, this life being one of those times. He also told me something else that took me by surprise: he said that he is living today in another body; he's a Catholic priest in El Salvador. "Does this priest know that he is you?" I asked.

"He has his suspicions," he replied; and I had to laugh, because this kind of information would shock the Roman Catholic Church.

But I suspect that St. Padre Pio revealed this because he wanted to introduce the concept of our multidimensional life, which I would be researching for the new book he said I would be writing; that's why the dream teacher Robert Moss, who is writing an autobiography of his own multidimensional life (*The Boy Who Died and Came Back*), was pulled into my field of gravity; because I'm ready now for the next stage of my journey through this world, which is learning how to live a karma-free life.

32. *Soul's Karmic Destiny*

It's all very mystical and complicated, and one wonders whether it's worth all the time and bother; but one really has no choice when he's in the grips of his karmic destiny. Like a writer possessed by an idea for his next book, he has to write it or suffer the anguish of not living up to what Jungian therapist James Hillman calls his "soul's code."

It took me years of reading and living the Way consciously to arrive at the simple realization that **our greatest need in life is to be who we are meant to be**. In a word, we are all born to be ourselves just as an acorn seed is born to be an oak tree.

In his book *The Soul's Code, In Search of Character and Calling* James Hillman calls this the "acorn theory, which holds that each person bears a uniqueness that asks to be lived and that is already present before it can be lived." This uniqueness is not a given, however, as Hillman maintains: "You are born with a character; it is given; a gift, as the old stories say, from the guardians upon your birth" (pp. 6-7).

The stories that Hillman refers to are the old myths; like Plato's Myth of Er at the end of his dialogue *The Republic*. Each person enters the world "called", says this myth, which Hillman explicates: "The soul of each of us is given a unique daemon before we are born, and it has selected an image or pattern that we live on earth. This soul-companion, the daemon, guides us here; in the process of arrival, however, we forget all that took place and believe that we come empty into the world. The daemon remembers what is in your image and belongs to your pattern, and therefore your daemon is the carrier of your destiny" (*The Soul's Code*, p. 8).

Hillman says our daemon is our calling, and that the Romans named it our *genius*, the Greeks our *daemon*, and the Christians our guardian angel; but I call it our karmic destiny, and it is not a given. It is created from lifetime to lifetime by the choices we make with each life we live. This is what makes our daemon unique (and by daemon I mean the archetypal spirit of our personal karmic destiny), because no two people live the same karmic life. We may live similar lives, but never the same karmic life.

Even parallel lives are dissimilar; like my two parallel lives. I am the same person as I was in my first life, but I am an entirely different person in my second life because I made a karmic choice to achieve a different outcome from my first life.

In my first life as Orest Stocco I did not get caught in the grips of my daemon as I did in my second life as Orest Stocco. My daemon was awakened from the deep recesses of my unconscious when I became possessed to do something one night in my early twenties that shocked my conscience awake; and once my daemon had me in its grips I had no choice but do its bidding and find my true self or die trying.

This was my "calling," and although it was not what one would normally refer to as a "calling"—like being called to acting, music, medicine, or writing for example—it was my soul's code to find the Way and align my karmic destiny with my spiritual destiny. It's no wonder that I heaved a big sigh when I learned that I had purchased my Seth book thirty-nine years ago—*because I could not believe how long I had been on my path!*

But here I am, back from my journey of self-discovery telling my life story in the literary conceit of my poem *Noman*; and although my journey has now entered a new phase, I'm happy to say that for all the personal sacrifices, humiliations, and life blood that I spilled along the way, I made it to my true self intact; and what I learned on my journey is that to BE our true self we have to BECOME our true self. And herein lies the mystery, because we cannot become our true self until we find the Way.

After I finished reading *Undiscovered Country* yesterday I was so nostalgic for my Gurdjieffian days of "working" on myself that

I went to my basement library and zeroed in on *The Unknowable Gurdjieff* by Margaret Anderson, founder and editor of *The Little Review* which between 1914 and 1929 published some of my favorite writers—James Joyce, Ernest Hemingway, and T. S. Eliot—and who was a devoted student of Gurdjieff; and for an added fix I also brought upstairs *Boyhood with Gurdjieff* by Fritz Peters, which I enjoyed reading the first time because it showed the enigmatic Gurdjieff through a boy's eyes.

Margaret Anderson was a prescient editor with a keen eye for originality who set out to present Gurdjieff's ideas with as much clarity as possible, and she skillfully captured the central idea of Gurdjieff's teaching—an idea so powerful that it affected everyone who bought into it, as she did (and I did also, but with reservations tucked away in the back of my mind). *"Man has no soul; he has only the potentiality,"* said Gurdjieff, and Margaret Anderson tells us how this powerful idea affected her life, which she had totally devoted to art before she "fortuitously" met the unknowable Gurdjieff.

"We have always assumed that man is born with a soul, that this is the endowment which distinguishes him from animals," Anderson writes. "But now in my vision I saw that you can't say a man is born with a soul any more than you can say a man is born with an art. A man may be born artistic—that is, with an art tendency—but he won't have an art until he has worked at art, developed it through an organic process of growth. He must live a life of Art. In the same way, a man can't have a soul until he has lived a life of the Soul" (*The Unknowable Gurdjieff*, p. 26).

This is a very hard teaching. Like an oyster that has a grain of sand to work with to create a pearl, so did Gurdjieff only accept students whom he felt had what he called a "magnetic center," because he could help them create the pearl of their own soul. "I cannot develop you," said Gurdjieff to the students that he accepted into his hermetic circle. "I can create conditions in which you can develop yourself."

Like Jesus' teaching of spiritual rebirth, Gurdjieff's teaching was all about creating one's own soul; and because I felt that

Gurdjieff drank from the same well of secret knowledge that Jesus did, I was forced to ask the all-knowing Ascended Master St. Padre Pio if Jesus also believed that not everyone is born with an immortal soul, to which he replied that it was *ipso facto* impossible because we are all a part of the divine Whole, therefore we are all sparks of God—which put the lie to Gurdjieff's basic premise.

But what anguish his students must have suffered under the misapprehension that they were not born with an immortal soul and had to stare into the face of their own nothingness every single day, especially given that their greatest need in life was to become who they were meant to be—as Louis Pauwels tells us in his book *Gurdjieff.*

Out of the thousands of acorns that an oak tree produces, perhaps one will take root and become an oak tree said Gurdjieff to young Fritz Peters in *Boyhood with Gurdjieff.* "Nature make many acorns, but possibility to become tree exist for only few acorns. Same with man—many men born, but only few grow," explained Gurdjieff , trying to illustrate his teaching of spiritual rebirth to the eleven year old boy. And the acorns that did not take root and grow, Gurdjieff called *"merde"* (fertilizer). That's so hard it's cruel.

"Many are called, but few are chosen," said Jesus, reflecting the same hard, cruel reality of the natural process of Soul-individuation; but having given birth to my immortal self in my mother's kitchen one fine day, I can verify that Gurdjieff and Jesus taught a system of spiritual self-realization consciousness that worked. I won't begin to explain the suffering that one has to endure to get there, though; that's why I was brought to tears as I reread Kathryn Hulme's and Margaret Anderson's life with Gurdjieff—and especially Louis Pauwels' stories of students that were brought to the brink of death because of the unbelievable demands made upon them by Gurdjieff's teaching.

By their own testimony however, Gurdjieff was a very compassionate man with boundless love for his students, and if he was hard on them it was only because he was creating the conditions for them to "work" on themselves—which Fritz Peters' *Boyhood with Gurdjieff,* and especially his sequel *Gurdjieff Remembered,* amply demonstrate, as do C. S. Nott's memoirs *Journey Through this World* and *Teachings of Gurdjieff.* In effect, Gurdjieff was helping them to create their own soul by teaching them how to transform the consciousness of their ego personality. This was the purpose of his esoteric school which he called the "Institute for the Harmonious Development of Man" in Fontainebleau, France where Fritz Peters lived as a young boy and C. S. Nott as a young man. A. R. Orage, the editor of the *New Age,* which G. B. Shaw called the best magazine of literature and ideas that England had produced since the eighteenth century, also lived there; as did Dr. Nicoll and Dr. Young, both well-known English psychiatrists and followers of C. G. Jung.

Gurdjieff sped up the natural process of self-individuation with his teaching, because he was aware that nature can only evolve man so far and no further; but the pressure to create one's own soul must have been unbearable for some of his students, and for all the love and respect and admiration that I have for Gurdjieff, I have to hold him accountable for all the heart-wrenching agony that his misapprehension caused so many followers.

The irony is that Gurdjieff's perspective is effective insomuch that it provides one with an all-or-nothing incentive to take evolution into their own hands and create their own soul, which is no different than the Christian perspective that unless we embrace Jesus as our savior we will suffer eternal damnation. This was the dilemma that Huston Smith, author of the bestselling *The World's Religions,* found himself in.

But he did find resolution. In his book *Why Religion Matters* he tells the story of how Father Lazarus, a missionary of the Eastern Orthodox Church whom he met in India, resolved his dilemma by using St. Paul's Second Corinthians to state his case.

St. Paul knew a man who twelve years earlier was caught up in the third heaven, whether in body or soul he did not know; but in that heaven he "heard things that were not to be told, that no mortal is permitted to repeat." Smith goes on to say: "Paul was speaking of himself, Father Lazarus was convinced, and the secret that he was told in the third heaven was that ultimately everyone is saved. That is the fact of the matter, Father Lazarus believed, but it must not be told because the uncomprehending would take it as a license for irresponsibility. If they are going to be saved eventually, why bother? That exegesis solved my problem and has stayed with me ever since. A number of years later I was pleased to find it confirmed by Sufis who (likewise quietly) accept at face value the verse in the Koran that reads, 'Unto Him all things return'" (*Why Religion Matters,* p. 270).

Unlike Huston Smith however, I could not live with that exegesis because I refused to accept St. Paul's arrogant presumption that he knew what was best for man by concealing the truth about soul's inevitable spiritual destiny; and not only St. Paul (whom I take to task in my novel *St. Paul's Conceit*), but the Gospel writers Matthew, Mark, Luke, and John as well who also imply that only through Jesus Christ can we be saved, and which I also take to task in my novel *Jesus Wears Dockers, The Gospel Conspiracy Story.*

If Gurdjieff honestly believed that man has to create his own soul (which I believe he did, because of all the books that I read on his life and teaching he never once wavered from this basic conviction), he can be forgiven for the anguish it caused his followers; but I had trouble with my old Roman Catholic faith however, and I had to vent my anger at Christianity's presumption that only through Jesus can we be saved; that's why I wrote *Jesus Wears Dockers* and *St. Paul's Conceit*. And that's why I had to go for a spiritual healing with St. Padre Pio, because I could not resolve my anger at Christianity.

I'm happy to say that St. Padre Pio healed me of my deep-seated anger that kept me from transcending myself, which I relate in *Healing with Padre Pio*; and I'm looking forward to our next book together because it will deal with the humble, but enlightened spiritual perspective that we are all born immortal, and that there is no time limit on spiritual self-realization consciousness; hence, no more reason to fear going to hell or being swallowed up by the consciousness of our own nothingness!

33. *Canned Opinions, Personal Beliefs, Prejudices and My Own Truth*

Tuesday, March 5, 2013 I had the following dream that brings my book to closure: *I feel that there is something wrong with my teeth. I look in the mirror to examine my teeth and they are all worn out and very dull looking. Something isn't right. Then I spit something out of my mouth and I have a little pile of dry enamel dust and a fragment of dental material in my hand, and I know that this is the remains of my worn-out teeth. Then I see that beneath each tooth there is a can full of something or other, like canned vegetables, fruits, and soups, but it's not that; the cans contain something else. And I get an empty plastic pail (the size of my drywall mud pails) and an empty cardboard box and I start taking all the cans out of my mouth. The cans are regular size vegetable cans, and I know that when I have taken them all out my mouth will be fresh and clean and healthy.*

I woke up puzzled, and I lay awake trying to figure it out.

I believe my dream is what Carl Jung would call a big dream. A big dream speaks to the whole psyche of man as well as the personal self; and my first impressions are that I have chewed and masticated the canned opinions, personal beliefs, and prejudices of the world (my own included) my whole life, and now that I have taken all the cans out of my mouth I can speak with a fresh point of view from my own gnostic wisdom of life.

The Sufis say that to learn the truth one must first unlearn what he knows; which is the most difficult part of the spiritual journey to wholeness, because one *is* what he knows. His knowledge is his ontological makeup. It is the *being* and *non-being* of his nature, and unlearning means letting go of what one is not; which is next to impossible to do.

"However much knowledge a man has," say the Sufis, "unless he has examined himself and confessed to himself that really he understands nothing, all that he has acquired will be as 'the wind in his hands.' One must 'die' before dying."

This reminds me of something that St. Padre Pio said. He told me that I had to learn how to write from my heart, because when I write from my mind "it's not real," which I took to heart because when I'm in the creative "zone" what flows out of me seems more real than real; "the truth above the facts of life," as Karen Blixen would say. That's how I wrote *Jesus Wears Dockers, The Gospel Conspiracy Story,* which I probably would not have published had St. Padre Pio not insisted; so what is my dream telling me, then?

Last month I "chanced" upon an infomercial on TV for a product called Nurti-Bullet, a juicer that breaks down the cell walls of fruits and vegetables and nuts and seeds and extracts all the nutrients to create smoothies called "nutriblasts." By extracting the nutrients one gets the most health benefits out of these foods, which goes a long way to improving one's health; and after drinking one nutriblast every morning for a week I no longer have cravings for snack foods, because my body is nutritionally satisfied; so on one level was my dream confirming the health benefits of our new extractor juicer, and on another level telling me that spiritual health depends upon the nutritional value of one's own truth extracted from the canned opinions, personal beliefs, and prejudices of life?

Dreams don't lie, and I feel that my dream is telling me that I have gone around a new bend in the river of my life with this book, because I specifically asked the Dream Weaver the other night for a dream that would bring closure to *The Summoning of Noman;* and my dream tells me that **I have extracted the goodness of life, and I no longer need to chew and masticate the canned opinions, personal beliefs, and prejudices of the world**—like Gurdjieff's teaching of self-transformation, Christ's teaching of spiritual rebirth, and the secret teachings of my spiritual path. These teachings, as remarkable as they are, have served their purpose; and it is time for me to stop chewing on them.

In effect, the Dream Weaver has given me symbolic permission to speak with my own authorial voice that has taken my whole life to realize; and I believe this summing-up dream brings closure to the quest of my parallel life—because I have scoured the "fourth corner of the abyss" and found my lost soul; I have achieved what I was reborn into my same life to achieve; I found the "strait gate" and lived the "narrow way," gave birth to my spiritual self, and broke the eternal cycle of karma and reincarnation; and I am ready now to learn the secret of how to live a karma-free life—*the next stage of human evolution!*

This is the truth that *The Summoning of Noman* has given birth to, and at long last I'm ready for my reckoning with God...

———♥———

About the Author

Orest Stocco was born in Calabria, Italy. He emmigrated to Canada and studied philosophy at university. A student of Gurdjieff's teaching for many years, his passion for writing inspired such works as *The Lion that Swallowed Hemingway* and *Healing with Padre Pio*. He lives in Georgian Bay, Ontario with his life mate Penny Lynn Cates. His personal dictum is: Life is an individual journey.

Visit him at: http://ostocco.wix.com/ostocco
Spiritual Musings Blog:
http://www.spiritualmusingsbyoreststocco.blogspot.com

ME AND MY SISPHYEAN ROCK

www.ingramcontent.com/pod-product-compliance
Lightning Source LLC
Chambersburg PA
CBHW021048090426
42738CB00006B/240